ROUTLEDGE LIBRARY EDITIONS BROADCASTING

Volume 36

TELEVISION AND THE POLITICAL IMAGE

TELEVISION AND THE POLITICAL IMAGE

A Study of the Impact of Television on the 1959 General Election

JOSEPH TRENAMAN
AND
DENIS McQUAIL

LONDON AND NEW YORK

First published in 1961 by Methuen and Co Ltd

This edition first published in 2024
by Routledge
4 Park Square, Milton Park, Abingdon, Oxon OX14 4RN

and by Routledge
605 Third Avenue, New York, NY 10158

Routledge is an imprint of the Taylor & Francis Group, an informa business

© 1961 Joseph Trenaman & Denis McQuail

All rights reserved. No part of this book may be reprinted or reproduced or utilised in any form or by any electronic, mechanical, or other means, now known or hereafter invented, including photocopying and recording, or in any information storage or retrieval system, without permission in writing from the publishers.

Trademark notice: Product or corporate names may be trademarks or registered trademarks, and are used only for identification and explanation without intent to infringe.

British Library Cataloguing in Publication Data
A catalogue record for this book is available from the British Library

ISBN: 978-1-032-59391-3 (Set)
ISBN: 978-1-032-60275-2 (Volume 36) (hbk)
ISBN: 978-1-032-60282-0 (Volume 36) (pbk)
ISBN: 978-1-003-45845-6 (Volume 36) (ebk)

DOI: 10.4324/9781003458456

Publisher's Note
The publisher has gone to great lengths to ensure the quality of this reprint but points out that some imperfections in the original copies may be apparent.

Disclaimer
The publisher has made every effort to trace copyright holders and would welcome correspondence from those they have been unable to trace.

TELEVISION AND THE POLITICAL IMAGE

A STUDY OF THE IMPACT OF TELEVISION
ON THE 1959 GENERAL ELECTION

BY

JOSEPH TRENAMAN

AND

DENIS McQUAIL

METHUEN AND CO LTD
36 Essex Street · London · WC2

First published 1961
© 1961 *Joseph Trenaman & Denis McQuail*
*Printed in Great Britain
by the Shenval Press Ltd
London, Hertford and Harlow
Cat. No. 2/6432/10*

'Military science, seeing in history an immense number of examples in which the mass of an army does not correspond with its force, and in which small numbers conquer large ones, vaguely recognizes the existence of this unknown factor, and tries to find it sometimes in some geometrical disposition of the troops, sometimes in the superiority of weapons, and most often in the genius of the leaders. But none of those factors yield results that agree with the historical facts. One has but to renounce the false view that glorifies the effect of the activity of the heroes of history in warfare in order to discover this unknown quantity, x.'

TOLSTOY, *War and Peace*

Contents

I · Election Television – an Unknown Factor	page	13
II · Method		17
III · Political Images		36
IV · The Nature of the Campaign		56
V · How the Campaign Reached the Electors		80
VI · Television Electioneering – The Viewers' Response		107
VII · Changes of Allegiance during the 1959 Campaign		123
VIII · Changes in Political Attitudes		142
IX · The Electors' Knowledge of Party Policies and National Issues		165
X · The Effects of Television and Other Media		182
XI · The Characteristics of the 'Changers'		207
XII · Some Implications		223
XIII · Summary of the Findings		227
Notes on the Chapters		237
Glossary		255
Reference Table of Sampling Errors		257
Appendices		
A · *Construction of Indices of Exposure*		259
B · *An Index of Political Change*		263
C · *Fieldwork and a Note on the Elusive Elector*		266
D · *Voting in the Sample and in the Constituencies*		269
E · *The Social Composition of the Sample*		271
F · *Estimates of Press Space devoted to the Campaign*		272
G · *Analysis Tables of Political Images*		273
Index		281

Illustrations

The receiving end of the campaign (*Roger Mayne*)	*frontispiece*
Views of the West Leeds constituency (*Roger Mayne*)	*facing pages* 18, 19
The opening Conservative Party and Labour Party election broadcasts	108
Mr Gaitskell in the studio (*Mirropic*)	109
'Election Marathon' rehearsal (*Granada TV*)	109
Views of the Pudsey constituency (*Yorkshire Post*)	184, 185

Acknowledgments

This election study could not have been carried out without the help of members of many interested departments at Leeds University, a collaboration which has been made easier by a Committee of Heads of Departments, under the chairmanship of the Vice-Chancellor, set up to advise the Television Research Unit. We should particularly like to thank Professor E. Grebenik for many constructive suggestions and for reading this book in manuscript, and Mr A. H. Hanson, Dr J. Rex, and Dr V. Wiseman of the Social Studies Department. We owe much to Mr W. H. Trickett for statistical advice, and to Professor G. P. Meredith and his colleagues. Although we have obtained a great deal of advice and assistance, we must take full responsibility for the conduct of the survey and for the conclusions drawn from it.

We should like to thank Dr A. S. Douglas, the former Director of the Computing Laboratory, Miss Winifred Ashton who steered most of our material through the computer, and Mr A. J. Mitchell and Miss M. Jowett for their help. Without it the preliminary studies would not have been completed in time and the final analysis would have been much smaller in scale.

The Chapter (No. IV) on the General Election campaign, which included a detailed analysis of the press and broadcasting coverage, was the work of Mrs M. E. Trenaman. We are much indebted to her for this and for help in many other ways. We should also like to thank the Unit Secretary, Miss Susan Mason, who with Miss Jill Rennie, Mrs B. Nancarrow, Mrs J. Dyson, Mrs J. Davies and Miss S. Handley, made up an enthusiastic and efficient operations team.

At many points in this study we have been influenced by the earlier work of R. S. Milne and H. C. Mackenzie of Bristol University. We are especially indebted to the latter for helping us in a more direct way with comments on the design of the study and the findings.

We wish to express our gratitude to Professor Sir Cyril Burt and Professor Philip Vernon for technical advice on a number of methodological points; and to Mr J. F. Scott of the Oxford University Unit of Biometry, and Dr David Butler and Dr Richard Rose of Nuffield College, Oxford.

Many other people have contributed to the work of this project, with advice, with information, and in other ways. We should especially like to mention: Dr Hilde Himmelweit, Professor H. J. Eysenck, Professor A. J. Brown, Professor G. R. Hargreaves, and Dr J. V. Loach; members of the BBC staff including Mr Harman Grisewood, Mr Kenneth Adam, Mr Robert Silvey, Mr F. Littman, Mr J. C. Thornton, Mr Kenneth Severs; Mr Noel Stevenson of the ITA; Sir Gerald Barry, Mr John Rayner, Mr Alan Pinnock and Mr Barrie Heads of Granada TV; Mr Geoffrey Cox of ITN; Mr E. W. Whitley of ABC Television; Mr N. L. Webb of Television Audience Measurement Ltd; Mr David Crouch, Mr J. Winning, Brigadier J. W. Hinchcliffe, Mr E. S. Adamson, and Mr C. J. Lindsey of the Conservative Party; Mr K. Peay, Mr Charles Pannell, MP, and Mr A. Wedgwood Benn, MP, of the Labour Party; Miss P. Preston of the Liberal Party; Dr Mark Abrams and Miss C. Seabrook of Research Services Ltd; Dr Henry Durant of the Gallup Poll; Mr R. M. Shields of the National Opinion Polls Ltd; Mr J. W. Droy of the Daily Express Poll; Mr John Beavan, Mr John McKnight; Mrs V. Grebenik, Mrs M. Mosley and Mr P. McQuail who, with others, helped to monitor the election broadcasts; the Institute of Practitioners in Advertising; The Editor of the *Daily Telegraph*; The Editor and the News Editor and Mr L. W. Hill of the *Yorkshire Post*; the Editors of the *Yorkshire Evening Post* and the *Yorkshire Evening News*; and Lord Reith and Mr Richard Crossman, MP, for permission to quote from their works.

Lastly, we are indebted to the forty interviewers who laboured, often in most trying circumstances, and to the thousand-odd electors of Leeds and Pudsey who so uncomplainingly volunteered the raw material from which this study was made.

Television Research Unit
(Granada foundation)
University of Leeds   J. TRENAMAN
October 1960   D. MCQUAIL

CHAPTER I

Election Television – an Unknown Factor

'This time it really makes sense to speak of a "television election",' wrote a Sunday newspaper with some trepidation on the eve of the 1959 General Election. In 1955 only 38 per cent of the population had regular access to television, and sound radio was still the dominant medium in broadcasting. In the four years between the elections, sound radio had been eclipsed and the party politicians, for the first time, literally faced an audience of tens of millions. With television debates and camera coverage of the campaign throughout the country, and the parties using the full technical resources of the television authorities to mount an onslaught on the susceptibilities of the elector, what might not happen? The purpose of this study was to discover what did happen during the brief interval of nineteen days between the opening of the campaign and the poll, and how far television was responsible for it.

The rate at which television has spread into British homes is itself a phenomenon. When this study was first mooted there were about 70 per cent of the households in the North of England with television. By the time of the election it was 75 per cent. When this report was written it had topped 80 per cent, and when it appears in print the proportion will be about 85 per cent, by which time it will have overtaken the corresponding American figure. In terms of television viewing, we are about to become the most heavily saturated nation in the world.

The political parties recognized the situation and prepared assiduously for it, by setting up television units to instruct speakers in the techniques of communication and generally to plan their broadcasts. The television authorities made their presentation facilities freely available to all three parties. The Labour Party took over the studio, part of the production team, and the style of the BBC's 'Tonight' programme. The Conservative Party made special films for use in their programmes but had decided on a more conventional discussion-style of presentation. The television campaign was, therefore, a conflict of method as much as of content.

Another new factor in the situation since 1955 was the presence of the Independent Television service. The Granada Network had already made an incursion into the Rochdale by-election of 1958 by presenting all three candidates in a special programme.[1] The Programme Companies were believed to be intending a full coverage of the campaign, apart from the Party election broadcasts. The BBC then announced their decision to make a clean break with their previous practice of totally excluding from programmes all material which might be held to influence the voter in recording his vote, other than the parties' own broadcasts.

Both television services were hampered, far more than is generally realized, by the Representation of the People Act 1949, under which any operation 'presenting to the electors the candidate or his views' should be charged to the candidate's election expenses. Newspapers were exempted by the Act from this provision but the broadcasting authorities were not mentioned and their position had not been tested in the courts. The Independent Companies suffered a further special restriction from a section of the Television Act 1954 which only allowed them to broadcast political material in the form of 'properly balanced discussions or debates'. Nevertheless, after taking legal advice, both services planned full news coverage of the campaign and a number of special programmes in which candidates presented their views, including the BBC's 'Hustings' and Granada's aptly named 'Election Marathon'.

It was not known how effectively television might influence public attitudes towards political parties and leaders. The full force of the medium had not previously been directed on to political issues. The Himmelweit report[2] had found that television 'influences the way children think' about social situations and 'affects [their] value judgments'. It was the personal and intimate quality of the image that was believed to be likely to have so powerful an effect. In no other medium could one virtually sit within fifteen feet of a political leader and watch his mind at work, study his manner and moods and assess his general qualities. Here, at last, was a medium where the speaker did not have to compete with conversation and domestic activities as a voice from the background, in an attempt to gain the attention of the elector. The television screen compels attention.

The new medium had taken over and maintained the prestige of sound broadcasting for impartiality and freedom of expression. It was not that the electorate knew that both the BBC and Independent Companies were required by Parliament to refrain from expressing any editorial opinion in matters of public policy. But this and other requirements had built up in the public estimation a reputation for objectivity and fair play which the Press, through its generally partisan editorial policies, did not enjoy. Was television, then, likely to replace the Press and the local political campaigns as a major electoral force, and if so, what would be the effect on electors?

In television, a new quality had entered British elections. The party manifestoes, which had once been shouted from public platforms by speakers well used to coping with hecklers, must now be directed to the family by the fireside. And the very people who would see no harm in a verbal scuffle at an open-air meeting or would rather enjoy reading in the newspaper about a boisterous exchange of views or a slashing attack on the policies of the other party, might bring a totally different set of expectations to what was being said through the screen in their own homes. It is true that sound radio had been used in previous elections, but its voice had been muted through the BBC ban on political comment and it had never possessed the compelling power of television.

In this situation it seemed important to those of us in the newly formed Television Research Unit at Leeds University, to undertake a study of the election actually in progress and the effect it was having upon the electorate. No previous investigation of the *collective* impact of the various campaign forces on electors had yet been made, weighing up the interactions of one upon the other, and partialling out the independent effect of each. The valuable studies which Milne and Mackenzie had carried out in Bristol during the 1951 and 1955 elections were not being continued, and, so far as is known, no other detailed surveys were being made of the 1959 election.

The parties themselves were changing in their attitudes to the electors. There was much talk of party images and even of creating or modifying images. The Conservative Party had conducted a nation-wide and extensive advertising campaign, first through the newspapers and, later, on public hoardings. No one knew what effect this would have, though it happened to coincide with a considerable improvement in the Conservative position, according to the opinion polls. What, then, is political allegiance and how is it projected in the thoughts and opinions of the party supporters? And in what units do we measure the strength of support? As John Beavan inquired in *The Twentieth Century*,[3] writing of the way individual attitudes are made up, 'if people had been asked not to vote but to express their opinion of the parties in the form of an appreciation index, [would many] have given 51 per cent to the party they marked to win and 49 per cent to one of the others?'

Because of this interest in the nature of political attitudes, we began, in July of 1959, to investigate the precise nature of the conceptions formed by the voters of the two main parties. A series of preliminary experiments gave us the material with which to make up scales of attitudes to the two major parties and their leaders. The campaign study itself took the form of two interviews with a cross-section of the electors in the neighbouring constituencies of West Leeds and Pudsey. The first round of interviews was completed immediately before the opening of the campaign on September 20, and the second visits were paid immediately after polling day. By comparing the two 'readings', we hoped to obtain a record of changes in knowledge, opinion and attitude. Detailed inventories of electors' viewing of the television programmes, radio listening, reading of the newspapers, and of what they had seen of the local campaign, could then be related to these changes.

We have divided our account of the findings into separate sections – one on the political images, a group of chapters on the various kinds of change noted in the electorate, an analysis of the contribution made by television and the other factors towards these changes, a close-up of the people who changed their political allegiance, an analysis of the content of the campaign, and so on. These chapters form a continuing story and the evidence is interlocking, though we have tried to make the chapters reasonably self-contained. Apart from the chapter on method which can be skipped by those readers who prefer to take what follows on trust, we have put technical details and footnotes together at the end of the book.

CHAPTER II

Method

THE SAMPLE SURVEY

This study used the panel technique in which the same sample of electors was interviewed immediately before, and again immediately following the General Election campaign. Had we anticipated large changes of opinion and response in which there would be no positive association between those opinions given before and those given after the campaign, it might have proved more reliable to have interviewed two separate but similar samples.[1] But there was every reason to believe, from the experience of many previous studies, that changes would be marginal. That being so, shifts in attitude could be estimated with much greater accuracy in a before-and-after study than by any other method.

The panel method certainly proved more economical than the alternative. The first set of interviews was not completed without losses on the way. It is reckoned that in most polling districts an electoral register will have only some 89 per cent of those eligible to vote still living at the registered addresses eight months after publication.[2] The registers used in West Leeds and Pudsey were compiled on October 10, 1958, and published on February 16, 1959. This rate of loss may have been exceeded in Leeds where very considerable slum clearance was being carried out during 1959. The finding of the houses selected – no easy task on a dark evening, especially in an area of straggling and incomplete development like parts of the Pudsey constituency, and the following-up of substitute names and addresses for those people who have moved away, took up more time than the actual interviews. A second round of interviews with the same sample met only a 6 per cent loss and took up much less interviewing time than the first. Apart from questions of cost, it was important to the study to have the second interviews completed as soon as possible after polling day.

If the results of a study of this sort are to have any wider application, one must know something of the method and circumstances in which they were obtained. These can be considered at three stages of the operation. First, one must know something of the constituencies in which the study was made. Secondly, the way the individuals who make up the samples were selected from the electorate, their number and their characteristics should be known. Thirdly, the method of actually obtaining the information from these electors must be considered. An account of the interviewing results is given in Appendix C.

Choosing the constituencies

We were looking for a constituency or constituencies in which the overall proportions of votes cast for the three parties were somewhere near the national distribution; where the major parties were fairly closely matched, because we wanted to assess the effects of television under conditions of heightened political interest. This, as it turned out from the results, was probably a mistaken assumption for it is likely that the impact of political broadcasting through television may be no less great in areas of comparative indifference. Further, we were looking for constituencies where urban development was mixed with suburban and some rural dwellings and where the economic status of the areas as a whole was near the national average. Finally, as there was always the prospect that the interval between the Prime Minister's announcement of the dissolution of Parliament and the opening of the election campaign would be as short as that of the previous election, there were advantages in choosing constituencies not far from Leeds. It turned out that the dissolution was announced on September 8, only ten days before the opening of the campaign and one calendar month before polling day. In 1955 the notice (between announcement and dissolution) was twenty-one days, in 1951 sixteen days, and in 1950 twenty-three days. As all our interviews had to be completed before the opening of the campaign, it was clear that we should have to choose constituencies that were close to Leeds itself; we could then effectively supervise the work of interviewers who would be operating over an area that was within easy access from the centre.

Very few constituencies came near to satisfying all these conditions. The two that were finally chosen, West Leeds and Pudsey, had the added advantage of being adjacent. West Leeds was the most nearly

WEST LEEDS

An area scheduled for slum-clearance

A view to the north of the constituency

Typical back-to-back houses in West Leeds

METHOD

marginal of the six Leeds constituencies. The choice of a second constituency was finally narrowed to Pudsey or Shipley, both of which were near-marginal at the 1955 election, both near Leeds, and both with a juror percentage near the average. The percentage of electors who are liable for jury service is a useful index of the economic status of an area, since there is in effect a property qualification for jurors. For any district or constituency the index can be calculated by counting the jurors in the electoral register for the area required and expressing this number as a percentage of registered electors in the area. The use of the juror index has been described by Gray, Corlett, and Jones,[3] who show that the higher the percentage of jurors the higher is household income, the occupational level, and the larger the house. Over the whole country in 1951 about 5 per cent of all electors were eligible for jury service. Shipley had a higher juror index which would have balanced the low figure of West Leeds, but Pudsey was chosen because of its convenience to Leeds. It lies between Leeds and Bradford, extending from the boundary of Huddersfield in the south to the escarpment overlooking the Wharfe Valley in the north. Pudsey Town is in the centre, but steep hills separate it from the pockets of old industrial development, like Guiseley, and Yeadon, that are dotted all over the area. At the 1955 election West Leeds had returned a Labour Member with a lead amounting to 13·4 per cent over his Conservative opponent and Pudsey had returned a Conservative Member with a lead of 10·4 per cent. There had been Liberal candidates in both constituencies. The aggregate of votes cast in the two constituencies divided between the two major parties in the ratio of 48·9 per cent for Conservative to 51·1 per cent for Labour, whereas the proportions for the whole country were 51·8 to 48·2 per cent.

The percentage of jurors in West Leeds was 1·48.[4] Two of the Leeds constituencies have juror-indices well above average (around 8 per cent) and four are well below. West Leeds was the third lowest but was chosen because its social composition and political balance were most suitable. The juror figures for its five wards range from 0·61 for Wellington to 2·01 for Bramley.

Pudsey has 3·71 per cent of jurors. Its twenty wards range in status from the unusually high figure of 17·62 per cent in Pudsey South to the national norm of 5·01 per cent in Chapeltown and down to 0·72 per cent in Hawthorn.

Drawing the sample
There were 112,554 names on the electoral registers in these two constituencies. It was decided to draw a systematic sample of names from each constituency by starting at randomly chosen points, and taking every 125th name throughout the Pudsey and every 150th name throughout the West Leeds registers. A total of 820 names were chosen by this means, 401 in West Leeds and 419 in Pudsey.

From this number 701 were satisfactorily interviewed before the campaign, a proportion of 85·5 per cent. It was known that some of the electors would have moved during the twelve months since the registers were compiled; some would have died; some would be in hospital or ill at home; and some would be away from home. If a person had moved within the area and could be found, he was interviewed at his new address. Substitute names were taken only for those electors who had moved out of the neighbourhood. The sample as a whole appears to be as representative as one could expect in a social survey conducted by interviews – in fact the distributions of age, sex and other characteristics fall within the margins of normal sampling errors. We were not entitled, strictly speaking, to put the evidence from the two constituencies together and to treat them as one sample, believed to be fairly typical of a large part of the population. We had first to establish that the things we were measuring – attitudes, intentions, knowledge – varied in the same way in each constituency. Of course the proportions of Conservative to Labour supporters were different in the two constituencies, but we needed to show that, for example, changes in attitude to Mr Gaitskell as a leader, among Labour supporters, in West Leeds and in Pudsey were not significantly different before we could put the two sets of data together and treat all Labour supporters as one population for purposes of analysis. This comparison of the two samples has been made in each of the factors we are examining, and figures for the combined samples are only given where no real differences have emerged. Where the findings do diverge, as in the voting behaviour of people who were undecided at the beginning of the campaign, they raise points of special interest.

Practically all social surveys have to make the best of imperfection in so far as they fail to reach every member of the required sample. One can usually only speculate about the people who have eluded the interviewer. Where this margin is small, any differences in their

METHOD

characteristics would have a negligible effect on the averages or other statistics for the sample as a whole. This is also true of the present study when we are dealing with *all* electors; one of the principal objects of an electoral study, however, is to isolate and examine that small minority of electors who change their intentions, and if such people have anything in common with the electors we failed to find it is important to know the sort of people they are likely to be. Here bias was undoubtedly introduced by the extent to which we failed to reach every elector in the sample who was capable of voting within the constituencies; in other words, those who could not be found or who refused to co-operate (some 11·3 per cent all told) were probably not representative, in political terms, of the bulk of the sample. The evidence of the small losses between the first and the second round of interviews suggests that such people were more likely to be Labour than Conservative and probably included a large proportion of non-voters. The fact that this elusive fringe also appeared to have a good deal in common with those who changed their minds during the campaign underlines the importance of accurate and full samples for electoral studies. Expressed in terms of the practical problem involved, if one were trying to measure a political swing of 2 per cent in a sample of 800, the sixteen individuals representing this movement might well be among the more difficult to approach. One careless or too-timid interviewer who failed to see, say, eight of the electors on his list could wipe out up to half of this vital fringe. (Appendix C sets out the interviewing results.)

Collecting the information

It remains only to report on the way the information was actually obtained from electors. The reliability of interviews may be much affected by the impression the informant gains of what the interview is all about, the wording of the questions, the length of the questionnaire and the circumstances in which it is presented.

At the first interview the elector was told that the survey was about 'things of interest to people during the coming General Election'. While the subject of television was mentioned in the course of the interview, no hint of any special interest in the medium was given, and care was taken to see that no reference was made to a second interview, either in the fieldwork or in the press reports.

The questionnaire was not long, by market research standards.

Most of it was taken up with four scales of attitude items and lists of policies and issues which had to be read over to the informant. These, too, were cut down to the minimum on the principle that it is better to have reasonably reliable responses to a few questions than doubtful responses to many. This may be particularly important in an election study where all the interviews have to be completed within a few days; and the interviewer may have to question his informants at rather inconvenient times, and often in inconvenient places.

A point that had to be watched carefully was the danger of having a wife's political opinion overshadowed by her husband's. Where the informant was believed to be a married woman, interviewers were asked to try to see her during the day, or, if the husband was present, to make it clear that it was the wife's personal opinions that were being sought. If there was any doubt about the independence of the responses, the interviewer was advised to seek separate interviews from both husband and wife, later discarding the husband's. As a check on this point, we looked at the voters whose political attitude responses pointed in a different direction from the way they said they voted in case there were a disproportionate number of married women among them; but there was not.

The lists of issues and attitude scales ran up to fifteen items. In case there was any likelihood of informants paying more attention to the earlier than to the later items, and as a check on the consistency of the responses, complete alternative sets of items, in reverse order, were printed on cards of contrasting colour. The sets were then used by each interviewer alternately. An analysis of the results showed no significant difference at all between the responses (see page 34).

Reliability of the sample

A question which should be faced squarely is: how far can these findings be said to be applicable to other parts of the country? In terms of strict statistical probabilities, only limited inferences about the electorate could be made from the evidence of two constituencies which had been arbitrarily selected. In every stage of the analysis, the results in the two separate constituencies have been compared. Where the same trends appear in both and are supported by the findings of other studies, rather more confidence can be placed in them. It is not always possible to estimate the degree of such likelihood[5] by putting forward any specific margins of error. Even a multi-stage sampling

METHOD

scheme which samples, first constituencies, then polling districts within constituencies, and finally types of individual within polling districts, is estimated by Professor M. G. Kendall[6] as liable to sampling errors of up to twice the normal standard errors. Some of the findings, such as those on political images, are obtained by methods which were designed for exact measurements of physical variables, and can only be applied cautiously to mental attributes. Their real significance can only be discovered by further research.

Any proportions or percentages quoted in the findings should always be seen to have sampling errors. The original sample was a 'probability sample' in the sense that every elector on the register had an equal chance of being chosen. It would follow that, in the case of any proportion such as the percentage of Labour voters, the probability of the value thrown up in the sample differing from the true value by more than an accepted margin (twice the standard error) is about one in twenty. But the incompleteness of the electoral registers and the deficiencies in the actual sample must increase this margin. A table of the normal confidence limits for several sizes of sample (or sub-sample) and for a range of percentages is given on page 257. But changes in proportion *among the same people* over a period of time (for instance, differences between before-and-after-effects) are here subject to very much smaller sampling errors.

THE ANALYSIS OF POLITICAL IMAGES

An investigation of political attitudes was carried out in Leeds in the two months before the 1959 General Election. Besides exploring the outlines of images of parties and their leaders, the enquiry set out to produce a scale which could be used to record movements of political allegiance too slight to be expressed as voting changes.

The matter needed an experimental approach. Assuming a minimum level of articulation in the population, one could probe these concepts by means of questions about what the parties stand for. If there are common elements in political attitudes, one might reasonably describe this commonality as the party image.

Finding the raw material

During the early part of August 1959, invitations were sent to 600 electors whose names had been drawn systematically from the electoral registers (taking every twelfth name from a randomly chosen starting point). Hyde Park Ward in Leeds North West constituency was chosen because it was conveniently near to the University for people attending group meetings and the juror proportion (4·4 per cent) was near the national average. The residents were invited to come to the University to see three films (a Conservative Party film about Mr Macmillan, a Labour Party television recording, including an interview with Mr Gaitskell, and 'Short Vision', an animated film about nuclear warfare). Four groups were convened, among whom 186 electors completed answer papers or gave written opinions. A further forty-eight electors who were added to the sample (totalling 234) were reached by a canvass of a Corporation housing estate in the area. In all, the political allegiance of the members of the sample was: Conservative 48 per cent, Labour 44 per cent, Liberal or uncommitted 8 per cent. The sample was, of course, highly self-selected as it was bound to be. The meetings took place during the fortnight of the August public holiday in Leeds when large numbers of residents were away. There is a tendency for invited audiences to include rather more of the better educated and articulate people than would be found in a random sample. To offset this tendency a little, all the names in a number of roads with high juror proportions were excluded. The sex, age, and school education distributions of the groups were not, however, seriously skewed. Indeed, the proportions of men and women were the same as in the later random sample; the age groups differed by never more than 3 per cent, and the proportion leaving school at 16-plus was 15·6 per cent compared with 16·6 per cent.

At the first group the sixty-eight members were asked to write down, as fully as they could, what they thought the major parties stood for, and to mention what they 'liked or respected' or 'didn't like' about each party. They were asked for the qualities they 'would look for in a good political leader', and what sort of a person they would expect the head of a Government to be. A further question ran: 'Suppose a foreign visitor were asking you about your views on the head of the next Government in this country, and he invited your candid opinion of both Mr Macmillan and Mr Gaitskell as political leaders, what would you tell him?' After the showing of the films, they were asked for any further thoughts on the political parties and leaders that occurred to them. As the opinions of this particular group played a formative part in the working out of the political attitude scales it was important that it should be fairly representative in its political allegiance; the proportions, in fact, were: Conservative 38 per cent, Labour 38 per cent, Liberal or non-committal 24 per cent.

A content analysis was made of the whole of this written material, noting the actual form of words used wherever phrases or adjectives recurred.

Sifting for attitudes

The second stage was more systematic. The analysis of this raw material produced twenty-three short statements of opinion, applicable to either major party, and representing the main trends of opinion. They were expressed, wherever suitable, in the form of words most commonly employed by the members of the groups. Sometimes this meant using colloquial and somewhat imprecise expressions, but it was more important to provide a frame of reference that could be used even by inarticulate electors than to produce very precise statements.

A similar list of thirty statements was drawn up for the two party leaders. Both sets were then presented to further samples of the electorate, who were asked to endorse the items they believed to be 'true of' the Conservative Party and then of the Labour Party, and similarly to indicate, by ticking, the items that 'apply to' Mr Macmillan and to Mr Gaitskell. The items are shown in Tables 60 and 61 in Appendix G.

A total of 166 electors endorsed the lists. The work was done carefully and without hurry, largely in group meetings similar to the first. To enlarge the sample, interviewers arranged for questionnaires to be filled in by forty-eight Corporation housing estate residents. Although objections can be raised to the method used, we had the impression that people were taking care to put down in their responses what they really believed.

One of the most pertinent criticisms of attitude scale questionnaires is what has been described by Cronbach[7] as 'response set'. This is the tendency for some people to respond to a long string of questions in a stereotyped manner, saying 'yes' even if there is only slight agreement with the statement, or saying 'no' when the issue is in doubt, or veering from one to the other. An authoritarianism scale produced in America by Adorno[8] has been widely criticized because all the items in the scale are so worded that affirmative answers point in the authoritarian direction. A number of writers have found that by reversing the items something different from a negative version of the original scale emerges. (See Eysenck, H. J., *The Structure of Human Personality*, Methuen, 1960, Chap. X.)

The difficulty of this sort of check is that while a statement and its opposite are mutually exclusive in meaning, a response to one cannot always be inferred from a response to the other, because there is often an intermediate position in which the response may be a state of doubt or some other alternative view.

As a check on the possibility of response set bias, two extra questions (negatives of items already listed) were included in the attitude items for political parties. The paired items were well separated from each other. If one found that a sizeable proportion of respondents endorsed both the item and its contrary, then one would doubt the validity of the answers. One such item was 'Would keep prices down' and its contrary 'Wouldn't keep prices down'. In fact, no member of any group endorsed both, either about the Conservative or the Labour Party. The proportions of endorsement for the two parties were: Conservatives, 'would' 35 per cent, 'wouldn't' 25 per cent; Labour, 'would' 26 per cent, 'wouldn't' 36 per cent. The areas of doubt between the two responses were therefore 40 per cent and 38 per cent respectively.

The other item was 'Would extend the welfare services', and its opposite 'Would cut the welfare services'. These two are not, of course, exclusive for there is the intermediate position of leaving the welfare services as they are. Two members of the groups endorsed both items concerning the Labour Party. Neither was an overgenerous 'ticker'. The negative item followed five consecutive favourable items and may have been misread as its positive form. In the Conservative Party list no member of any group endorsed both these items.

The weight of endorsement for each item is of some interest, but it is not the most important thing. We were looking for common factors behind the individual opinions. The exploratory method for this purpose seemed to be a variant of factor analysis suitable for electronic computer calculations. Several techniques might have been tried but they would not have answered the question we put, namely, how can we reduce a mass of correlated measured responses to a small number of independent (uncorrelated) tendencies. Factor analysis is a quantitative method of classification and it seeks first the principle that

METHOD

accounts for most of the individual variation, then the principle that accounts for the next greatest share, and so on. Such principles are mutually independent. The first step is to inter-correlate all the items. A coefficient of correlation measures the extent to which two tendencies agree or coincide, namely, in this context, the tendency to endorse one item and the tendency to endorse another. Since there were twenty-three items for each party and thirty for each leader, the computations involved the working out of 1,376 correlations between items. When all this material was further broken down into separate sets of answers for Conservative and Labour supporters, the total number of correlation coefficients to be calculated came to 4,128 in all. The further stages of the analysis were more complex and only the use of a computer made it practicable.

Product-moment coefficients were used for the correlations. Before these could be calculated, weights had to be given to the responses. The common practice was followed, attaching a weight of 1 to an endorsement (indicating that the informant believed the item to be 'true of' the party or leader) and 0 to non-endorsement. The correspondences between endorsements had then to be counted. This meant that we needed to know how many persons had endorsed, say, item 1 and also item 2, from which we could compute from the marginal totals how many had endorsed neither, or 1 and not 2, or 2 and not 1.

The assumption behind product-moment correlations of two-by-two tables (or point correlations, or Yule's phi), is that there are two distinct categories of response, neither varying in degree, such that those who approve of the statement and those who disapprove do so with equal strength or confidence. This is often not the case with attitude data which tend to be distributed as a continuous variable. Nevertheless, the product-moment coefficient was considered more suitable than the tetrachoric for our purpose.

The correlation matrices were analysed into their principal components. Each matrix was first analysed into latent roots and vectors. For this purpose, unity was inserted for the self-correlations between each item along the leading diagonal, following Hotelling's method. The process of iteration was stopped after the third root had been extracted; in the earlier analyses the fourth root was produced but it was not considered significant enough to be used. The vectors were converted into Hotelling's[9] principal components by multiplying each element by $\frac{\sqrt{\text{Latent root}}}{\sqrt{\Sigma \text{Sqs. components}}}$. Taking the whole sample, one finds that the first four factors account for 50 per cent of the variance, and the first three for 45 per cent. It is shown below that when the Conservative and Labour sub-samples were analysed separately, further components appeared. In all, perhaps two-thirds of the political opinions expressed could be put down to common factors. This means that, of the great mass of opinions which make up political images, about two-thirds can be resolved into three or four general tendencies. The proportions are much the same for both parties and both leaders. Responses to some items were governed more than others by the common factors, some being almost completely 'saturated' by them, others hardly at all. A factor variance or communality of 100 per cent (in Tables 60-65) would mean that the item had no unique meaning, and merely acted as a release mechanism for the common factors. A figure of 0 per cent would mean that the item was judged only for its specific meaning and was untouched by the common factors. Tables in Appendix G show the first factor loadings, or the degree to which answers to a given item correlate with the underlying tendency denoted by the factor, and the communalities or the proportions of the variance of each item accounted for by the three factors.

As we were looking primarily for a single dimension along which to measure the more sensitive movements in attitudes to the major parties, the analysis might have stopped at this point, for we had only to choose items most heavily loaded with the common factor to produce the necessary scales. But if there were secondary factors it seemed sensible to try to represent them, and only by further separate analyses of the responses within each group of party supporters could we discover any distinctive features in the party and leader images.

In this first analysis we had differentiated a factor which marked off very clearly Conservative from Labour supporters, which we have called the 'traditional-versus-radical' factor. It seemed to follow that if we divided our sample of electors into two groups, according to their party allegiance, one Conservative and the other Labour, and analysed each separately we should hold the traditional-versus-radical factor constant and be able to see what features, if any, of the political images were peculiar to the party supporters themselves. The Conservative group would, for example, have a considerable degree of loyalty to traditionalism in common which would not show up as a

METHOD

separate factor in any further analysis of their responses. Or, putting it the other way round, if it did show up it would disprove our inference about the traditional-versus-radical component.

We therefore applied the same method of factorization to the correlations obtained for the material from Conservative and Labour supporters separately. As had been anticipated, the factor in the first analysis disappeared because, by dividing the sample according to the interpretation of the first analysis, we had virtually eliminated the factor in question, and new sets of features emerged which took us some way further towards an explanation of the character of the party and leader images. The analysis results are shown quantitatively in Tables 60-65 in Appendix G and an interpretation of their meaning in terms of each image is attempted in Chapter III. We are only too conscious of the subjective nature of such interpretation, and more extensive studies will, we hope, throw more light on some of the features. Some elements are strongly identified, and these we have tried to distinguish from others which, because of the limitations of the raw material, are weak.

The factor loadings, as they stand in the tables in Appendix G do not show the components very well. The reason is that they represent vectors of varying length, each along a different hypothetical dimension. The true item values can often only be seen if all three (or more) dimensions are plotted out in relation to each other and the axes along which they lie rotated in order to obtain a better fit. Two factors could be related to each other by plotting out the corresponding loadings for each item on a two-dimensional surface. Three factors can be represented by the three dimensions of ordinary space, but for convenience, and following Thurstone's suggestion the factor loadings were transformed into angular notation and plotted out on a spherical surface. Three planes at right angles (or orthogonal) to each other can be drawn on a spherical surface and, by extending the vector lengths proportionately, the three factor loadings can be plotted on the surface. The advantage of Thurstone's method[10] is that a *single* point can represent *all three* factor loadings (although only two, any two, are needed to locate the point). Once the factors are plotted out it becomes an easy matter to rotate the three axes to obtain a better fit. All eight analyses for the parties and leaders were transformed into angular notation and plotted on to a spherical surface in this way. Some rough idea of the distribution of the factors can be obtained by looking at all three factor loadings for any one item. In the Conservative Party attitudes, for instance (Table 62), it can be seen that item 4 (factor loadings, ·46, ·54, −·04) and item 8 (·51, ·53, −·03) are very similar and would occupy similar positions in a three-dimensional space. Figure 1 shows, by way of illustration, how the items in the Labour Party image (endorsed by Labour supporters) are distributed on a spherical surface. The three arcs represent the rotated axes, forming a spherical triangle (or what Thurstone calls a 'positive manifold'). The points of the triangle are the maximum loadings. They represent 'the underlying properties or simplifying parameters in terms of which the correlations of the whole test can be understood.'[11] Items distributed along an arc would therefore represent various loadings of the factors depicted at either end of the arc, and zero loadings of the third (opposite) factor.

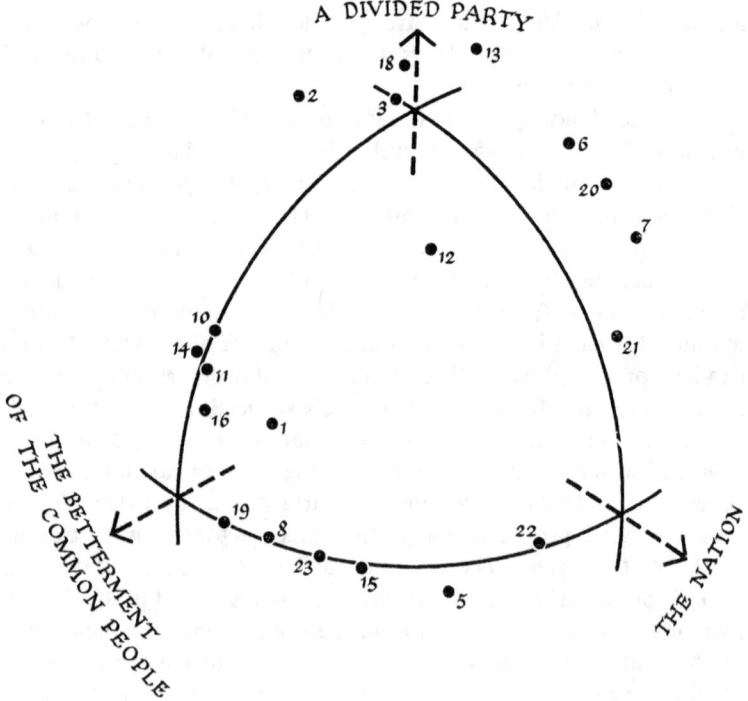

Fig. 1. – *Labour Party image (among Labour supporters). Distribution of factor loadings of attitude items as represented on a spherical surface. The numbers refer to items listed in Table 63, Appendix G.*

METHOD

In attitude analysis it is often difficult to discern the precise meaning of a group factor when the number of statements being investigated is strictly limited. One could increase the number but the labour of analysis would prove prodigious. Perhaps the most satisfactory procedure would be to carry out further experiments, using new sets of attitude statements, designed to explore any factor that begins to emerge from the original analysis. Clearly the choice of statements for the original scale is vital, especially in a study like ours which had to be completed within the few weeks preceding the election, and for which there were no previous studies on which to build.

Scalogram analysis

In scalogram analysis, Louis Guttman[12] claims that an attitude scale is more than a collection of opinions representing a universe of belief; he argues that the items have a natural order, ranging usually from extreme 'pro' to extreme 'anti' such that any one person will endorse adjacent items somewhere along the scale line. The most favourable respondent will endorse a group of adjacent items at the favourable end of the scale. A somewhat less favourable respondent will endorse a group, overlapping the first, but a little nearer the unfavourable end. Each alternative position along the scale represents a 'scale type'. The effect of this is that the endorsements pile up in the centre and thin out towards the ends of the scale, rather like a 'normal' distribution. Thus extreme views are defined as those opinions held by fewest people.

The practical value of scalogram analysis is that it suggests a hierarchy of meaning in attitude items; it can disclose items which do not fit into the scale pattern and can sometimes indicate a single item which will alone discriminate between respondents above and below a given point on the scale. Its theoretical foundation is plausible but arbitrary. By itself it would be an inadequate means of exploring party images. Scalogram analysis of attitudes to the Conservative Party and the Labour Party, before and after the campaign, was carried out in order to see whether they could add anything to the principal component analyses.

For this purpose we used a specially constructed piece of equipment (a single, transparent scalogram board) which has been described elsewhere.[13] One hundred sets of answers were drawn systematically from the main sample, and the party attitude responses were analysed.

A fairly close fit to a Guttman scale emerged. Some 85 per cent of the pre-campaign items fitted into 'scale types' (=a coefficient of reproducibility of ·85), and 89 per cent of the post-campaign items.

This consolidation, as a probable effect of the campaign, appeared in attitudes to both main parties. It does not necessarily mean a consolidation of opinion *within* the ranks of party supporters because the sample was drawn from all electors. It does suggest a slight lessening of tolerance at the end of the campaign.

The central item in the Conservative scale, linking, as it were, supporters and opponents, was 'Out for the nation as a whole'; the item 'Out to raise the standard of living for the ordinary man in the street' was at the favourable extreme and therefore least commonly endorsed. In the Labour Party scale the order of the items was almost reversed. 'Out to raise the standard of living for the ordinary man in the street' became the central item, and 'Would make the country more prosperous' was at the extreme position and was least endorsed.

Selection of attitude scales for the main election study

Once the dimensions of political attitudes had been explored, it became a fairly simple matter to choose a compact scale of items for the fieldwork of our main study. In the preliminary experiments, we needed the largest number of items that could conveniently be presented to groups of electors and handled in the analysis. For the main study we needed a list that could be presented at the door. It was an economy to have items that were valid for both parties, and similarly a list that would apply to both leaders.

This arrangement would also give the elector the impression that he was judging both sides by a common standard.

The chief purpose of the scales was to register movements in political allegiance that were too sensitive to be recorded in voting changes. It was, therefore, essential to select items that were heavily loaded with the traditional-versus-radical factor in the initial analysis. We also wanted roughly equal numbers of favourable and unfavourable items so that respondents would feel that they were being offered a balanced selection of opinions. And since it had been found, in the principal axes analyses, that the items for the leaders were often grouped separately into those expressing personal qualities, leadership qualities, and aspects of policy, it was felt important to include representative items from these three groups. It was also thought

METHOD

likely that television appearances might unduly affect a leader's personal standing as compared with his leadership or policy aspects, which was another reason for a balanced choice.

To represent these various categories it was found necessary to have fourteen items in the final leader scale, but only nine in the party attitude scale. Despite this limited size, both scales proved to be sufficiently reliable. No attempt was made to choose items which could be arranged in some progressive order of intensity. An ordered sequence was not necessary for our purpose, nor did we attempt fine gradations of weighting. Measurements of attitude, in our experience, have not yet reached a degree of precision where much, if anything, would be added by weighted systems of scoring. The scales used in our study were scored by counting one mark for each favourable item and minus one for each unfavourable item endorsed. Of course, the real criterion was not 'favourableness' which would have been a subjective and arbitrary standard, imposed by the authors, but the positive or negative loading of the item in the traditional-versus-radical component. For what we were trying to measure was movement along that axis.

Reliability of the scales

If a list of items is used as a means of estimating a single quality, in this case political allegiance, one needs to be sure that all the items are measuring the same thing. Clearly there is not much point in retaining items that are not. The question is really whether the items are a good representation of the attitude universe we were sampling.

One way of putting this question to the test is to divide the scale into two halves, to work out separate scores for each half and then compare them. If they are much the same we can assume that the two halves are measuring the same dimension.

Using the Spearman-Brown split-half formula, we tested the two attitude scales on each party and each leader, with the following results:

Scale	Reliability Coefficient
Conservative Party	·89
Labour Party	·87
Leader (Mr Macmillan)	·87
Leader (Mr Gaitskell)	·86

The similarity between these coefficients is quite extraordinary. They were based on responses in the main study. If anything, they underline the universality of the traditional-versus-radical factor. If there are subsidiary factors which would not divide equally between two halves of the test, as was the case here, the split-half reliability measure would be reduced.

A further indication of the general reliability of the measures is given by a comparison between the attitude scores and the item endorsements before and after the General Election campaign. We very much doubt whether one person in a hundred would remember the particular items he had endorsed three weeks before, not having any expectation of being asked a second time, and with the whole Election campaign intervening. Yet the close similarity of the two groups of scores (see page 145) is quite remarkable – evidence both of the stability of attitudes and the broad reliability of the measures.

As a check on the possibility that items which appeared early in the scale would be given more attention than those at the end, interviewers were instructed to use two lists of attitude (and also national issue) items, one being in reverse order to the other, and to present them alternately. Thus, half the results were obtained from scales running in one order, and the other half from scales running in reverse order. A comparison of the two affords some check on scamped work by interviewers or hasty responses by electors. The lists were printed on cards which were handed to each informant. The interviewer then read out each item from his check sheet while the informant read it on the card and decided whether or not he believed it to be true. It was found that there was no significant difference between the two sets of items – in fact the ratio of items placed at the extreme where possible differences would be greatest, and those in the centre of the scales, was $1 \cdot 03:1$. Even the most discrepant item was well within the normal probability fluctuations: χ^2 (corrected) for the most discrepant item was $1 \cdot 65$ ($P = \cdot 20$) or a one-in-five chance of a random effect.

One important difference did appear between the evidence of the pre-election attitude studies and that of the main study, and one that is methodologically interesting. It was found that the percentages of endorsement of the items obtained by the doorstep interviewing method in the main study were consistently higher than those obtained within the groups. The ratio was exactly $7:5$ and was constant for high and low endorsements, for favourable and unfavourable items, and for those concerning each party. The regression is strictly linear. There is probably a tendency for a person who is being interviewed on the doorstep to give the benefit of the doubt to an item over which there may be uncertainty, whereas the member of a *group* would probably leave the item if he was not sure of his answer. A comparison between the two sets of figures provides some considerable check on the reliability of the group material. Half the figures are within 2 per cent of each other, allowing for this regression factor, and few are widely discrepant.

The validity of the scales

The acid test of a scale of political attitudes is whether it can accurately predict voting behaviour. Or so it might be thought. In practice, people have been known to vote aberrantly or to vote against their fundamental convictions because of some temporary dissatisfaction. Certainly this might be true of by-elections. But it is hard to believe that at a General Election such people are more than a tiny minority.

We have compared attitude scores recorded immediately before the General Election campaign with the voting on polling day. Each person in the sample recorded one score for the Conservative Party and another for the Labour Party. As a basis for prediction, we compared, in each case, the party receiving the higher score with the party for which the person voted. The correlation between the two, taking the *post*-election attitude scores, being ·98 (r_t) or ·92 (r_{phi}). What this amounts to, in practical terms, is that out of every hundred voters whose attitude scale pointed to a Labour vote only one would vote Conservative, and out of every hundred with a Conservative attitude seven would vote the other way. The two party leader scales correlate with voting behaviour to the extent of ·93 (r_t).

The predictive value is really greater than is indicated by this division, for we could put a probability value on likelihood of voting in a certain direction according to the *intensity* of the attitude score. In the case of those electors with borderline scores we would be doubtful about their voting, and in most cases the few errors in prediction would be found to lie within this group.

CHAPTER III

Political Images

The term 'party image' has been on the lips of the party leaders, of the newspaper columnists, and of the many political commentators who have been discovering the reasons why Labour lost the 1959 election. The image was regarded as a projection cast by the party persuaders or by circumstances on to the minds of the electorate. A false move, or an inappropriate slogan, could distort the image and might even lose an election. 'We dinted our own image by this attempt to defend ourselves against the accusation of increasing income tax', said Mr Crossman[1] in a broadcast.

The concept is not new. Milne and Mackenzie[2] were discussing it at the 1951 election; Benney and Geiss[3] were speaking of the 'class image of a party' in 1950; Lazarsfeld uses it in *The People's Choice*, and as long ago as 1908 Graham Wallas[5] was referring to a 'party image'. What is new, it seems, is the extent to which the image is now regarded as something capable of being created, through all the channels of information and persuasion. In this respect it carries over the assumptions of advertisers who study the delineation and creation of 'brand-images'. A brand-image is defined by one motivation-researcher as 'a characteristic set of feelings, ideas and beliefs associated with a brand through its presentation, including advertising, and its performance'.[6] Research enables one to bring 'the product more nearly into line with the non-user image'.[7] The criterion of success is not the creation of an image which perfectly represents the product, but the adaptation of the image and, if necessary, the product to what the public will buy. The application of this principle to politics is, of course, opportunism. The new departure is, perhaps, the widespread use, over the years leading up to the 1959 General Election, of advertising media and other means of mass communication to produce a party image that would be acceptable. Butler and Rose[8] observe that 'before the election the Conservative Party engaged in a public relations campaign on a scale that was altogether new to British politics'. To be effective, they argue, such a projection must play upon those aspects of a party's 'personality' which are already known, and, in part, accepted, leaving unnoticed the less satisfactory features. They claim that the Conservative Party modified its advertising campaign, before the election, to conform to particular interests among the electorate, as revealed in market research surveys. In a post-election broadcast discussion,[9] R. H. S. Crossman said: 'He [Mr Gaitskell] had created his own image. All we did was to make quite sure that there was room for the image to develop. What we did quite consciously work on was the image of the party.'

Advertising techniques seek to merge the appeal of a product into some basic human need, in such a way that potential customers may be inclined to believe that the product is to some extent satisfying the basic need. For example, most women want to look beautiful. Advertisements for a certain soap will claim that it offers 'a beauty treatment'. Many women will buy the soap without necessarily believing its claims. A woman who has just used the soap for the first time might look in the mirror and, seeing a clean and well-towelled face, feel that her skin is a little more attractive, perhaps as a result of some ingredient in the soap. She will then continue to buy the soap. She may even forget why she first gave it a trial. Whether there is anything in the advertiser's claims or not, so long as the product is associated with the satisfaction of a need in such a way that one can never be sure that it has *not* contributed to that satisfaction, it will very likely continue to sell. In much the same way, people want to be prosperous. They may believe that they are not noticeably worse off than they were five years ago, and will be willing to take on trust the assumption that they are on the way to prosperity.

The advertising of marketed goods does produce results, and advertisements on television appear to have been highly successful. It is often assumed that the projection of political images could be no less successful. This assumption overlooks one vital difference between brands of goods and political parties. Public attitudes towards advertised products are fairly tolerant; on political questions they are protected by deep convictions and resistances. This is not to suggest that the defences could not be breached or that political attitudes may not be modified by persuasion and even advertising. But the process of attrition would presumably have to be a long one.

The present study can throw little light on the modification of political attitudes over a long period of time. It is concerned with shifts of opinion during the short and highly abnormal period of the

General Election campaign. In order to record movements of that sort, an attempt was made to explore political attitudes and to construct scales representing some features of the party and leader images.

How do people 'see' their party? In terms of a set of principles? As an organization pledged to carry out a certain programme? As a social movement to which one belongs by birth or by adoption? As an organization behind a group of leaders in whom one has confidence? As a projection on a national scale of people one knows locally? Or as an organization whose values happen to coincide broadly with one's own? No doubt the concept varies widely between individuals. And no doubt so-called subjective and objective factors enter into it. The chances are high that the son of a miner will support the Labour Party and that the son of a company director will support the Conservative Party. And although the criteria by which judgments are formed may largely be conditioned by background and upbringing, people are willing to view a party's record and programme dispassionately, if only in occasional moments of revelation or despair!

A person's decision to support a particular party is not changed often, or overnight. Previous studies in religious, political and social fields have produced evidence of the stability of attitudes. They have also shown that where an attitude exists aggregations of ideas and associations are accumulated around it. For most voters, a considerable body of associations appears to have been built up around the chosen party; loyalty is generated, which may also be linked with other loyalties to one's class, one's neighbours, one's workmates, profession, family or friends. How, then, can an amalgam of so many deep-seated experiences and often unconsciously felt associations be described as an image?

Our attempt to find an answer to this question was an empirical one. We did not set out to test any theories about social attitudes, or about the new status expectations of the upper working class, or to look for evidence of what the political parties were trying to project. We started with a clean slate, taking down the evidence from electors, individually and in groups, of their impressions, opinions and beliefs about the political parties and the two principal leaders. All our subsequent analysis stemmed from this source. Of course, empiricism is itself an attitude and we were very conscious that at many stages in the investigation decisions had to be taken, systems of analysis selected and interpretations made, all of which were bound to be subjectively affected. In the later stages of the analysis, when we were searching for underlying unitary elements in the great network of verbal expressions of opinion, we depended on a form of factor analysis. All that such a method can produce is a set of constructs or hypotheses, which still have to be interpreted. We lay no claim to having discovered general truths about the nature of political images which would stand comparison with the firm findings of research in the physical or biological sciences. We have simply identified tendencies for groups of opinions to be associated with each other in the expressions of electors. Nevertheless, this is not an impressionistic study; its raw material is entirely derived from the electors themselves; and its exploratory methods, though open to objection from some quarters, are capable of verification and, judging by the predictive powers of the resulting scales, they are to be preferred to introspective or subjective classifications. A fuller account of the actual methods employed is set out in Chapter II, and we will now turn to the findings.

We are assuming then that party images are sets of mental associations common to given sections of the population. They may constitute attitudes which, as Thurstone said, 'lie behind opinions and behaviour'.[10] If they do, they will be relatively stable and will have what Allport described as a 'slippery propensity of accommodating themselves'[11] to rational attack. What such attitudes represent in terms of mental processes is not known. They remain inferences, however much their description is clothed in scientific terminology, but unless they are admitted, as Allport says, 'it becomes impossible to account satisfactorily for either the consistency of any individual's behaviour, or for the stability of any society'.[12]

Some general attitudes

At the preliminary stage of the analysis, one began to notice features that recurred in almost identical form in each subsequent phase of the inquiry. One was the tendency for electors to express some criticism and some appreciation of both major parties, and at the same time to hold firm to a deep loyalty to one party. Another was the habit of downing the opposing party with a single phrase: 'too much nationalization' about Labour, or 'looking after the rich' about Conservatives. A third was the demand for a clear, consistent and firm policy from any party.

The qualities expected in a political leader were much the same among supporters of all parties. They may be classed under three heads. First, personal qualities like 'honest and sincere', 'intelligent', 'a good speaker', 'well educated' and 'straightforward'. Secondly, leadership qualities, such as 'strong willed', 'able to speak out', and 'not afraid to make unpopular decisions'. Thirdly, aspects of general policy were mentioned, including 'fair to all classes', 'interested in the welfare of ordinary people', 'peace loving' and the like. This threefold division was later confirmed and extended by the computer analysis.

The outlines of the political images were derived from analyses of electors' endorsements of selected lists of opinions about the parties and their leaders. The extent of these endorsements can be seen in the percentages listed in Tables 60-65 in Appendix G.

The traditional-versus-radical component

In the whole sample, with both the Conservative Party and the Labour Party material, the largest common factor appears in the endorsement of the majority of the favourable items and the avoidance of the majority of the unfavourable items. At a first impression it seems to be a measure of blind loyalty or morale, indicating either support for or opposition to the party concerned and separating party supporters from party opponents. But a second element cross-classifies the first, as though it were arranging the items along a second dimension. This provides clues to the meaning of the analysis. When we compare the Conservative Party with the Labour Party factors we see the same pattern, as it were, in reverse. In the Conservative Party image the attitude statements converge on to item 5 ('Really respects British tradition') with item 9 ('Stands mainly for the upper class') not far away.* This, then, we have called a *loyalty to tradition* component. We are not using the term in any evaluative sense, favourable or unfavourable. Attitude analysis has to work on approximations, and the term 'traditional' is the best we can find to express a complex of ideas. These include continuity in the social order, and respect for those who appear to be at the top of the social hierarchy.

In the Labour Party image these same items are at the far end of the distribution, and the point of convergence is represented by item 14 ('Stands mainly for the working class'), item 11 ('Would extend

* The item numbers refer to those in the tables in Appendix G.

the welfare services'), and item 1 ('Would try to abolish class differences'). We may call this a *loyalty to radicalism or reform* component. 'Radical' is not a very satisfactory term for a complex that seems to imply changing or challenging the established order, principally for the benefit of what is described as the working class, but its use has strong precedents in earlier work on social attitudes.

As the two components may be regarded as opposite poles of a single system, they are described as a *traditional-versus-radical axis*, but we must remember that to a large extent they represent blind allegiances. In the reactions to the two leaders we also find a similar component. This group of factors accounts for about 45 per cent of all the variability in response.

This, then, is a general tendency which is common to most if not all of the expressions of opinion about the parties and the leaders. As well as identifying the underlying unitary factors, the analysis was able to show how far any particular statement of opinion was 'loaded' with the factors, for they may vary quite considerably. In this case, all the items are fairly strongly identified with the first and largest factor and there is little point in going into small differences in the subsidiary factors. When we turn to the further features of political images *within the separate groups of party supporters* we shall find considerable variation, on the basis of which we were able to select some items and reject others for our final scale.

As the same items convey both the traditional and the radical aspects, according to whether they are endorsed or not endorsed or are favourable or unfavourable, they have the advantage of being able to serve as one single scale which could be used, and was used, to measure attitudes to either party. In the same way the leader items were used to measure attitudes to both party leaders.

Does this common element in the party images only affect Conservative and Labour Party supporters? And if they change their allegiance to one or other of the major parties, do their attitudes strengthen correspondingly in the appropriate direction? On a scale used at a later stage in this study, ranging from $+5$ down to -4, the average Conservative attitude towards his own party is recorded at $+3 \cdot 1$, and towards the Labour Party it was $-1 \cdot 2$. The average Labour supporter is more moderate in his support and less sharp in his hostility, his position on the scale being $+2 \cdot 7$ to his own party and $+0 \cdot 2$ towards the Conservative Party. If we take these two spans as frames of reference the average *Liberal* attitude to each major party is almost exactly one third of the score of that same party's supporters, being $+1\cdot4$ to the Conservative Party, and $+0\cdot8$ to the Labour Party. This does not mean that the Liberal Party has no separate entity in the public mind. But taken with the other evidence (on issues and policies) it suggests that the lines of force in the political field run between two poles and not three, and affect those outside the major party groups no less than the supporters.

This finding has some affinity with the work of M. Johnson, H. J. Eysenck,[13] and M. Sanai, though there are important points of difference. Eysenck's analyses have produced a common factor which he calls 'radicalism-conservatism' as basic to general social attitudes. A second factor of practical-versus-theoretical attitudes (William James's 'tough-minded' and 'tender-minded') does not appear directly in our data, though there are suggestions of something like it in Conservative attitudes to Mr Macmillan.

M. Johnson,[14] working as did Eysenck and Sanai in a group at University College, London, under the direction of Professor Sir Cyril Burt, analysed some attitude material and found a 'Radical-Conservative' common factor which 'included moral and religious as well as political and economic beliefs'. M. Sanai,[15] factorized thirty statements on social, political and religious topics given to 250 students. His first and strongest factor he described as 'heterodoxy-versus-orthodoxy', or, as suggested by Burt, 'alterationism' and 'preservationism'. He showed that a person who was orthodox or traditional in politics tended to be much the same in religion, ethics and other social problems. The value of such related studies is that they help to fill out the meaning of the factor.

Those who are accustomed to thinking of party images as single, clear-cut profiles, may find some difficulty in accepting two or three separate elements, each with its distinctive meaning, and sometimes apparently contradicting each other in the sense that one is favourable and the other unfavourable. Psychological analyses of abilities and personality traits commonly reveal patterns of this sort. Closer examination will show that any contradictions are only apparent; the factors are quite independent of each other.

The Conservative Party image (*among its own supporters*)

The Conservative Party image that emerges can be described in terms of three factors or components, the strongest being the first, accounting for 19 per cent of the variability; the other two represent 9 per cent each.

1. *A national component*
This idea comes out most strongly in statements like: 'Out for the nation as a whole' (15), 'Fair treatment for all races and creeds' (19), 'Would extend the welfare services' (11), and, oddly, 'Stands mainly for the working class' (14).

2. *A strength component*
This element is examplified by negatives of critical statements implying that the Conservative Party has no internal squabbling (3), a clear policy (20), keeps its promises (18) and does not talk too much (2). The statement 'would really work to prevent a nuclear war' (10) also comes within this group.

3. *Individualism*
This component implies that the Party 'will give more chances to the individual who wants to better himself' (8), 'would get things done in a forthright way' (4), and 'would try to abolish class differences' (1). It merges, not illogically, into statements concerned with the material well-being of the individual: 'out to raise the standard of living for the man in the street' (16), 'would make the country more prosperous' (23) and 'would keep prices down' (17).

It is not suggested that the elector is at all conscious of these three elements or that every party supporter necessarily expresses them equally. In all, they account for about 37 per cent of the variation in opinions. Even after allowing for the considerable effect of the traditional-versus-radical element this still allows some freedom for individual opinion, and, therefore, for the items to have some specific meaning.

A further analysis of electors' individual reactions shows that all three elements in the Conservative Party image are very widely distributed among its supporters. This means that most Conservative supporters express all three elements in their projections of what the party means to them. Five attitude items most closely associated with each factor were examined for the analysis. The second element, representing strength, was expressed only through the non-endorsement of critical items, but as some of the people who did not endorse these items would have been undecided about them, the component is certainly less widespread than appears from the figure of 99 per cent in the following table:

TABLE 1

Percentage of Conservatives endorsing one or more items strongly representing each component of Conservative Party image

Conservative Party image component	%
National	79
Strength	99
Individual rights	92

It happens that some of the items which convey these common factors are also those which are most widely endorsed by Conservative supporters. Common opinions are usually part of the common 'image' but it would be a mistake to regard the most common opinion as epitomizing the image. The meaning of a heavily endorsed item could be quite specific and have no implication which it shared with other items.

The Conservative Party inverse image (among Labour Party supporters)

We carried out a separate analysis of the attitudes of Labour supporters towards the Conservative Party. Again, as we had supposed, the traditional-versus-radical feature disappeared through being controlled by the selection of the sub-sample. Three distinct groupings can be seen when the three factors are plotted out. Again, the first is much the strongest.

1. *A strong national element*
This finds expression in such statements as 'Out for the nation as a whole' (15), 'Would really work to prevent a nuclear war' (10), 'Would get things done in a forthright way' (4), 'Will give more chances to the individual, etc.' (8).

2. *An upper class party*
In a sense, this is a critical element. It is conveyed in statements like

'Stands mainly for the upper classes' (9), (*Not*) 'Stands mainly for the working class' (14), 'Has no clear policy' (20), 'More interested in people abroad than at home' (7) (which is probably read as 'not interested in people at home' in this context), and 'Don't keep to their promises' (18).

3. *For prosperity*
Three items convey this element: 'Would make the country more prosperous' (23), 'Out to raise the standard of living for the man in the street' (16), and 'Would keep prices down' (17). Associated with it is the view that the Conservative Party 'Would extend the welfare services' (11). The Labour man's image of the Conservative Party is seen to have favourable features. There is no suggestion here that it is primarily prosperity that attracts, though it does play a small part. The image has features in comon with what Conservative supporters see in their own party. In brief, it implies that the Labour voter regards the Conservative Party as an instrument of the upper classes, acting in the national interest to a large extent.

The Labour Party image (among Labour supporters)

The analysis produced three component features within the image of the Labour Party.

1. *The betterment of the common people*
This, the strongest element, accounting for some 27 per cent of the variance, implies that the Labour Party is 'out to raise the standard of living for the man in the street' (16), stands for 'fair treatment for all races and creeds' (19), 'will give more chances to the individual' (8), 'stands mainly for the working class' (14), 'would extend the welfare services' (11), 'would keep prices down' (17), and 'would make the country more prosperous' (23). As will be seen in Table 2 these are also some of the most frequently endorsed items.

2. *A divided party*
Although this may be regarded as an expectation of unity and, to some extent, strength, this component produces strong criticism of the party. From so few statements it is difficult to delineate the feature with any precision: on the face of it, the items represent a striving for unity, and some sense of disillusionment, but they may also represent

an authoritarian trait within the make-up of the ordinary man which also appears, to some extent, among Conservative supporters. The items concerned are: 'Too much internal squabbling' (3), 'Don't keep to their promises' (18), 'They have a bad past record' (13), and 'Talks too much' (2). Notice that items 6 ('Too much afraid of America') and 20 ('Has no clear policy') are also within this component.

3. *The nation*

A third component is inferred from the analysis. The distribution of the items in Figure 1 (conforming so closely to the sides of a spherical triangle) suggests a further component beyond item 22. As one moves away from the corner identified with the first factor, which is pretty closely associated with improved conditions for the working class, one finds item 15 ('Out for the nation as a whole'), item 5 ('Really respects British tradition') and finally item 22 ('Keeps too rigidly to the party line'). This seems to express national, as distinct from class, expectations.

As with the Conservative Party image, the items most frequently endorsed by supporters of the Labour Party were often those that are strongly identified with common factors in the attitude:

TABLE 2

Percentage endorsement of Labour Party attitude items by Labour supporters

	%
'Would really work to prevent a nuclear war'	82
'Out to raise the standard of living for the man in the street'	81
'Stands mainly for the working class'	78
'Would extend the welfare services'	75
'Fair treatment for all races and creeds'	72
'Would try to abolish class differences'	70

The question arises, how are these three image components distributed? Are they universal among Labour supporters or are they confined to different groups of people, or both? We can find the answer to this question by looking at the endorsements of those items which are most strongly identified with each common element. It turns out that all three factors are rather widespread, as the following table shows:

TABLE 3
Percentage of Labour Party supporters endorsing one or more items strongly representing each component of Labour Party image

Labour Party image component	%
Betterment of common people	87
Divided party	61
The nation	74

The second, critical element, although not very strongly expressed, is fairly widely distributed throughout the Labour voters. Like other critical factors, it is inversely related to the positive ones. Those who voice it more strongly endorse fewer of the items in the main element, and this tendency is consistent.

One wonders who these more critical supporters are. An examination of the results of the main study shows that they are in no way unrepresentative of the Labour supporters as a whole. The distribution between men and women, over the age range and in occupations, is completely normal for this population. Even when one isolates the 8 per cent of the main sample who endorse both of the two most critical items in this component, no trend appears. It has been suggested that the Labour Party is losing support from the status-seeking upper working class, especially those in the new housing areas, but there is no evidence here that such people are the ones who are critical of the party. All grades of occupations of electors living in all types of housing are represented. A few jobs, taken at random from the 'critics', will illustrate the point: night boilerman, leather dresser, bricklayer, worsted mender, a retired driller, a railway labourer, an oxygen dispenser, a clerk/accountant, a schoolteacher, a blacksmith and works inspector.

The Labour Party inverse image (among Conservative supporters)

Among Conservatives, the Labour Party has a rather blurred image. There are common factors, and they account for about 34 per cent of the variation between endorsements. Again, one must not forget the underlying traditional-versus-radical element which is eliminated here. Two broad groupings can be discerned:

1. *Weakness*

This comes out in items reflecting the absence of a clear policy (20), failure to keep their promises (18), too much of the party line (22), too much talk (2), and fear of America (6).

2. *Not a national party*

This factor has positive and negative aspects. Positively it identifies the Labour Party with the working class (14), being too free with public money (21), and taking nationalization too far (12); negatively it regards the Labour Party as not respecting British tradition (5 negative), suppressing the individual (8 negative), not representing the nation as a whole (15 negative), and not being fair to all races and creeds (19 negative). Some favourable items are endorsed by minorities, but no favourable feature appears in the general image.

Here again, the representative items are also endorsed very widely: against nationalization, 80 per cent; too free with public money, 76 per cent; and too much squabbling, 75 per cent.

The Gaitskell image (among Labour supporters)

The traditional-versus-radical factor is as evident in the attitudes to the leaders as it is to the parties. As much as 42 per cent of the variation in response towards Mr Gaitskell, and 48 per cent towards Mr Macmillan, come under this head. The leader becomes identified with the party and to that extent wears its coat.

As with the parties, too, totally different patterns of response are seen in the attitude factors for Labour as compared with Conservative supporters.

1. *The complete leader*

An array of nine qualities makes up the strongest element in Mr Gaitskell's image. He is here regarded as strong (6, 20, 23), clever (5), well educated (14), great himself (2), concerned with Britain's greatness (28), and concerned with rich and poor alike (25).

2. *Personally trusted*

A separate group of descriptive qualities also contribute to the picture of the Labour leader: kindly (15), humorous (21), straightforward (7), fairminded (11) and honest (19).

3. *An unsuitable person*

This component appears to fall into two groups. Both are critical. One, which is at the opposite end of the axis producing the leadership factor, suggests that Mr Gaitskell is unsuitable (10), not strong enough (4, 22), relies too much on those around him (29). The other group is more hostile and speaks of him as: not sincere (18), not pleasing (9), out of touch (26), looking to the past (24), and too full of his own importance (17).

Are all three components of the Gaitskell image present in every Labour supporters' response or are some confined to limited groups? One can get some idea of the way they are distributed by taking the five items most strongly associated with each component (through its factor loading, not its proportion of endorsement), and seeing how far they are endorsed by Labour supporters in the sample.

TABLE 4

Percentage of Labour supporters endorsing one or more items strongly representing each component of Gaitskell image

Gaitskell image component	%
1. Complete leader	88
2. Personal trust	75
3. Unsuitable	27·5

The critical factor is seen to be confined to a minority of Labour supporters, and it increases in intensity as the others decrease. The three out of every four Labour supporters who do not share any of the critical views endorse over half the favourable items towards their leader. Those who endorse 70 per cent of the critical items only endorse, on average, 28 per cent of the favourable. And those who endorse all the critical items support none of the favourable ones.

The Gaitskell inverse image (among Conservatives)

Two elements can be distinguished. The first, which is much the stronger, accounting for 29 per cent of the variation in response, is critical and describes him as weak (4, −6, 22, −23), narrow in outlook (12, 13, 24), and personally unsatisfactory (17, 18). It does give him a point or two, however, as practical (8), clever (5), and a good speaker (16).

The second element in the Conservative view is favourable, on the whole, regarding him as honest (19), straightforward (7), humane (15), and concerned with the welfare of the people (1).

The Macmillan image (among Conservative supporters)

Of all the political images, Mr Macmillan's has the largest common components. Apart from the traditional-versus-radical factor which is here held constant, the three common factors account for 50 per cent of the variation. Again, three quite distinct features emerge.

1. *A strong leader*

The concentration of five 'tough' items at one end of the axis, when the underlying factors are plotted out graphically, makes this component clear. 'A strong leader' (20), putting the good of his country first (30), 'strong enough to make even unwelcome decisions' (23), strong willed (6), 'practical and down to earth' (8) and the negative of 'not really strong enough' are the items concerned.

2. *A man of culture*

In this component, Mr Macmillan tries to restore Britain's greatness (28), he is humane (15), 'has wide political interests' (27), is 'well-educated' (14) and 'speaks very well' (16). These last two form the centre of what may be described as a 'cultural' factor. And item 14 is the most widely endorsed among Conservative followers, as many as 91 per cent supporting it. With them are associated qualities of honesty (19), straightforwardness (7), a concern for all classes of the community (25) and an interest in their welfare (1). These two factors produce something not unlike Eysenck's 'tough-tender' social attitude.

3. *An unsuitable person*

This third component is similar in its composition to the third feature of Mr Gaitskell's image. At the extreme of this axis is found the statement 'not the best man in his party for the job' (10), and close by are statements about relying too much on others (29), being only interested in one class (12), full of his own importance (17), looking too much to the past (24), and out of touch (26).

What is the source of this criticism, and is it confined to a disgruntled minority in the Conservative following, or is it a general undercurrent throughout Conservative attitudes? The two items most widely endorsed among the several identified with this component give some indication. They are 'only interested in one class' (12) and 'out of touch with the needs of ordinary working people' (26). Possibly Mr Macmillan's following is weakest on the working-class fringe of his supporters. A further attempt to isolate the source of this critical element was made by an analysis of the questionnaires completed by Conservative supporters.

The five items most closely associated with each of the three components of the Macmillan image were endorsed as follows:

TABLE 5

Percentage of Conservatives endorsing one or more items strongly representing each component of Macmillan image

Macmillan image component	%
1. A strong leader	90
2. A man of culture	98
3. An unsuitable person	29

Thus, it is only a minority (as with the Gaitskell image) who represent this critical component and they do not endorse many of its items. There is an inverse ratio between support for the favourable components and endorsement of the critical one, as was found in the Gaitskell image. The three out of every four Conservatives who do not endorse any critical item, support 68 per cent of the favourable items, on average. Those who agree with 70 per cent of the critical items only endorse 17 per cent of the favourable, and the few who endorse all the former endorse none of the latter.

The Macmillan inverse image (among Labour supporters)

A novel feature arises in the Labour supporters' image of Mr Macmillan. Here the appreciative element is dominant, totalling 21 per cent of all the variance, and finds expression in such statements as 'practical and down to earth' (8), 'really honest' (19). He is seen as a straightforward (7), humorous (21), humane (15), peace-loving (3) and patriotic (28, 30) figure.

A second, critical element is hostile, regarding Mr Macmillan as puffed up (17), insincere (18), looking backwards (24). There is also more than a suggestion that he is not the best person in his party to be the leader (10), and is not strong enough (22, 29).

Political attitudes in general

Out of the considerable mass of material that was fed into the computer, some general features of the images have emerged, which suggest profiles of the parties and their leaders and recur in one image after another. The image is still far from a sharply defined outline. The evidence is still too slight to permit anything like a general theory of political attitudes being put forward, but it may be worthwhile reviewing some of the common features.

Basically, responses to most political situations appear to be governed by the position of the individual on a single traditional-radical scale. The positions of Liberals and uncommitted electors can be found in an intermediate position on this same line. If the elector is of Conservative bent he will look for national unity, strength and cultural features in his party and its leadership. He will expect to find disunity and a narrow, class preoccupation in his opponents. He will also believe their leaders to be culturally inferior. Conservative supporters, for instance, voted Mr Macmillan as 'well educated' to the extent of 91 per cent; Mr Gaitskell only 59 per cent!

If the elector is a Labour supporter he will think primarily of a will to improve the lot of the common man and of unity (or strength through unity). When he looks at his political opponents he will see strength and national unity, as it seems to him. Their leaders may represent a class to which he does not belong and which he resents, but he will grant that they are culturally well endowed if not superior. 77 per cent of Labour supporters believe Mr Macmillan to be 'well educated', but only 68 per cent suppose as much of Mr Gaitskell.

To the ordinary elector, prosperity means more than creature comforts; it means something approaching security of employment and the means of obtaining a reasonable minimum of food, shelter and clothing for himself and his dependents. Yet, contrary to what many political commentators suppose, the means of obtaining such physical benefits do not figure as main determinants in political attitudes. They appear, but only as weak elements in the Conservative Party image. The basic factors are associated with what the elector believes to be the needs of the community as a whole and of the under-privileged in particular; they are related to the traditions of social justice rather than social benefits.

How does it come about that political attitudes in the two major party groups are so different from each other? Labour attitudes to their opponents are often appreciative, whereas Conservative attitudes to Labour are almost invariably hostile. The easy answer would be to say that each side gets what it deserves, but an impression that is strongly borne in on one when meeting a cross-section of electors or studying their reactions is that the difference is deeply rooted, perhaps in the structure of society itself. The Conservative Party, in all its works, is identified with society as we find it, with its industrial framework, its cultural inheritance, its history as a major power. It does not put forward any programme of large radical changes in the social order; indeed its policies are often general reflections of social attitudes ('Stress the greatness and unity of Britain,' etc.) rather than concrete proposals for change. This is both its source of strength and its limitation. The natural forces of cohesion within society, working through the many agencies of communication, project and perpetuate such traditional values. Through countless channels, including television and the Press, the national and cultural values are daily circulated through the whole body of society.

One must expect a radical party to be socially ostracised to the extent that it challenges this system of traditional values. As is seen in the Labour Party, it may want to retain the values but challenge something of the economic system behind them. But the two are inextricably mixed in the minds of the average elector, or so it would seem from our findings, and radical campaigners are left with the problem of how to separate them and to create an alternative system of loyalties that is not automatically vetoed by the existing sanctions within the attitude field, as anti-national, anti-unity, or anti-culture. Yet they cannot move too far from their radical position for the centre of gravity of the Labour attitude, as it is seen in this analysis, lies in radicalism and is rooted in working class support. It is perhaps for some such reasons that the Conservative supporter sees in the Labour Party only ideas that challenge his own political faith, whereas the Labour Party supporter sees some elements in the Conservative Party with which he identifies himself (i.e. national and traditional appeals) and some which he rejects.

We have seen more than once, in the analysis of the political images, features indicating some degree of appreciation of points in favour of the party which electors do not support, and some considerable self-criticism within the body of party supporters. Although general self-criticism as represented in the images is usually confined to a minority of party supporters, some element of toleration and of a realistic acceptance of one's own party's limitations is probably characteristic of the British elector. On average every elector endorses at least one item in every nine either against his own party or in favour of the other.

This willingness to acknowledge virtue in the opposition is fairly equal in the two major parties. In the following table, five items, all appreciative, have been selected from the party attitude scales with the percentage of party supporters endorsing each item in *favour of the other party*:

TABLE 6

Endorsement of attitude items favourable to the opposite parties

Item	By Labour about Conservative %	By Conservative about Labour %
'Really respects British tradition'	51	17
'Will give more chances to the individual who wants to better himself'	15	15
'Would really work to prevent a nuclear war'	31	46
'Out for the nation as a whole'	21	15
'Fair treatment for all races and creeds'	19	33

The self-criticism is more evident in the ranks of Labour supporters and finds expression in the second main feature of the party image. The following items show the extent of this candour, among supporters of the two parties:

TABLE 7

Endorsement of attitude items critical of the party supported

Item	By Labour about Labour %	By Conservative about Conservative %
'Talks too much'	17	16
'Don't keep to their promises'	19	21
'Keeps too rigidly to party line'	22	12

POLITICAL IMAGES

What the parties were trying to project

To see whether the images the parties themselves were consciously attempting to project differed from those revealed by this study, three assessors analysed the scripts of the Party election broadcasts and agreed on a number of broad intentions which appear to lie behind the propaganda. These differed from the images in the minds of electors in two or three important respects. What the Conservatives were trying to project included two of the components of the Conservative Party image as we found it in the views of electors, but also stressed experienced leadership, capable of commanding respect abroad. The appeal to individualism in the electors' image was not stressed by the party.

The Labour Party projection included two of the three components from the electors' image, but excluded the important unity factor, which usually took the form of criticism of disunity. They stressed youth and vigour, and high ideals, which do not figure prominently in the image we have delineated. The traditional-versus-radical distinction which separates supporters of the two parties appeared only explicitly in the Conservative emphasis on tradition and continuity. To some extent, the Labour Party's case for improved social services might have complied with this radical requirement, but radicalism in the sense of an alterationist approach was not stressed.

In political communication, as in all perception, we tend to see only what we are looking for. In the short run it is idle for a party to put forward claims or to describe itself in terms which are greatly at variance with the picture the elector already has of its image. One can only build on what is already there. After all, the components of the images may represent realistic assessments.

CHAPTER IV

The Nature of the Campaign

As soon as the dissolution of Parliament was announced, the parties chose political programmes to put before the electors. Any analysis of the progress of the campaign must naturally be related to these programmes. For this purpose we took the Conservative Party's manifesto 'The Next Five Years', the Labour Party's 'Britain Belongs to You', and the Liberal Party's 'People Count'. The Conservative document dealt with twenty-two broad issues, grouped under the headings of:

  I. *Sharing Prosperity*
      The Pound   Unity
      Trade opportunities
 II. *Employment and Economic Change*
III. *Policy for Progress*
      Technical advance   Nationalised industries
      Modern roads   Public administration
      The Land
 IV. *Opportunity and Security*
      Education   Security and retirement
      Good housing   The use of leisure
      Good health   Liberty under the Law
  V. *Our Duty Overseas*
 VI. *Policy for Peace*
      United Nations   Armed forces
      Relations with Russia   Disarmament
      Our alliances   Nuclear tests

The Labour Party manifesto also rested on twenty-two issues described as:

The truth about production	Taxation – and Planned expansion
Ending poverty in old age	Local unemployment
Widows	The countryside
Education	Scotland, Wales and Northern Ireland
Housing	
Health	Who goes to the Summit
Leisure	The Rule of Law and the United Nations
Youth	
Private industry	The arms race

Public ownership Two worlds
The cost of living War against want
Consumer protection Our Socialist ethic

The Liberal Party's document stressed the point that the people's 'first desire is peace' and listed fourteen points in Liberal Policy:

The British H-bomb The countryside
Bring down taxes Spend on the roads
Cut prices Aid the pensioner
Invest in education Help the sick
Opportunity in industry Scotland and Wales
Industrial democracy Commonwealth partnership
Ownership for all Britain must lead

How far were the parties and the communication media successful in conveying these programmes to the electorate? The Party election broadcasts on radio and television were in the hands of the parties themselves and if what was said there did not adequately reflect the messages of the manifestoes, there must have been some reason for the divergences, or they have only themselves to blame. There were, in fact, one or two important differences between them, particularly in the broadcast emphasis on peace, but in general the programmes cover all the points of the party documents and with much the same degree of emphasis on particular items.

There is, of course, a great deal more to report during an election campaign than the messages of the original manifestoes of the parties, including the progress of the campaign itself. Speeches, press conferences, new disclosures of policy, criticism and counter-criticism are all part of the campaign, and by the time the contest is under way there seems some danger of the original declarations being swept aside in the swirling tides of controversy. Many of the irrelevances, the disputes between candidates and the personal aspects are swept up in the capacious columns of the Press. It is, perhaps, surprising that when these more trivial matters are left aside the newspaper coverage falls into much the same pattern as that of the two broadcasting services.

We reviewed the entire television campaign in the North. We covered every Party election broadcast, the special 'Hustings', 'Election Marathon' and other public debate programmes broadcast in

England, and the daily news bulletins throughout the period on both BBC and ITV. Six monitors, based on London, Nottingham, Oxford and Leeds, viewed the entire output in shifts, reporting on content, treatment and relevance from lists of policies and issues being used in the survey. Scripts of the party political broadcasts were made available by the BBC and the Granada TV Network and used for detailed analysis. The news bulletins, for which no scripts were available, were recorded on tape.

A similar analysis was made of the Party election broadcasts on sound radio, and of the reporting of the campaign in the national and local Press (see p. 75).

The main emphasis in the three media

Table 8 shows the proportions of time or space given to the various issues or policies raised during the campaign in the Press, television and sound radio. The newspaper analysis is based on all national daily, and three local, newspapers over three days (averaged per day). For this purpose the newspaper reports of purely personal stories, constituency news and the progress of the campaign itself have been excluded. The 362 column inches devoted to the *political* comment on 'the Jasper affair' are not included in the figure of 5·7 per cent shown against Press coverage of 'Productivity and economy' issues below. A total of 2,470 column inches was devoted to political items per day, in the Press. The percentages below for issues referred to in the TV Party election broadcasts, the Hustings TV programmes and the Sound Party broadcasts are based on the number of lines of script devoted to each, whereas the figures for the Other (special) TV programmes and the TV news bulletins are based on the number of references to each issue as percentages of all references.

Of the several issues on which the parties focused much attention, the question of peace was most discussed. It was only in the Press that it did not occupy the largest share of the space. The question of pensions did not stand out in the party manifestoes in the same way as it does in the table – it was one of the principal planks in the Labour Party platform and it was their emphasis, especially in the Party election broadcasts, which brought it to the front.

Since the Party election broadcasts were entirely controlled by the parties and were planned as a complete series, we can take it that the order of priority they show is what the parties themselves intended. A

TABLE 8

Issues reported and discussed in BBC and ITV television broadcasts, sound broadcasts and newspapers during the General Election campaign (in percentages of total time or space given to political items within each category)

Issue	TV Pty. el. b'sts %	Hustings TV %	Other TV %	TV news %	Sound pty. b'sts %	Press %
Permanent, peaceful settlement	15·2	19·9	14·9	16·6	13·2	11·1
Pensions	14·3	10·4	11·3	15·0	9·0	11·8
Foreign C'wealth & Colonial	13·1	12·1	11·3	7·0	14·5	11·1
Productivity & economy	10·0	8·4	11·3	16·0	7·7	5·7
Education	9·9	6·7	7·7	2·3	7·7	9·6
Employment	8·5	4·4	9·9	8·9	5·7	6·2
Agriculture	8·1	0·0	0·0	0·5	2·3	5·2
Housing	7·0	10·2	6·3	7·5	7·7	8·5
Prosperity	5·6	8·1	0·7	2·3	10·0	11·2
Social services	2·6	0·9	6·3	2·8	3·5	0·8
Cost of living	2·4	10·9	6·3	9·9	9·8	8·1
Transport, roads, etc.	1·6	0·0	1·4	0·0	1·0	1·3
Nationalization	0·9	0·1	5·6	6·1	4·0	5·5
Industrial relations	0·6	3·0	4·2	4·2	2·8	3·4
Others	0·2	4·9	2·8	0·9	1·1	0·5
	100·0%	100·0%	100·0%	100·0%	100·0%	100·0%

little more time was available on television than on sound radio (215 cf. 180 minutes), and it was known that the television audiences would outnumber by several times the radio audiences, so one would have expected the television output to receive the most careful attention and balancing. Elsewhere, in the 'Hustings' programmes, the news bulletins and in the Press, their messages had to submit to the prompting of an audience, or to a screening for 'news value'.

In the television Party election broadcasts the subjects of nationalization and industrial relations, which in our classification included strikes and the powers of the trade unions, were hardly developed at all. If these questions were decisive in turning the tide against the Labour Party, as some critics have alleged, it was not because of any emphasis in the parties' campaigns.

In the 'Hustings' programmes, where there was an audience of local constituents in the studio, and perhaps for that reason, the cost of living and housing are among the issues most discussed, whereas they were given less prominence in the parties' own broadcasts.

Differences between the television and sound radio Party programmes are odd. It is difficult to see why, if prosperity and the cost of living received so much more attention on sound radio, the subject of pensions should receive less, when the principal difference between the two audiences is that the sound (only) public includes more elderly people and more than twice as many retired people,[1] as the television audience. One would therefore have expected the pensions issue to have been stressed in this medium. The sound broadcasting pattern is remarkably close to that of the Press, perhaps because the contributions there were more easily changed from day to day and therefore reflected the ebb and flow of the campaign, much as the Press did. The sound broadcasts had some topicality. Scripts could be changed and rewritten up to the last minute. The television contributions were evidently taken more seriously by the parties, being planned more as a whole, and were less susceptible to day-to-day pressures. The theme of prosperity accounted for 11·2 per cent of newspaper space, and 10 per cent of sound Party broadcasting time on the radio, but it only occupied half this proportion in television Party broadcasts, only 0·7 per cent in special television programmes and 2·3 per cent of television news time. Was the subject more welcome to some audiences than to others? As the television news editors were under considerable pressure to be scrupulously fair (because of the Representation of the People Act and public scrutiny of their first election coverage) it is likely that the time allotted by them to prosperity was proportionate to the actual attention devoted by the party spokesmen in the field. The Press emphasis was no doubt the result of editorial decision and perhaps the radio speakers followed suit.

In the course of the campaign a challenge from one major party will often be met by a new line of attack from the other, and the real significance of some of the issues in the conflict only emerges in this way. The Press plays an important part in this development, probably more so than broadcasting, for the greater space it devotes to political matters and its topical approach provide a suitable forum for controversial debate. In the following outline sketch we trace something of the way the four main issues were developed and treated by the parties, by way of illustrating the nature of the campaign. In the case of the prosperity issue, the quotations are mostly taken from pro-Labour newspapers, and with the pensions debate they are drawn from the Conservative Press, because in both cases the positive arguments are probably familiar.

Prosperity

In his introductory message in the first paragraph of 'The Next Five Years', Mr Macmillan said 'Our policy can be simply stated: Prosperity and Peace'.

The Labour manifesto raised doubts about the genuineness of Tory prosperity in these words: 'The businessman with a tax-free expense account, the speculator with tax-free capital gains, and the retiring company director with tax-free redundancy payment due to a take-over bid – these people have indeed "never had it so good" .' (In the first budget of the newly elected Conservative Government, the Chancellor of the Exchequer, Mr Heathcoat Amory, attempted to meet some of these Labour criticisms by introducing new legislation to overcome tax evasion in the City.)

The Opposition and Liberal papers were quick to point out that present prosperity and content was a materialistic, and indeed an ignoble issue on which to fight an election. As *The Guardian* said in its leader on October 6 (shortly before Polling Day) 'We should not vote simply for our stomachs, but for a fair distribution of extra wealth.' Another typical comment from this newspaper was the report of an interview with Dr W. D. L. Greer, Bishop of Manchester, advising the electorate that 'simply to vote for our pocket is less than Christian', and adding, 'better austerity with freedom than security in a golden cage'.

In a leader on September 28 the *News Chronicle* said 'Mr Macmillan's great claim that we owe our prosperity to his party is downright over-sugaring of the pill we are asked to swallow. It is largely due to influences from outside which would have helped any party in power.'

The *Daily Herald*, in its rôle as the official Labour newspaper, ended its appeal to readers on October 6 by saying, in an editorial headed 'Prosperity', 'Put Britain straight and see right done to the British people. Let's have no second-class citizens here. Give *all* their fare share of expanding prosperity.'

Although at the time an impression was given that prosperity was stressed to the exclusion of other issues, in fact the amount of time and space devoted to this issue in the various media was only about 6·5 per cent. This proportion includes both the pros and cons of the 'prosperity and content' propaganda.

Immediately after Polling Day, the following question was put to West Leeds and Pudsey electors: 'Can you think of anything that has been in the news during the last three weeks which you think might have some effect on the way people voted?' It is unlikely that these answers, as they stand, represent the real factors in the situation. We can only, at best, say that they may serve as a guide to the thoughts that were in people's minds at the time of the election. Of the 60 per cent who answered this question wholly or in part, only 8 per cent of the Labour voters and 7·5 per cent of the Conservative voters specifically mentioned present prosperity and content as a factor affecting voting behaviour. Four other reasons were quoted more often, which were, in order of frequency: 'rash Labour promises', nationalization, strikes and trade unions (industrial relations), pensions in general (including support for an increased old age pension).

Electors in our sample were asked, both before and after the campaign, which national issues they thought were most important. In the list which was shown to electors, there was no actual reference to prosperity, but an item entitled 'Keep the cost of living down' was clearly relevant. The cost of living was the issue selected as of first importance, 67 per cent endorsing it in the pre-campaign interview and 74·8 per cent after Polling Day.

Second in importance was the question of peace (taking the two items 'A permanent peaceful settlement' and 'Control H-bomb production and testing' together). Pensions was third in order, being selected by 53·5 per cent.

The Press is a sensitive thermometer for gauging public reactions, except when editorial policies bias the selection of reports. On this occasion, the morning newspapers accurately and sensitively reflected these three major issues of the moment.[2]

Peace

'Prosperity and Peace', said Mr Macmillan, was the Conservative policy. But peace rather than prosperity was the single item given most space in political programmes, and was second only to Foreign, Colonial and Commonwealth questions in sound radio broadcasts. One notices that in the 'Hustings' programmes, where the presence of an audience of electors asking questions was likely to direct the attention of the candidates towards those on which the more interested party supporters felt most strongly, the peace question dominated the programmes with 19·9 per cent of time devoted to it (see Table 8).

In our analysis of the campaign coverage, the heading of 'A permanent peaceful settlement' included such topics as the Summit talks, Mr Macmillan's and Mr Gaitskell's visits to Moscow, disarmament and the Geneva talks on the possibility of ending the testing of nuclear weapons.

The total percentage of West Leeds and Pudsey electors who endorsed this issue of peace in its broadest sense was 64 per cent in the pre-election interview and 68 per cent afterwards.

Differences between the party arguments on this subject were largely confined to discussion as to who was most likely to succeed at the Summit talks. The subject was one on which the party leaders were understandably reluctant to introduce controversy. In the main, the Conservative argument, most often expounded by Mr Selwyn Lloyd, was, in the words of the party manifesto, 'Do you want your present leaders to represent you abroad?' On September 30, following the apparently successful Khrushchev-Eisenhower talks in Washington, Mr Macmillan stated that the date of the Summit meeting would be announced in a 'few days', and the *Daily Express* headlined the news from America as 'Macmillan's triumph'. A report from Washington that no date for the Summit had yet been agreed gave Mr Gaitskell the opportunity to claim that the Conservatives were using the Summit negotiations for political ends.

Pensions

The Labour Party's election programme included a number of pledges for social reform. These pledges perhaps created more problems than support, but were an expression of the Labour Party's view of itself as 'a party of conscience and reform'. This phrase was first used by 'Cassandra' of the *Daily Mirror* in one of the television Labour Party political broadcasts, and was picked up later by Mr Gaitskell who said he liked the phrase and thought it well expressed what the Labour Party stood for.

The main plank in the Labour platform was the promise immediately to raise the retirement pension by ten shillings a week. Labour discussion and elaboration of this issue, Conservative reaction and Press comment made pensions second only to peace as an election issue.

Other proposals on which the Labour Party committed itself were the working out of a universal superannuation scheme, the promise that £50 million a year would be spent on hospital building and development, and a scheme for other improvements and extensions of the Health Service.

Backing this programme of social reform, the economists of the Labour Party claimed that it could be achieved by a planned expansion of the economy, by reducing tax evasion, imposing a Capital Gains Tax, and by a diminution of waste in the armed forces. The Labour Party undertook not to increase taxation to meet the additional expenditure.

This promise not to increase taxation provoked a quick reaction from the Conservatives who were able to raise the cry of 'irresponsibility'. From this point onwards in the campaign, the Conservative speakers and Press stressed the two themes of 'rash Labour promises' and the danger of financial chaos and national bankruptcy which they claimed would result from such an increase in spending on the social services. The Conservative Research Department put the cost of Labour's programme to be found from revenue at a minimum of £750 million a year.

Typical statements on this subject from both sides of the political arena were: Mr Macmillan on September 27, reported in *The Sunday Times* as saying 'In many ways they (the Socialists) outbid us. They seem to have a lot of money to spend – your money of course. Don't be misled by the slick operators who offer you a scheme to get rich quick.' And again in the *Telegraph* on September 25 in a speech reported from Swansea, Mr Macmillan said he would 'make no auction of election pledges'.

On September 26 Mr Gaitskell said 'By dealing with expense accounts which involved £500 million a year, and with capital gains which totalled £2,000 million in the last six months and by a tax on expense accounts, a Labour Government could finance increases in the social services and at the same time cut taxation where the shoe pinched most'.

By this time the newspaper comment on the take-over bids and 'the Jasper affair' was at its height. Over the three days included in the newspaper content analysis (see below) more space was devoted to 'the Jasper affair', even in its limited political implications, than to any single issue in the party manifestoes. It was often suggested in the Press that political capital might be made of these events. The Labour Party speakers commented, particularly on the take-over bids, and the Conservatives also managed to turn the situation to account with such phrases as the 'Socialists want to make a take-over bid for Britain'.

At the same time it was suggested that the weight of authority behind the Conservative criticisms of 'rash Labour promises' was having some effect on the electorate. The *Daily Telegraph* said on September 28, 'the Labour promises may well defeat themselves, as more and more people come to enquire how they are to be paid for'.

On September 25 Lord Hailsham said, 'Labour's programme bore no relation to reality when the cost was added up. Which of the pledges is going to be broken? Is it their pledge not to put up taxes, or is it the pledge to carry out their programme, because they can't have their programme and their pledge not to put up taxes.'

And on October 7, Mr Maudling returned to the same point: 'Labour had produced a range of promises so expensive that to fulfil them would undermine our national resources.'

Foreign, Commonwealth and Colonial policies

The Labour manifesto, under the heading 'Two Worlds', summed up the Party's foreign, Commonwealth and colonial policy as follows: 'Two worlds, one white, well-fed and free, the other coloured, hungry and struggling for equality, cannot live side by side in friendship. In their attitudes to the colonial and ex-colonial peoples of Asia and Africa the Labour and Tory records stand in sharp contrast.'

Countering this statement, the Conservative manifesto, on the same theme, said, 'Our central aim in multi-racial countries is to build communities which protect minority rights and are free of all discrimination on grounds of race and colour.'

On television the parties devoted 13·1 per cent of time to discussions of these issues, and the Labour Party, in its programmes, included speakers like Father Trevor Huddleston to comment on the dangerous and difficult situation in South Africa.

The more serious papers gave the party policies on the subject an equal amount of coverage. In a long article on September 28, the *Telegraph* summed up the 'Colonial Challenge' as follows:

'A Conservative Government would be more aware of the economic and political dangers of forcing the pace. A Labour Government would be embarrassed by pressure from a section of its own members to go too fast. A Labour Government might win greater confidence from nationalist leaders in the colonies and have more influence over them. On the other hand, the same nationalist leaders might equally be tempted to expect too much too soon.'

The Times on September 25 set out the contrast between the past record of the party policies in Africa as follows:

Labour	*Conservative*
1. Local government reform	1. Introduction of qualified franchise in multi-racial societies
2. State controlled economic development	2. Suppression of Mau Mau
3. Publication of Watson Report	3. Exile of the Kabaka
4. Initiation of Central African Federation	4. Implementation of the Central African Federation
5. Exile of the Khamas	5. Return of the Khamas

In a television Party election broadcast on October 6, Mr Gaitskell represented the Labour Party's attitude as: 'putting on one side the old ideas of racial and national supremacy and recognizing that whatever a man's colour or race – be he African, Asian or European – the claim to equal status and equal consideration can't be denied any longer.'

As can be seen in Table 8, Foreign, Commonwealth and Colonial policy ranked high in the comparative analysis of all the means of communication. It was third in rank order in the television Party election broadcasts (13·1 per cent of the total), and in the Press coverage.

The television and radio coverage of the election
Political broadcasting in Britain began in the General Election of

1924 when the three party leaders, Baldwin, MacDonald and Asquith, gave single speeches. The decision to put on the broadcasts was taken by Reith (now Lord Reith) under considerable opposition from all sorts of institutions and interests. He argued that 'the utility of broadcasting as a medium of enlightenment is prejudiced owing to the ban upon such matters'.[3]

Three factors have shaped the development of political broadcasting. One, largely the achievement of Reith, was the idea that broadcasting was an agency for the service of the public and as such was concerned with all matters of public interest, and that absolute impartiality and safeguards against abuse were to be its unwritten law. As early as 1924, Reith wrote:

'It is probable that more debates will be held so that people may have an opportunity of listening to outstanding exponents of conflicting opinions on the great questions, political and social, which are today understood by a mere fraction of the electorate, but which are of such vital importance.'[4]

This principle, so hard at first to establish against an unimaginative departmental control and vested interests in other means of communication, was accepted, cautiously by the Crawford Committee, and later fully by the 1935 Ullswater Committee.

The second factor was the rule, laid down in 1927, that 'the BBC must not express in broadcasts its own opinion on current affairs or on matters of public policy'.[5] This same restriction was stated explicitly in the Television Act 1954 governing the conduct of Independent Television: 'the exclusion . . . from the programmes broadcast by them, of all expressions of their own opinion as to . . . matters of political or industrial controversy or relating to current public policy.'

The third determining factor is the Representation of the People Act 1949. The relevant part of this Act is Section 63 which states that no expenses shall be incurred 'with a view to promoting or procuring the election of a candidate' except by the candidate himself, his election agent and persons authorized 'in writing' by the agent. It states that the prohibition extends to expenses incurred in such activities as 'presenting to the electors the candidate or his views, or the extent or nature of his backing'. There is a proviso that this clause shall not be held to 'restrict the publication of any matter relating to the Election in a newspaper, or other periodicals'. Thus, exemption from the restrictions of this Section of the Act is expressly given to the Press, but not to broadcasting. There was clearly a danger that the television and sound broadcasting authorities might find themselves exposed to legal proceedings initiated by any candidate for having promoted the election of any other candidate who appeared in their programmes. It was, and still is, impossible for the BBC or the Independent Companies to act with the same freedom enjoyed by the Press. All they could do was to obtain legal advice on exactly how far they could go and to see that they went no further.

Because of the Act, candidates could not appear on television or radio unless all the other candidates in their constituencies were present. Even this arrangement was an expedient suggested by legal advisers as unlikely to provoke legal proceedings. On this basis Granada's 'Election Marathon' challenged the Act on a massive scale (see below). The BBC 'Hustings' programmes included speakers from three parties but they were chosen by the parties themselves, not the BBC, and were not announced as candidates for any particular division. It was even impossible for radio and television spokesmen to interview any election candidate, however eminent. With three minor exceptions noted below, the Act also prevented the television authorities from recording the speeches of any candidate (even the Prime Minister) in his own constituency. An amendment to the Act, exempting the broadcasting authorities from the provisions of Section 63, is clearly desirable.

The Party election broadcasts, by an arrangement going back to 1939, are worked out by agreement between the three main political parties, the BBC, the ITA and the Programme Companies. So much time is made available and it is then left to the parties to fill it as they choose, using the technical facilities of the broadcasting authorities as they wish. Any minority party qualifies for a broadcast only if it has fifty or more candidates in the field. The Government of the day, by custom, speaks first and last in the sequence. It was also agreed that one clear day should elapse between the last election broadcast and Polling Day.

A total of 215 minutes was allotted on television to the parties, to be divided between twelve broadcasts varying in length from ten to twenty minutes. In sound broadcasting 180 minutes of time were divided between nine broadcasts of fifteen minutes in the Home Service, and nine of five minutes in the Light Programme.

The 1959 General Election marked a new departure for the BBC.

Hitherto they had omitted from their news broadcasts any reports of election speeches and of the election campaign, and had excluded from their programmes all other material which might be held to influence the voter in the recording of his vote. On this occasion, possibly because of the challenge of a new situation with television so widespread, possibly because of support from political circles for a bolder policy, and possibly because of the plans which some of the Independent Companies were known to be making, they put on a series of controversial broadcasts and provided for full news coverage.

The BBC put out twelve controversial 'Hustings' programmes of forty minutes each, two per Region, in sound and television, in the 'Tonight' placing at 6.45 p.m. Questions were put to speakers who appeared as representatives of their parties. Parties contesting at least one-fifth of the constituencies in any given Region were entitled to be represented. In fact, only the Welsh Nationalist Party, apart from the three main parties, qualified. The audiences were made up of equal numbers of supporters of each party represented on the panel of speakers, with a sprinkling of uncommitted people. The groups of questioners took turns to put their questions. Precautions were taken to see that the meeting was orderly and that its proceedings conformed to the interpretation of the 1949 Act.

Another BBC innovation was the broadcasting of three 'Any Questions?' programmes within the campaign period. On these occasions the parties were consulted about representative speakers, and the questions had a political slant.

As a variant of the 'Hustings' technique, Granada staged 'The Last Debate' in its largest Manchester studio. Three party spokesmen, Mr Selwyn Lloyd, Mrs Barbara Castle, and Mr Arthur Holt, delivered short speeches and then answered questions addressed to them by the audience. For some reason, perhaps because of the size of the audience, or the form of seating as in a galleried public meeting, or the absence of preparatory briefing, the audience interrupted and heckled on such a scale that at times the speakers were shouting to try to make themselves heard, but the outcome was a lively and memorable broadcast.

The campaign was reported daily in BBC sound radio and television news bulletins, in 'Radio Newsreel' on the Light Programme and in a daily Press summary on radio. The main political news came on at about 10.15 p.m. when a fifteen minute bulletin gave an account of the day's happenings in the campaign. On ITN there was coverage in the bulletins and a special late bulletin 'The Election Day-by-Day', from 10.50 p.m., reported the day's news.

Both BBC and the ITN coverage were carried out on the principle of what was 'news value'. No specified proportion of time was made over to political affairs, nor was there any pre-arranged balance of news from the several parties. The election was treated as a national debate, like reports on Parliamentary debates, and news stories were put out as they came in. The coverage went on until midnight before Polling Day. On Polling Day only reports on the progress of the Poll were broadcast.

This news coverage included reports from the television services' own correspondents, recordings from speeches by party leaders, interviews with spokesmen of party headquarters, talks on the way the election worked, reports giving local impressions of the way the campaign was going, and filmed surveys of particularly interesting constituencies. The reporting of the speeches of candidates in individual constituencies ran close to the prohibitions of the Representation of the People Act and it was not until late in the campaign that the Independent Television Authority took the risk of authorizing ITN to use sound cameras for this purpose. Consequently only one constituency, Scotstoun, Glasgow, was reported in this way in the Independent network. The BBC confined their reporting of the candidates' local campaigning speeches to silent shots (with equal time for each candidate) overlaid by the reporter's voice giving brief biographies and the line of campaign. A news reporter's version, even when superimposed on a silent picture of the political speaker, is a poor substitute for the original. Part of the nature of the television medium is its apparent authenticity. A still picture of a dumb speaker always seems inferior to the live image. Both television news services are evidently capable of selecting from candidates' speeches in such a way as to ensure a generally fair and impartial coverage. What they still need is the legal right to do so.

To the principle of 'news value', the Editor of ITN has added the need for 'parity of technical resources' during the election. Since sound film cameras were still few in number, it was clearly necessary to try to distribute them so that their use would not confer an unfair advantage on one side or the other. ITN therefore tried to include sound recordings of two representative Conservative and two Labour speakers each day, and to bring in sound reports of Liberals and other parties over the period roughly in proportion to the number of their candidates in the field. As the election got under way, and became more and more a contest between the party leaders, they had to try to allocate sound cameras fairly in covering the speeches of Mr Macmillan and Mr Gaitskell. Because of the prohibitions of the Representation of the People Act 1949, however, no sound film report was shown of candidates speaking in their own constituencies, except for the Scotstoun ITN report and two brief extracts from candidates speaking at street corner meetings on the BBC news.

The practical difficulties facing the television news departments were rather greater than those of the Press. Reports had to be on the air by 10 o'clock or 10.50 p.m.; political speeches were not usually made earlier than 7.30 in the evening, and often in out-of-the-way places, though such requirements of the medium undoubtedly affected politicians' local arrangements. There were only about half a dozen places outside London where sound films could be developed and cut to the required lengths. The film crews had to make their selections from unscripted speeches as they went along, since the limited time available made it impossible for the news editors to process, view and select more than brief extracts in time for the same evening.

A remarkable tribute to the fairness of the selection of items is seen from a count of the amount of BBC bulletin space given over to news of each of the parties. The Conservatives had been given 1,875 lines of space, the Labour Party 1,850 lines, and the Liberals 507 lines. The ITN coverage, judging by our monitors' reports, was no less fair. Our own scrutineers, who were viewing critically, could find little or nothing to complain of. One important omission from the television coverage of the campaign was the views of electors themselves. The impression given was one of considerable activity on the part of candidates and political parties, but the electorate was seldom seen and never heard in the news bulletins. They made an important contribution to the 'Hustings' and 'Last Debate' programmes. One hopes that another time they will also have their place in the news.

Granada's 'Election Marathon'

The boldest experiment in television coverage of the campaign was Granada's 'Election Marathon'. It was the first attempt in the history of broadcasting to present the candidates to their own constituents as local claimants throughout every constituency in the North. It was not the first broadcast of its kind, for the same network had presented the three Rochdale candidates in a programme when the 'Ludovic Kennedy' by-election was fought in 1958.

For the candidates it was an opportunity to speak directly to the electors whose votes they were seeking, and to reply to points made by their opponents, who appeared with them. Of the 229 candidates taking part, 98 were Conservatives, 100 Labour, 25 Liberal, 3 were Welsh Nationalists, 2 Communist and 1 Lancastrian; 'for the minority candidates it was a rare opportunity of equality in political broadcasting'.[6]

When plans were maturing for the mounting of this first attempt fully to cover all the constituencies in the North, various uncertainties within the strict legal interpretation of the Act made it necessary to seek Counsel's advice and Sir Ivor Jennings, Master of Trinity Hall, Cambridge, finally gave his opinion of the proposed programme. 'Marathon', he said, was legal under the Representation of the People Act and he recommended:

1. 'No candidate should appear on television unless all the other candidates in his constituency are prepared to appear;
2. All such candidates should appear in the same programme, each of them speaking for X minutes in an order determined by lot;
3. Candidates should be instructed that they must speak judiciously about the "issues" of the election, which appear to them to be important on the national plane, and must not address their constituents direct;
4. Granada should make it plain, preferably through the announcer at the beginning of each session, that the candidates are explaining their opinions to viewers generally, because it is just as important to have good back-benchers as it is to have good front-benchers.'[7]

On the Television Act, Sir Ivor said Section 3 was not to be interpreted as a legally enforcable set of duties but rather as a code of behaviour.

Thus reassured about the Representation of the People Act, Granada decided to change the form of 'Election Marathon' to a series of short debates between candidates. This would remove any possibility of contravening the requirements of the Television Act.

THE NATURE OF THE CAMPAIGN

As will be seen in the next chapter the brevity imposed on the speakers by these legal restrictions was the main criticism levelled against the programmes by those who viewed them in West Leeds and Pudsey. It is doubtful whether the audience realized the difficulties that had to be overcome before a programme of this kind could receive official permission to be heard at all.

The first recommendation (that no candidate should appear unless all the other candidates in his constituency are prepared to appear) limited the programme. 348 candidates were invited, of whom 294 accepted. Of these 294, sixty-five did not appear, two owing to illness, the rest because their opponents could not appear. Fifty-four candidates refused – thirty-four Conservative, seventeen Labour, and three Liberal.

'Marathon' was on the air for a total of eleven hours forty-one minutes – six hours three minutes in Lancashire, and five hours and thirty-eight minutes in Yorkshire.

After the programmes were over, Granada invited the candidates and their agents to give their opinions on the series. A summary of their reactions, printed in Granada's report, shows that eighty-one letters were received from MPs and ex-candidates. Forty-one commented on the favourable reception of 'Marathon' in their constituencies; thirty-two felt the time allotted had been too short; twenty-six said the hours of transmission had been unsuitable; thirteen praised 'Marathon' for giving viewers the chance of seeing their candidates; ten were surprised at the wide coverage of the programme; eight thought the programme had been well worth doing; seven were amazed at how much could in fact be said in one minute; six said the programme was boring and that there had been too much repetition; four were convinced 'Marathon' had increased public interest in the election; three complained of uncomfortable seating; three complained of bad make-up and lighting – said they were made to look old; three felt there should have been a different system for the order of speaking – the last person to speak having a distinct advantage; three said 'Marathon' was of no benefit to those who had already been MPs – it gave their opponents an advantage in getting themselves known; two felt that advance publicity had not been good enough – they would have liked to include times of appearance in election addresses (the arrangements were completed after the *TV Times* had gone to Press, so that only 'Marathon' was mentioned and the names of the constituencies and candidates could not be shown); two would have liked a rehearsal; one would have liked a clock with a seconds hand; one complained that the Chairman did nothing but keep time; and one would have liked a drink of water or preferably something stronger, before and after the programme. (A report on the impact of this series is included in Chapter V.)

The Press coverage of the election

This analysis of the Press coverage of the election campaign was made in order to see just how far changes recorded in knowledge of policies, choice of issues and in attitudes to the parties could be related to what the newspapers actually wrote, and how the Press coverage compared with the television campaign.

It was decided to make a content analysis of a sample of the election material published during the campaign (September 19 to October 7) in the national dailies and three local Yorkshire papers (the *Yorkshire Post*, the *Yorkshire Evening Post* and the *Yorkshire Evening News*).[8] Three dates were chosen at random within the period September 19 to October 7. These were September 25, September 28, and October 7, and all newspapers issued on these days were analysed. All references to the election, both direct and indirect, were then measured in column inches.[9]

All this mass of published material was classified according to subject into five broad categories: national issues, party policies, local constituency news and comment on election procedure, personality sketches (descriptive), and personality sketches (trivia).

A limited amount of duplication in classifying was unavoidable. It was found impossible to separate the two categories 'Immediately increase old age pensions' which was listed as a party policy and the issue headed 'New approach to the question of old age'. The column inches devoted to this general topic were therefore placed under both headings. In the classifications 'Spend more on education' and 'Abolish the 11-plus exam' it was easier to divide the material and there is little over-lapping in these two categories. Apart from these two exceptions all the counts are independent.

Issues and policies

In general, the issues in the election were well reported. The space

TABLE 9

Editorial space, in column inches per issue (average of three days), devoted by national and local (Leeds) newspapers to General Election campaign (September 25, 28, October 7, 1959)

Newspaper	Issues %	Policies %	Personalities Descriptive	Personalities Trivia	Personalities Both %	Election procedure & constituency news %	Totals Total election coverage	Totals % of total space per paper
Times	81 (27·5)	19 (6·4)	0	11	11 (3·7)	184 (62·4)	295	(11·1)
Guardian	92 (34·9)	28 (10·4)	4	15	19 (7·3)	126 (47·4)	266	(10·0)
Daily Telegraph	205 (45·1)	45 (9·8)	45	6	51 (11·2)	154 (33·9)	455	(17·0)
Yorkshire Post	85 (28·2)	46 (15·7)	7	7	14 (4·8)	149 (51·3)	294	(8·5)
Yorks. Ev. Post	21 (11·7)	7 (3·9)	5	12	17 (9·4)	137 (75·1)	182	(6·9)
Yorks. Ev. News	3 (7·1)	0 (0·0)	0	0	0 (0·0)	39 (92·9)	42	(1·8)
Daily Mail	50 (28·8)	15 (7·9)	15	14	29 (15·1)	99 (51·2)	193	(7·8)
Daily Express	32 (18·6)	0 (0·0)	26	68	94 (55·2)	45 (26·2)	171	(5·4)
News Chronicle	54 (29·5)	11 (5·8)	50	16	66 (35·5)	54 (29·2)	185	(9·6)
Daily Herald	85 (30·7)	24 (8·8)	36	10	47 (16·9)	120 (43·6)	276	(16·9)
Daily Mirror	38 (25·8)	3 (1·7)	41	16	56 (38·5)	60 (34·0)	147	(5·2)
Daily Sketch	13 (11·4)	0 (0·0)	0	59	59 (54·0)	38 (34·6)	110	(5·5)
Totals (all papers)	759 (29·1)	196 (7·5)	228	235	463 (17·7)	1194 (45·7)	2613	

devoted to individual issues is given in Table 58 in Appendix F. The issues represent the basic problems confronting the country both in the views of the political parties, as shown in their manifestoes, and in the eyes of the electorate, as seen from the weight of their responses to our survey questions.

The editorial space given to issues varied a good deal as between newspapers, from 45·1 per cent in the *Telegraph* to 7·1 per cent in the *Yorkshire Evening News*. In case the three days selected for analysis were, by an odd chance, quite unrepresentative of the coverage of the *Yorkshire Evening News*, we took three other issues during the campaign period (September 24, 29 and October 6). With these included, the proportion of space devoted to issues increased to 14 per cent, mostly as a result of a long report of candidates' election messages on September 29. The number of column inches devoted to any aspect of the election only increased from forty-two to fifty per day as a result of this further count, or 2·1 per cent of the total newspaper space available.

We found that the larger questions, like pensions and peace negotiations, were covered by practically every paper, so that the number of separate newspaper reports is roughly proportional to the total space devoted to any one national issue. The *Telegraph* covered all seventeen national items listed, the *News Chronicle* fourteen, *The Times* thirteen, *The Guardian* eleven, the *Daily Mail*, the *Daily Herald* and the *Daily Mirror*, nine each, and the *Daily Sketch* one. The largest single item was an article of 103 column inches on employment in the *Daily Telegraph*.

The large aggregate of 474·5 column inches on the political implications of the financial 'scandals' in the City of London, set off by reports of 'the Jasper affair', was only the political part of this vast 'story'. The Press seemed to think that these affairs were news and that they were likely to influence the electoral decision. The politicians on both sides tried to turn the news to account, but as far as our evidence goes, the electorate did not seem to be much affected.

The only important issues not included in the survey list which figured at all prominently in the Press were roads, agriculture, trade unions and trade disputes. The last subject was not discussed by the parties in their manifestoes or broadcasts. It only boiled on to the front pages during the episode of the British Oxygen strike, though the *Express* on October 7 printed a main story on the front page headlined 'Wildcat Strike in Car Industry'. In fact this threatened strike did not materialize.

The Press reports on the policies listed in our Knowledge of Policies index are analysed separately (see Appendix F, Table 59).

It is perhaps surprising to find that the old age pension proposal was the only party policy in the campaign to receive any widespread attention from the Press. In fact, it occupied more space than that given to policies on education, housing, colonial development and the anti-nuclear club put together. Out of the total editorial space given over to the election, only 7·5 per cent was concerned with these specific policies.

Constituency news and election procedure proved to be the largest category and filled 45·5 per cent of the total election editorial space. This is partly because newspapers normally cover regional events in their local editions and have far more space available for detailed reports of local campaigning than television or radio. Further, the terms of the Representation of the People Act prevent any radio or television programme from dealing with local events except in the most restricted way.

Items listed as 'procedure' include descriptions of the way the candidates were selected, how the election campaign was organized and carried out, notes on postal voting, use of cars on Polling Day, work of the Returning Officer, and so on.

'Personalities' reporting was divided into two sections. The first, generally descriptive, gave a straightforward, and in the main, an unbiased account of many of the parliamentary candidates and the leaders of all the parties. The second section listed as 'Personalities (trivia)' included such items as reporting of barracking and heckling of various well-known candidates, candidates accusing each other of unethical conduct, humorous articles, accusations by both sides of 'smear' tactics, reports of and reactions to Lord Montgomery's remark that 'those who voted Labour should have their heads examined', and the large mass of 'woman's magazine' chat on the wives of candidates, how to give an election party, and even an article by a doctor on the hazards to health involved by over-much canvassing. A description of Mr Gaitskell's chauffeurs in which it was pointed out that one used to drive a hearse and the other was a convinced Liberal, and references to Mrs Bessie Braddock's birthday bouquet are typical examples of what we have classified as 'trivia'. The amount of space devoted by the newspapers to personality items of both types on the three days selected, varies from nil to as much as 55 per cent.[10]

Anyone trying to look objectively at the Press representation of the election campaign and at the television representation must be struck by the contrast in partiality. The television approach was impersonal, as near impartial as could be, and never expressed any editorial policy of its own. The Press approach also included much reporting of an equally high standard in which comment might be free but the facts of the political scene were still regarded as sacred. No doubt, too, the 'trivia' helped to enliven what might otherwise have been a dull campaign. But in some newspapers the selection was so one-sided and the facts selected were so coloured that the readers were not getting anything like a fair picture of the issues which the political parties were trying to place before them.

The difference cannot be put down to the nature of the two media. It has been said that the absence of a monopoly in the Press is protection enough against any serious abuse of editorial power. This argument assumes that an elector can and will buy more than one newspaper and, by comparing them, become aware of their several limitations. We know that relatively few people do read more than one daily paper. It is true that people often take a newspaper whose editorial views roughly coincide with their own, but, as we shall see in Chapter V, this is not altogether the case and with the introduction of new standards of impartiality, first by sound broadcasting and later by the television authorities under Parliamentary direction, public attitudes to editorial selection of news may be changing. As we shall see in this study, people have developed extraordinary powers of resistance to propaganda, and there is even a suggestion that they are beginning to react away from the exhortations of some Press editorials. There was a time when the appearance of a statement in print in a newspaper was popularly regarded as a criterion of truth. There are grounds for believing that this confidence is shifting over to the more ephemeral medium of broadcasting.

The long struggle through two centuries for the freedom of the Press is part of our inheritance and editors are rightly jealous of any suggestion that it should be curtailed. The first principle in the objects of the Press Council is 'to preserve the established freedom of the British Press'. We are not concerned here with freedom but with partiality. If television were likely to take over many of the functions of the Press, as it has done with the cinema and sound radio, it might not matter so much that their standards in political reporting were so different. But the function of the Press remains certainly undiminished, if not unaffected, by television. The printed word is still the only form of communication in which the receiver can have full freedom of reference, reading as and where he chooses, and when he chooses. Only the Press can adequately report the detailed and local aspects of the campaign and set before the elector a full and accurate account of what the parties are saying. If the results of this study show anything, it is that in the short run the effect of a partisan editorial approach is to gain nothing. A more responsible presentation of the several sides of a case might increase public confidence in the Press as a whole, and, paradoxically, extend its political influence.

CHAPTER V

How the Campaign Reached the Electors

How far was this considerable outpouring of propaganda successful in reaching the whole electorate, and which medium reached the largest audience? If we look back at the studies of other elections we see a change taking place in the importance of the different media. Back in 1948 Lazarsfeld was commenting that, 'in recent years, the radio has taken its place beside the newspaper as a distinctive medium of communication', and he noted that as a specific source of influence 'radio plays a relatively stronger rôle than the newspaper'.

In the 1950 and 1951 General Elections in Britain radio receivers were installed in well over 90 per cent of homes and as many electors heard the parties' messages through this medium, either directly or through the news bulletins, as read them in the newspapers. In 1950 the authors of the Greenwich Survey[1] reported that nearly all of their sample of electors were reading a newspaper, and that 62 per cent mentioned newspapers as a source of political information. But 61 per cent referred to radio. Milne and Mackenzie estimated that 'about 80 per cent of the voters were reached by *each* of these sources' in 1951.

By 1955 the pattern had changed. Radio, still the only source of broadcasting for 60 per cent of the public, had markedly weakened as a political source. Although the Party election broadcasts in 1951 and 1955 went out at much the same time of evening – for audience size is a fairly strict function of time – audiences, as measured by the BBC Audience Research Department, fell from 36 per cent in 1951 to only 15 per cent of the population in 1955. Milne and Mackenzie reported that in Bristol the average number of radio programmes heard fell over the period from just over three to only one per elector. D. E. Butler[2] commented that 'if the enthusiasm for politics on the air was low in the 1955 election, it was surely due to the nature of the election rather than to the allegedly deadening social effects of the TV age'. Although television was only in 40 per cent of the Bristol homes (cf. 38 per cent in the whole country) the Party broadcasts on TV were reaching slightly more electors than those on radio. The difference is largely caused by the greater use made by the public of the visual medium or what in a moment of resignation the BBC[3] describe as 'the inertia of the audience'. Already in 1955, D. E. Butler was reporting that the contest was being hailed as 'the first TV election'.

By 1959, television had taken the place formerly occupied by sound radio as an instrument of political communication, equal in penetration, if not in volume of output, to the Press. Three-quarters of the households in the North owned a receiver at the time of the election, and most of them, or 57 per cent of the electors, heard a Party election broadcast. Nearly every viewer, or 90 per cent of those with television, saw some political programme or political news reports during the campaign.

It might be useful to set out some roughly equivalent statistics from the 1950 election Greenwich study, the Bristol studies of 1951 and 1955, and the present survey. All the figures are liable, through sampling errors, to deviate by at least 2 to 5 per cent away from the 'true' figure, according to the percentage quoted, and the 'true' figures represent different constituencies. But the sampling methods were rigorous. The two Bristol columns are, of course, more closely comparable.

TABLE 10[4]

Exposure to propaganda through various sources in four British General Elections

Source	1950 (Greenwich) %	1951 (Bristol) %	1955 (Bristol) %	1959 (Leeds) %
Election addresses (at least one copy 'read' by electors)	40	56	63	69
Campaign meetings (electors attending)	7	10	6	11
Party election broadcasts (electors hearing at least one)				
(a) Radio	69	68	36 ⎫ 70[5]	16 ⎫ 67
(b) Television	—	—	38 ⎭	57 ⎭
Proportion of opposing party's supporters in election broadcast audiences				
(a) Radio	—	43	45	—
(b) Television	—	—	46	49

The steady rise in the proportions of electors reading something of the election literature may be significant. If it is, it probably reflects an all-round improvement in the quality and format of election addresses and an increased distribution of other leaflets rather than any real rise in political interest.

The only conclusion to be drawn from the figures of attendances at political meetings is that there is no evidence here to suggest that this form of propaganda has declined or increased in public support over the past ten years. H. G. Nicholas,[6] writing in 1950, claimed that there were fewer large mass meetings in 1950 partly because of 'the substitution of the radio talk for the public appearance'.

The inference of the broadcast audience figures is that, through one broadcast medium or both, an audience of nearly 70 per cent of the electors has been reached by the parties direct. To these figures we could add the numbers of those hearing political news bulletins on radio or television outside the Party broadcast audiences. As it is suggested below that rather more than half of these audiences were viewing the Party broadcasts voluntarily, the ratio of 51:49, supporters to opponents, in the total audiences among the West Leeds and Pudsey electors must represent a fairly high degree of toleration.

It was not possible to find statistics of the reading of political news in the Press over all four election periods, but some comparisons can be made between pairs of studies; the proportions mentioning newspapers as a chief source of political information in 1950 and 1951 can be compared, and the proportions of readers habitually looking at the political news in 1955 and 1959. The inference is that newspapers have played much the same part in the campaign over the whole period. As was suggested in Chapter IV, the newspaper, as a source of political news, serves several purposes which broadcasting cannot challenge.

The only possible conclusion to be drawn from the figures in Table 10 is that over the past ten years there has been scarcely any change in the extent of political participation. The dominance of television is the only new factor. Against this background we shall look at the new features in the process of communication that occurred in 1959.

The television audiences

Nine out of every ten of the West Leeds and Pudsey electors with television sets saw something of the political campaign through that medium. The proportion with television was 76 per cent and altogether 68 per cent of the electorate saw either news reports or Party election programmes during the campaign. The amount of viewing of political material varied between one type of person and another. Married people saw more than single, men rather more than women, and the elderly least of all.[7] The Party election broadcasts reached 57 per cent[8] of the electorate in our samples. Among those who saw any Party broadcasts at all on television, the average number of programmes received was 5·5, but if we consider viewing in relation to the whole sample the average reduces to 3·1. One rather surprising point that emerges is that as many as 6 per cent of the electors received both the television Party broadcasts and the separate broadcasts on sound radio.

As in earlier elections, the amount of viewing of these programmes varied very widely from one individual to another. Some saw only one or two, rather more saw five or six and there were others who saw nearly all. The wide variation from light to heavy viewing is only partly a product of the widely ranging interest in politics to be found in the electorate. It is also, in part, a carry-over of general viewing habits, which also show great variation.[9] Since the motive for a certain amount of the viewing of political television broadcasts was no more than a reluctance to switch the set off before its appointed time, people who were normally heavy viewers would naturally see more political material too.

Viewers in our West Leeds and Pudsey sample were asked which of the Party election broadcasts they had seen. They were reminded by a list of speakers and subjects when they were in doubt but as they had to cast their minds back over a period of up to one month, it is remarkable that their evidence tallies so closely with the BBC Audience Research figures. The sample percentages, compared with the BBC estimates for the North (reconstructed from the separate figures for ITV Band III and BBC audiences), and the TAM ratings are given below.

TAM ratings are estimates of the percentages of sets in homes able to receive ITV which were switched on for the broadcasts. As some 70 per cent of the homes in the North of England were receiving Band III and Band I (ITV and BBC) programmes at that time, an average of 49 per cent set-usage for the Party election broadcasts would mean that nearly 35 per cent of all households contributed to the total

TABLE 11

Party election broadcast audiences

			Sample %	North Population (BBC est.) %	TAM Rating %
Sep. 19	(Con.)	Macmillan and Cabinet discussion	29·5	22·7	48
Sep. 21	(Lab.)	Pensioners, Bessie Braddock, etc.	15·5	23·0	53
Sep. 22	(Lib.)	5 speakers, John Arlott, Robin Day, etc.	28·0	28·5	51
Sep. 23	(Con.)	R. A. Butler, story of young couple, Keith Joseph	20·0	19·2	47
Sep. 26	(Lab.)	Housing conditions, comprehensive schools	27·9	21·3	53
Sep. 28	(Lab.)	Jack Hylton, John Osborne, Bevan: industrial	18·0	19·5	48
Sep. 29	(Con.)	Factory and farm: Macleod	23·6	25·4	52
Oct. 1	(Lab.)	Humphrey Lyttleton; Harold Wilson	21·5	22·0	50
Oct. 2	(Con.)	Chataway, Selwyn Lloyd, Lennox-Boyd	26·2	19·3	44
Oct. 3	(Lib.)	Grimond	28·6	22·6	51
Oct. 5	(Lab.)	Youth and Gaitskell	31·9	23·6	39
Oct. 6	(Con.)	Macmillan	40·2	25·4	56
		Averages	25·9	22·7	49·3

audience. There are 2·23 persons aged twenty-one and over in the average household with a television set.[10] If we take the BBC average audience as an estimate of individual viewers and the TAM figure as an estimate of set-usage, then the average number of viewers per set was one-and-a-half.

Television Audience Measurement Ltd have recorded figures of separate estimates of the numbers of homes in ITV areas able to receive both networks that were switched on to the Party election broadcasts for the first minute and the last minute of each programme. There was an average loss of 13·5 per cent from beginning to end of the broadcasts, which was fairly consistent over all the programmes and with no difference at all between Conservative and Labour broadcasts. Audiences are shrinking fast between 10 and 10.30 p.m. and this rate of loss is no greater than usual. Discussing this point, TAM conclude: 'for the Northern area at least the drop in audience during the election broadcasts was the sort of drop one would expect at that time of the evening with any broadly comparable programme'.[11] It follows that although there was some switching off by uninterested viewers before the programmes came on, there was no abnormal loss after they had started – which is both to the credit of the parties and producers and also an indication of the serious interest of the electors who decided to view them.

The TAM system shows percentage losses in audience for the Party election broadcasts of 8, 11, 9, 11, 5, 10, 9, 5, 8, 4, 13, 10, in date order. There is no evidence of satiation here. Had there been any such tendency it would have increased progressively as the campaign went on. In fact, the average loss for the first six broadcasts is 9·0 and for the second six it is 8·2. The two closing programmes attracted larger audiences than the others and might be expected to suffer greater loss but the difference between these two figures and those for the preceding ten broadcasts is not statistically significant.

The BBC published figures which show the changes in total audience between the preceding programmes, ending at 10 p.m., and the Party election broadcasts starting at 10 p.m. The average ratio among BBC viewers was 100:99 (before the election campaign it had been 100:93), and among ITV viewers it was 100:58 (whereas before the campaign it had been 100:77). Some variation is to be expected between BBC and ITV viewers for it is known that there are consistent differences between them. BBC viewers are generally slightly better educated,[12] and more interested in serious programmes. They are also more Conservative.[13]

We see from these figures that the television election broadcasts slightly increased the BBC's 'expected' audiences at 10 p.m. but decreased the ITV's. It does not seem very likely that all these 'additional-to-expected' BBC viewers had been looking at the preceding BBC programmes or had just switched on for the occasion. Probably some switched over from ITV to BBC as they did for the election results on polling night. But the same Party election broadcasts went out on both networks. Did viewers regard the BBC version as more authentic?

From the same source we see that news bulletins on television and radio obtained slightly larger audiences, where measurements were comparable, over the campaign period compared with the weeks before. Such comparisons at least assure us that election politics are of comparable interest to other programme material. The inclusion and the priority of placing for such programmes cannot, of course, be made on mere considerations of 'box office'.

Was it an interested audience?

We tried to estimate the size of the more serious audience for the Party election broadcasts. There was no alternative to the Party election programme. All other campaign programmes, including the news bulletins, were put on at a time when non-political alternatives were available on the other wavelength. We assumed that viewers who saw some of these other political broadcasts, presumably by choice or as the preferred of two alternatives, since they could always have tuned in to something else, were relatively selective where political material was concerned. Of those who saw one or more Party election broadcasts, 64 per cent also saw the late election news bulletins three or four times a week, or at least two of the 'Election Marathon' programmes or a 'Hustings' programme. These relatively selective viewers also saw more Party broadcasts than the unselective viewers and if we allow for this difference we estimate that 70 per cent of the total audience for Party broadcasts was reasonably interested.

This estimate is probably an upper limit. Viewers could see the election news and still not really want to have twenty minutes of party electioneering. An alternative estimate was based on the proportion of viewers who had shown a recognizable interest in political news *before* the election campaign.[14]

To give some idea of what is meant by this criterion of an interested political viewer, we have counted all electors who obtained the minimum 'interested' score on pre-election exposure. Such a minimum standard would include viewing of 'Tonight' on BBC Television, 'fairly often' viewing broadcasts dealing with party politics, reading 'nearly all' of, say, the *Yorkshire Evening Post* every day and hearing the morning news on sound radio at least three times a week. This count showed 52 per cent of the audience as likely to have a fairly definite interest in politics before the campaign.[15]

If we regard this figure of 52 per cent as a lower limit and 70 per cent as an upper limit we can take a middle estimate of 60 per cent of the Party election audiences as viewing voluntarily. It should be remembered however that these were often the same people viewing several broadcasts. Selectivity in viewing of political programmes is not just a distinction between those viewers who are interested and those who are not. There are degrees of selectivity. We plotted out the total amount of viewing of Party election broadcasts for all electors in terms of their normal (pre-election) interest in political broadcasts or current news. There is a constant ratio between them, so that one increases with the other (measured as a correlation of $\cdot 34$; $P = \cdot 001$). In terms of numbers of electors we could reckon that about 5 million electors were viewing in this way, while another 5 or 6 million were seeing them without particularly wanting to do so. As we shall see with the 'changers', it was this less interested section which learned most from the broadcasts and were the most likely to change their voting intentions. The logical extension of this argument is that perhaps no other single step would serve the interests of politicians better, and perhaps the electoral process itself, than to place Party election broadcasts at a time when the maximum number of unselective viewers could be tempted to keep their sets switched on.

Television as a forum for political debate

One of the most remarkable features of the Party election broadcasts on television was the composition of the audience they attracted. In the two constituencies our estimates show 47 per cent of the electorate viewing one or more Labour Party programmes and 53 per cent viewing a Conservative programme, with very considerable overlap between these two groups (for 57 per cent saw *any* election broadcast).

We have divided the viewers according to their dominant party attitude into Conservative or Labour partisans. If we consider all the viewers towards both sets of broadcasts we find that 49 per cent were looking at programmes put out by a party they did not support, but here the sample underestimates the Labour strength in the country as a whole. By weighting the Labour representation to bring it up to the national proportions, according to the balance of votes cast, we can arrive at an estimate of the composition of the audience. We also have to take into account the number of Party election programmes seen by each type of elector. Those Conservative viewers who saw any election broadcast saw, on average, 2·8 of Conservative and 2·3 of Labour broadcasts. The Labour viewers who saw any broadcast averaged 2·4 of Conservative and 2·5 of Labour broadcasts. The estimates for the average audience are, therefore:

TABLE 12

Composition of Party election broadcast audiences

Party election broadcasts	Conservative voters %		Labour voters %	
Conservative	57·5	+	42·5	(=100%)
Labour	50·6		49·4	

Some considerable part of this phenomenon must, it seems, be a willingness to see both sides of a public debate, and if so, it is an important extension of the democratic process. For, apart from broadcasting, there is no comparable opportunity for general public debate. An elector will continue to read the same newspaper through the campaign, and unless it is one of the three or four journals that attempt to put all sides of the political debate before their readers, he will have only a highly selected and tendentious version of what is being said. For comparison, we give the proportions of voters reading newspapers of one or other party leaning. For this estimate, the *Guardian* and the *News Chronicle* have been classed with the *Daily Herald* and the *Daily Mirror* as pro-Labour papers. The figures are derived from our sample.

TABLE 13

Newspaper readership in terms of voting

	Conservative newspapers %		Labour newspapers %	
Conservative voters	89	+	11	(=100%)
Labour voters	33		67	

In all, 22 per cent read a newspaper whose editorial policy runs counter to their own political allegiance. The figure would be enlarged a little, but not much, by including overlap between readership of the *Daily Mirror* and other journals, not accounted for here.

The implication of social differentiation for the propagandist

At a general election the parties have a duty to the electorate to present their propaganda and to bring to the public notice the principal views and problems confronting the nation. Speaking of the need for political education, Mr R. A. Butler in his Foreword to *Marginal Seat*, 1955, said, 'political parties must do everything they can to interest and educate the electorate, not only in their own policies but in the basis of democratic government'.

They will use every method of communication to these ends, but the new media, especially television, present them with new problems largely because of the social divisions within the groups of party adherents which have been described. As an instrument of communication the Press has the advantage of a differentiated audience. A party spokesman knows what the temper of the readership of the *Daily Telegraph* or the *Daily Mirror* will be and he can modify what he has to say accordingly, just as a speaker will vary his matter and manner according to whether he is addressing an audience of chartered accountants or one of boiler-makers. The television audience is largely undifferentiated, and any appeal to it must be a broad one, finding common factors of interest and comprehension. At first sight, this might appear seriously to limit the purposes of the political propagandist, which are to rally supporters as well as convert opponents. On the other hand, the new medium may compel him to shift his emphasis from persuasive appeals directed at particular levels of the electorate to a more objective statement of his programme and intentions.

The television news

The campaign was fully reported in all BBC and ITN news bulletins. Exactly one-third of our whole sample (33 per cent) saw the bulletins on one or other network fairly regularly, or 44 per cent of those with television. The BBC Report[16] estimates audiences of 7·3 per cent, 7·1 per cent and 10·1 per cent for the three bulletins at 6 p.m., 7.25 p.m., and 10.15 p.m. They also estimate daily audiences of 4 per cent to 5 per cent for the ITN news bulletins at 5.55 p.m., 9.25 p.m., and 11 p.m. By and large, these audiences were no less than those for general news bulletins in the preceding week.

The special programmes on television

The BBC 'Hustings' programmes were extensions of the well tried 'Who Goes Home' series in which an MP from each party answers questions from the floor. The audiences ranged from 6 per cent to 9 per cent, varying a little between Regions. There were two Northern programmes, and also one from Wrexham, broadcast in the North. One or other was seen by 22 per cent of our sample.

Granada's 'The Last Debate' broadcast on October 6 was a large-scale political meeting of the old style, far removed from the politeness of the party broadcasts. Mrs Barbara Castle, Mr Selwyn Lloyd and Mr Arthur Holt spoke in turn and tried to answer questions against a mounting barrage of interruption. It had all the atmosphere of a public meeting in a large public hall. As many as 22 per cent of our local electors saw it.

Other ITV election programmes in the North were:

'Fast Focus' (Granada), a five minute commentary by three party spokesmen immediately after each election broadcast.

'How an Election Works' (Granada), two programmes on the procedure and management of elections.

'Now is the Time' (Granada), a programme on parliamentary procedure stressing the importance of the poll.

'On Your Doorstep' (ABC), and 'First Results' (ABC), reported on the progress of the campaign in various places.

'ABC's Election Time', a regional survey of election matters.

The Granada 'Election Marathon' series

As this ambitious project introduced a new factor into television electioneering we considered its impact on the electorate in some detail. Despite Granada's own trailing of the series and their advertisements in local newspapers all over the North, only about one in five (18·5 per cent) of our informants could give a tolerable description of it within a week of the last programme. This implies that either the title did not make much impression on them, or, more likely, that many people did not fully understand the difference between one form of election broadcasting and another. Comparisons with Granada's 'Fast Focus' and even with 'People and Places' were common. As the programmes went on the air before 5 p.m. or after 11 p.m. they were not in a position to attract any large part of the mass audience. The characteristic description of the series was, 'all the local candidates had a chance', which shows some understanding of the situation if only among a minority of viewers. All told, 22 per cent of the informants saw something of the series (including a few who had not been able to describe it). As a percentage of that part of the public able to receive ITV, this audience would represent just over 30 per cent. The TAM estimates of the numbers of homes viewing 'Election Marathon' show averages of about 6 per cent of Northern homes with ITV reception for the afternoon series, and 9 per cent in Yorkshire, going up to a peak of 14 per cent, for the late evening series. The BBC estimates for the evening programmes were an average of 4·5 per cent of the adult population of the North per programme.

The proportions of Conservative, Labour and Liberal voters, as well as non-voters, among the audience were almost the same as those in the whole sample. And the age, sex and educational distributions were also normal. So it seems that the 'Election Marathon' reached a typical cross-section of the electorate. This fact, coupled with the fairly heavy rate of viewing (65 per cent of those who saw anything of the series viewed three or more programmes), points to an audience which habitually views at that hour, rather than a selective minority of keenly interested followers of the campaign.

There is no evidence to suggest that interest was chiefly focused on the opportunity to see one's local candidates, though the fact that the West Leeds and Pudsey speakers appeared in the first two programmes before the publicity arrangements had made their full effect may explain why our local viewers were not particularly looking out for their own candidates. There must have been considerable difficulties in marshalling a 'cast' of over 200 speakers, at short notice, and under restrictions (Representation of the People Act) which automatically knocked out two or three other candidates if one dropped out, and put the whole organization under the strain of uncertainty about the legality of the operation. No doubt for this reason, advertisements in the local Press usually only appeared on the afternoon before the evening of the broadcast, and candidates were seldom able to make their appearances known. In fact, 36 per cent of those who viewed anything in the series said they had seen their own candidates. The separate figures for West Leeds and Pudsey differ by only 2 per cent.

When we asked electors what they thought of the series, we had in mind the possibility that some of the candidates might appear inexperienced and inadequate by comparison with the 'professionals' in the national broadcasts, and informants were invited to compare the speakers with 'politicians in the national party programmes'.

Of those who expressed any opinion, nearly half thought the 'Marathon' speakers as good as (or no worse than) the national politicians. If to these are added the verdicts of those who regarded the series as 'satisfactory', the responses fall into a ratio of about 5:4, favourable to unfavourable. Some impression of the favourable reactions may be given by quoting one or two actual comments:

(From a railway timekeeper) 'They were level-headed sort of chaps – knew what they were talking about. The talks more forthright than the national.'

(From a fireman) 'They put over an honest programme. The others put in what they were told.'

(From a housewife) 'I thought it was better for local people to see their own candidates than national ones.'

For some viewers there were noticeable differences between their own candidates and the party leaders:

(From a housewife) 'They were not as used to TV as national politicians. National politicians are more relaxed. I suggest the locals try too hard and don't get it over because they are too stiff.'

(From a technician) 'The quality of speakers varied. A hotchpotch. The time was too short for them.'

The time factor was the real ground for criticism. Looking over the evidence as a whole, it does not seem that the local candidates suffered any loss of prestige through having to make an all-too-brief appearance under conditions that are exacting, to say the least, for all but experienced broadcasters. For a television appearance is always, in a sense, a performance. The glare of lights, the difficulty of knowing what is happening in the rest of the programme, the visual distractions in the background, the sense of separation from the receiving end, all inhibit the first performer. It was a novel experiment but it was a programme that needed a network of local transmitters. The series was split between Yorkshire and Lancashire and if it could have been further sub-divided there would, no doubt, have been time for the programmes to have taken on the more expansive 'Hustings' form in which the speakers answer questions in turn, perhaps after short opening statements.

The value of the 'Election Marathon' idea was that it transferred the political focus for a time from the party headquarters in London and from the metropolitan centres to the local constituencies, even if, as we have shown, such programmes had no effect on people's voting decisions. Of course, national issues are always paramount and the principal strength of any candidate lies in his identity with a national party. But the process of centralization has been taken a long way further forward by the development of broadcasting, and any initiative on the part of the television authorities to restore something of the status of the local man and the local situation is important. Unfortunately, the Representation of the People Act, in effect, restricted any references to local issues because any candidate who stressed them might well have been accused of using the opportunity to further his own election.[17] Despite this restriction there were some lively local passages in the talks, from references to Derbyshire cricket to the Quarry Hill flats in Leeds. Some speakers gave potted biographies, like the Conservative from Blackpool South who went over his twenty-four years in the House in sixty seconds. A number, far too many, recited the hackneyed Party slogans and jibes at their opponents. Some fumbled with all-too-obvious notes which, though concealed from themselves under their desk tops, were in full view of the cameras. One speaker tried to get through a history of national insurance but was stopped by the light when he had still only reached 1949. Mr David Crouch, the Conservative candidate for West Leeds, commented: 'Potted politics of this sort are somewhat boring. On the other hand, I did find that my own constituents, the people who were personally interested in me, were interested in the few minutes we were on . . . I think that is the way the programme should be judged. It was an opportunity for reaching probably more of one's constituents in a few minutes than one could meet in the whole of an election campaign. I certainly found that a lot of people I canvassed had seen me on TV.'[18]

In another General Election, with amending legislation to give to broadcasting the same privileges as the Press in campaign coverage, perhaps some agreement could be reached between all the television authorities to include a fuller representation of *local* debates. Something more than two-minute appearances would be necessary, and it might be better to select a proportion of constituencies by ballot until such time as local transmitting facilities make it possible for every elector to see his own candidates.

Viewing on the evening of polling day

Before the election some concern was expressed about the danger of well-established serial programmes tempting viewers to stay at home when they might be recording their vote. Butler and Rose[19] report: 'The idea that the lure of television would discourage voting in the evening (Labour's best time) was widely voiced during the campaign.' The programme which excited most apprehension was 'Rawhide', a Western series, filling an hour from 7 p.m. to 8 p.m. In fact, the normal audiences for 'Dotto', the programme that followed immediately after it, were larger, but the argument of those who felt that 'Rawhide' should be taken out of the eve-of-poll programmes was that it filled a particular hour when many working-class people normally vote; the ITV audience was known to be predominantly Labour and this particular programme was expected to hold the attention of a quarter of the electorate. To leave the programme in the schedule – they argued – was to be responsible for a situation that was likely to interfere with the democratic process and damage the Labour Party's chances. The circumstances in which the British people choose their governments – it was argued – should not be regarded as an event 'external' to broadcasting.

On the other hand, it could be held that the only logical conclusion to this argument would be to exclude any programme that was likely to attract an audience, and that there was no good reason for picking on 'Rawhide' beyond its timing. If it were established that the effect of such an exclusion would be to send more Labour Party supporters to the polls, then one might think of a number of other exclusions which would help the cause of one party or another, and if one exclusion were made to suit the Labour Party, should not another be made to suit the Conservative Party in the interests of impartiality? The problem is not an easy one to solve. The answer must ultimately lie with the political parties themselves. At present they can only try to persuade the television authorities to comply with their wishes, for they have no powers of compulsion.

'Rawhide' went on as usual, and about a quarter of the population looked at it, as usual. The proportions of our sample viewing the four relevant broadcasts on October 8, and the BBC Audience Research figures, in brackets, are:

TABLE 14

Polling-day viewing

p.m.	BBC	Sample %		p.m.	ITV	Sample %	
7.45	'Spy-catcher'	10	(10)	7.00	'Rawhide'	28	(21)
8.15	'Black and White Minstrel Show'	25	(20)	8.00	'Dotto'	25	(21)

HOW THE CAMPAIGN REACHED THE ELECTORS

Over 70 per cent of the electors with television in our sample were looking at some programme or other on the evening of Polling Day between 7 p.m. and 9 p.m. There were rather more Labour than Conservative viewers. Among non-voters the proportion was 79 per cent but the difference is not significant, and with such small numbers it is quite impossible to draw any conclusions about non-voting and viewing. Among all viewers there was a good deal of switching from one service to another. The ratios between the numbers seeing some ITV programme and those seeing some BBC programme that evening were: Labour voters, 100:63 (ITV:BBC); Conservative voters, 100:92; Liberals, 100:75; Non-voters, 100:95.[20]

Sound broadcasting

The great majority (92·5 per cent)[21] of our electors had sound radio in the home. But nearly all of those with television turned to the newer medium for their political news and addresses. Altogether 16 per cent of the sample heard Party election broadcasts on sound, and, among these, 5·8 per cent also saw some Party broadcasts on television, leaving 10·3 per cent relying entirely on sound.

The news bulletins contained about 20 per cent of election news, on average, rather more being included as the campaign developed, especially in the 10.30 p.m. Light Programme news and the 8 a.m. Home Service bulletin. The audiences, as estimated by the BBC, ranged from 2 per cent to 12 per cent, the latter being the average for the morning 8 o'clock news. These figures were a fraction higher than the corresponding audiences just before the campaign opened.

The Press

It is estimated[22] that 80 per cent of the population read a morning daily newspaper (though over 90 per cent read a Sunday newspaper). In West Leeds and Pudsey the sample proportion is as high as 95 per cent. The difference is largely explained by the extensive sales of the *Yorkshire Evening Post*. As many as 63 per cent of our sample read it regularly (73 per cent in West Leeds and 53 per cent in Pudsey). Even the *Daily Mirror* readership looks small by comparison.

The following diagram shows the readership[23] (not circulation) of the morning newspapers with estimates of the three local papers derived from the election study.

Fig. 2. – Readership of daily newspapers – IPA estimates of percentages of the N. and N.E. Region adult population reading national newspapers, with sample estimates for the three local newspapers.

How much of the political pages in a newspaper do electors read? About a third say they do not read any at all. 42 per cent read the reports fairly regularly, and there were intermediate degrees of interest, as shown in the following table.

TABLE 15

Percentages of electors reading election speeches in the newspapers with corresponding proportions seeing political programmes or reports on television

Reading of election speeches	%	
Fairly regular reading	42	of whom 74% see politics on TV
Occasional reading	27	of whom 61% see politics on TV
None	31	of whom 56% see politics on TV
	100	

We can also divide readers into two groups – those who read election speeches in their newspaper at least 'just a little, two or three times a week', and those who do not. We can similarly divide viewers into two groups, above and below a campaign viewing score (see p. 260) of at least six out of thirty-eight, which would be equivalent to seeing, say, a late evening news bulletin three or four times a week and viewing two Party election broadcasts. A comparison of the two divisions gives us an indication of the overlap.

TABLE 16

Election television viewing

Reading election speeches in the newspaper	Higher %	Lower %	Totals %
Higher	32	19	(51)
Lower	27	22	(49)
Totals	(59)	(41)	(100)

The overlapping between the effects of the two media is greater than this simplified table suggests. Rather more electors were in touch with the campaign through television than through the Press, but only just over 13 per cent of the electorate saw nothing through either medium, the bulk of these being found in less skilled occupations.

We can similarly look at the people who saw the late television news bulletins fairly regularly (the bulletins giving full campaign reports) and see whether there are many electors among them who did not read the election news in the Press. Dividing these viewers into the same two categories as shown in Table 16 above, we find 12 per cent of all electors viewing but not reading.

The conclusion we draw from these three comparisons is that there is overlapping between exposure to the campaign through the two media, and that increasing exposure to one is related to increasing exposure to the other. Some read about the election in the newspapers and do not see television. More see the television campaign and do not read the Press accounts.

It is not only viewing of television and newspaper reading that overlap. The same process of overlapping and reinforcement is found with the other campaign activities – attending meetings, reading election addresses, listening to the radio election broadcasts etc. In fact, this is a phenomenon common to almost all intellectual pursuits.[24]

Exposure to the three mass media

We have been considering television, sound radio and the Press separately, but if we regard them as alternative or supplementary sources of information we can see how far the electors were affected by one or other of them or by none. For this purpose we combined our measures of exposure to the campaign through television, radio and newspapers. Figure 3 shows the proportions of electors exposed to varying amounts of the campaign through any medium.

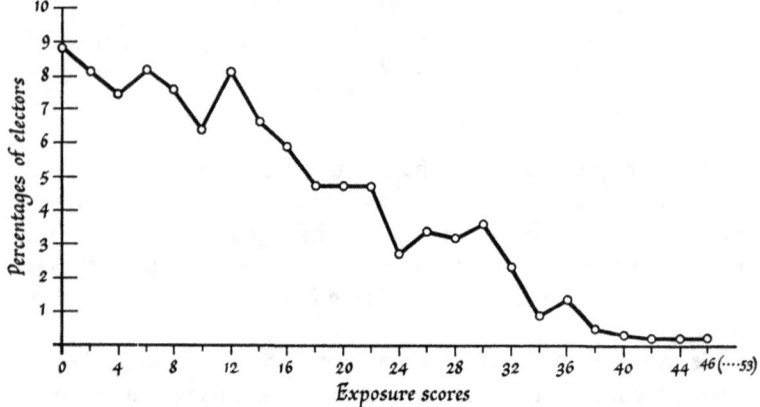

Fig. 3. – Percentages of electors with varying levels of exposure to the election campaign through the mass media.

The maximum score was fifty-three, which would have indicated that an elector read nearly all the political news in a more serious newspaper, saw the whole television campaign coverage, and heard most of the sound radio campaign – clearly an almost impossible task. The average score was just over thirteen out of fifty-three, or about a quarter of the total possible. A score of thirteen could represent, to take one example, reading a little political news fairly regularly, seeing three Party election broadcasts on television, seeing the television election news most evenings, and hearing election news on sound radio occasionally.

The exposure pattern varies for different sorts of people. Men, for example, saw rather more than women (incidentally, they see more television and read more of the newspapers in normal times). The following table sets out the average exposure scores for electors in each social group.

TABLE 17

Exposure to the political campaign (TV, radio and the Press); average scores for social groups

Men	14·3	Married	13·7	More skilled	14·3
Women	11·9	Single	10·3	Less skilled	11·6
		Age group	21-29	12·5	
			30-44	13·5	
			45-65	13·3	
			Over 65	10·6	

The largest group differences are found among single people and the elderly, both of whom saw a good deal less of the campaign than other electors. People in low grade jobs, too, saw less than people in more skilled occupations.

Electors' own impressions of items of news that may have influenced the election

All our informants were asked after the Poll whether they could think of anything that had 'been in the news during the last three weeks' which might have had 'some effect on the way people voted'. About 60 per cent of the whole sample mentioned something. It was not expected that this question would throw any light on the real reasons why people voted as they did; its aim was to discover whether any items in the news had made any outstanding impression during the campaign.

The question would better have been asked immediately before Polling Day, for the knowledge of the result was bound to affect electors' approaches to the answers they gave. They were likely to try to find reasons for the Conservative victory, but in so far as these reasons reflected what had appeared in the Press and in broadcast news, they were of interest.

Most of the answers were critical of Labour; this might be taken to imply that the public could find no other good reason for the Conservative victory, but in fact it is probably a good deal easier to criticize a failure than to explain a success. No doubt, too, after eight years of Conservative government, Conservatism is a familiar fact and the more novel element was Labour's attack on it and its profferred alternative.

TABLE 18

Percentages of electors mentioning items in the news which may have affected the election

Item	All (392) %	Labour (129) %	Conservative (198) %
'Rash Labour promises'; cost of new pension scheme; 'bribery' of electorate	32	22	44
Nationalization	26	30	25
Strikes, damaging to Labour (especially British Oxygen strike)	10	7	11
Pensions, in general	9	12	7
Present prosperity and content	8	8	8
Summit talks, peace, visits to Moscow	7	8	6
The conduct of the campaign in general	5	11	3
'Jasper affair'	4	4	4
Montgomery's speech	3	5	2

The heading 'Rash Labour promises' includes all comments implying that the Labour Party promised more than it could achieve. A fairly common view was expressed by one Labour voter who said, 'Most people think Labour tried to buy their way in'. The number of electors referring to nationalization schemes as a reason for Labour's loss is only a smallish minority of the whole sample, but it is interesting that it should rank second in the whole list. The issue of nationalization (pro or con) was not regarded as among the most important by our informants (judging by their choice of issues), either before or after the campaign, nor did it come up at any stage in the exploration of party images. The inference is that here, as in the other items, electors are echoing the explanations put forward by party leaders and political commentators for the Conservative victory; to this extent the answers are an indication, though a limited one, of the successful communication of the mass media in which these arguments were most commonly quoted. Our analysis of the Press campaign showed that, on average, thirty-seven column inches per day in the daily newspapers were devoted to nationalization. As many as

HOW THE CAMPAIGN REACHED THE ELECTORS

128 column inches per day dwelt on the theme of 'Rash Labour promises'. We can best illustrate the individual reactions by looking first at the comments of Labour voters and then Conservative voters.

Typical of the *Labour* voters' comments on other aspects of the campaign were:

'Running the other side down did not help the party';
'Labour did not work hard enough to put it over';
'Labour's policy is not clear enough'.

There were no strongly held opinions about the reasons for the Conservative victory. Some people expressed the view that there seemed no great reason for change, and that the Conservative Party 'was managing all right'. A housewife remarked: 'Working people vote for those who look after them, and the Conservatives have raised family allowances.' Another spoke of the 'idea that most folks have never been as well off before – so they're not bothered. They don't want a change.' Another mentioned the advertising campaign: 'Quite a lot of posters about how good you've had it; it had an effect on voters, but they haven't lived long enough to know it.' Another Labour view was 'Everybody is happy with the present Government.' A more critical one ran 'People have been kidded into a glorified world which there isn't.' One man believed that the reduction in the price of beer, 'a godsend to a lot of people, had swayed electors'.

The general tone of these Labour voices is that of acceptance; there is little recrimination of the Labour Party or of its leaders, and little animosity towards the Conservatives or alarm at the prospect of another five years of Conservative government.

Conservative voters were merely more critical of the Labour Party. A typical reply was 'Labour, and Gaitskell in particular, made a lot of ridiculous promises they could not fulfil, so sensible people voted accordingly'. A coalman added: 'There's a limit to what the working man can afford.' There was also criticism of Labour's nationalization plans ('This here taking things over has turned folks against Labour'), and occasional comment on what was regarded as 'Labour keeping quiet' about it during the campaign.

Another fairly common theme was that the Conservative Party is more business-like and efficient and better equipped to run the country's affairs. One sixty-two year old woman said 'I voted Conservative because they are better educated and know their job, and how to run the country, and the others are ignorant'. Another

Conservative voter remarked that 'in Yorkshire wild promises like those made by Labour would make anybody think twice'.

There is no evidence in the opinions summarized above that any particular item of news, external to the political campaign, weighed heavily on people's decisions.

The importance of the local campaign

In looking for the effects of a campaign carried out at a national level, and based on national issues, there is some temptation to under-rate the campaign as it is carried out in the constituencies. One is inclined to compare the eight million electors watching the Prime Minister on television or the headlined story in the national daily with the earnest, but sometimes unrewarding, efforts of the local agent and candidate to bring politics to the doorstep, and inject an element of local relevance into the campaign. The work in the constituency is the oldest, and still theoretically the most important, activity in an election. The party organizations depend on the support and enthusiasm of area and constituency workers, who themselves must feel that the part they play is a vital one. Our study of voting movements in West Leeds and Pudsey showed that strong pressures are exerted by the local community, and by the fairly limited world from which most people derive their impressions.

The propagandist function of the local organization during a general election may, however, be less important than its rôle as the agent of the central party machine. In West Leeds and Pudsey the message of the man on the spot reached a rather more limited audience than that which was nationally disseminated. It also appears that the local campaign touches only those who are also being informed by broadcasting and the Press. It has not been possible to assess the importance of the local candidate as a person. Previous estimates have not placed it very high,[25] but no systematic study has been made of the possible advantages of a vigorous organization and a good candidate. Contacts made at the constituency level and the impersonal contact made through the communication media are two different things, different in purpose and possibly in results.

Because of the limited aim of the survey, no attempt was made to assess in detail the success or failure of the candidates in reaching their constituents, or to compare the efforts of one candidate with another. Accurate and comparable figures are not usually available for attendances at meetings or for canvassing results. We have relied, therefore, on the account given by electors in our sample of the part they took in the campaign, without distinguishing between the efforts of the three parties. In both constituencies, Labour and Conservative candidates followed traditional campaign procedure, holding a series of indoor meetings in schools and halls, and addressing open-air meetings through loudspeakers. These activities were supported by door-to-door canvassing, as much of it as possible by the candidate himself, and by a distribution of election leaflets.

How successful were the candidates in contacting electors?

We asked electors, after the Poll, what part they had taken in the campaign. There was an average participation of about 40 per cent of the total possible – an estimate based on attendance at meetings, reading election addresses and talking to canvassers.

For most people the only contact with the local organizations was reading their election addresses, or being canvassed, and altogether 73 per cent of the sample said they had been involved in one way or another, without taking into account any local election posters or other signs of local political activity. Attendance at political meetings was not high; nor was the number of electors who had seen or heard their candidate at the many open-air meetings, held by candidates on fine evenings and at lunch hours. In all, 15 per cent claimed to have seen their candidate somewhere during the campaign, less than half this number at open-air meetings. And 8 per cent of voters also saw their candidate appearing on the Granada 'Election Marathon' programmes.[26]

69 per cent claimed to have read some or all of the addresses delivered by the parties, though the figure is probably a gross over-estimate of the extent to which the local election literature was seriously examined.[27] A higher proportion of Conservatives (73 per cent) than of Labour voters (65 per cent) claimed to have read some, a function no doubt of the educational differences between party supporters. Non-voters took a less active part in the campaign than the others; they went to fewer meetings, and were less inclined to have read the candidates' addresses. One point of some interest is that non-voters were not more neglected by canvassers than actual voters. In the sample as a whole, 49 per cent said they knew of a canvasser calling at their homes, probably an under-estimate of the calls

actually made. Between the constituencies there was quite a large difference in the numbers who said they had been canvassed – 58 per cent in Pudsey, and 40 per cent in West Leeds – though there is no sign of any difference between parties in this.

The extent to which the local candidates were known after the election

One very rough index of the success of the local campaign is the extent to which electors are familiar with the names of their own candidates. During the week after the Poll, we asked people the names of the candidates in their constituency. Only 9 per cent of the sample could not name *any* of the candidates, and two out of five of these did not vote. The proportions among the two groups of voters for the two major parties who could not name the candidate they had voted for were precisely the same (9 per cent of each). The great majority of electors could name all the candidates. Lack of knowledge here is almost certainly a reflection not of relative success or failure on the part of the party organizations but of other factors influencing ability to recall, or to take in, information in the first place.

Factors governing local participation

The parties themselves are aware that the constituents who take an interest in the local campaign are not representative, and that unless they make strenuous efforts they will be largely preaching to the converted.

Correlations were found between local participation and other political activities (see Chapter X), which bear out the belief that the local campaign is most successful at reaching those electors who already make use of other sources of information and persuasion. In both West Leeds and Pudsey, reading of political reports in the Press was associated with local participation in the campaign. In Pudsey there was a correlation between the two of ·28 and in West Leeds of ·43. A parallel correlation exists between participation in the local campaign and listening to or watching political broadcasts. The same overlapping was found by Lazarsfeld *et al* in their 1940 study. They[28] described it as 'the concentration of exposure' and went on to say that exposure in one medium '*supplements* rather than complements' exposure in another medium. While this is still largely true of the effects of the local campaign, which are almost completely confined to those who receive a lot from other sources, the contrary is no longer true. Television appeals in particular and, to a much less extent, the Press, are able to reach an audience which is not motivated by political interest and even to add to their stock of knowledge.

Although the difference is not quite significant, it is interesting to notice here that the electors who changed their allegiance from one party to another in the campaign saw rather more of the local activities than did the consistent voters (31 per cent, cf. 23 per cent above average in local participation). This is in line with the general tendency for inter-party changers to be more than usually involved in the election (see Chapter XI).

Did television interfere with the local campaign?

A much debated question was whether television would, in a variety of ways, diminish the importance and effectiveness of the constituency campaign. It was suggested that the greater attraction of national political figures on television would keep politically interested people at home, and that the normal heavy viewing of the uncommitted and the moderates would keep them away from meetings, and make the work of canvassers difficult.

Our findings do not support these fears, though the evidence is largely negative. It shows that a high degree of television viewing is accompanied by a high degree of local participation. One cannot conclude that television actually created interest in the local campaign or the local candidates, but it leaves it still an open question.

TABLE 19

Local participation and viewing of political broadcasts

	Not viewing %	Medium viewing %	Heavy viewing %
Percentage with high local participation	18	22	30

The table (a summary of a larger scatter diagram) shows that local participation increases progressively as political viewing increases. Of those who took a fairly active part in the local campaign (that is to say, they must have talked to a canvasser or seen the candidate or attended a meeting) exactly three-quarters saw something of the television political output. But, again, we must be careful not to infer a cause from what is only established as a significant association.

None of the comments given by candidates runs counter to the evidence produced in the survey. If anything, they confirm the opinion that television stimulated rather than stifled political interest. The candidates were realistic about the numbers to be expected at meetings, and were satisfied rather than disappointed at attendances. Mr David Crouch,[29] Conservative candidate for West Leeds, felt that political broadcasting in no way interfered with the canvass or meetings, and that viewing in general did not interfere with calls by canvassers, since most people are quite accustomed to interrupting their viewing to receive visits. He also believed the public preferred to meet a politician in the flesh, even if he was not famous. Mr Crouch found a higher attendance at meetings than he had expected, particularly later in the campaign, and suggested as a possible cause a distrust of the television message or a heightened interest in the election issues brought about by the election broadcasts. The Labour candidate in West Leeds, Mr Charles Pannell, did not believe television viewing had inconvenienced his constituency workers in any way, or that there had been any decline in attendance at meetings. The Conservative Party agent for the Yorkshire Area, Mr John Winning, confirmed the views given by the West Leeds candidates, that television was certainly not a serious hindrance, and had no adverse effect either on the number of workers volunteering to help during the campaign or on attendance at meetings.

CHAPTER VI

Television Electioneering–The Viewers' Response

The aim of this part of the study was to examine the reactions provoked in an audience by the election television of the two main parties, and to find at least partial answers to a number of questions about this form of propaganda. How far are these broadcasts effective in conveying information? Were the broadcasts successful in creating the impressions aimed at, and in avoiding any adverse impression? How far do the views expressed by politicians and professional critics accurately represent those of the average viewer? Our own evidence is based on the views expressed by invited audiences who were shown telerecordings of election broadcasts and asked to answer a number of general questions after each one.[1]

The material obtained can therefore only be treated as a rough indication of the general effect of the programmes, but as the sample was reasonably representative it can be used for purposes of comparison, as between one broadcast and another, and one method of presentation and another. Recordings of the two opening election broadcasts of the campaign were chosen for the study and were shown to audiences in the second week of the campaign. The programmes could have been seen earlier, but it was hoped that this would have a minimal effect on the opinions expressed.[2] In both cases the broadcasts were slightly shortened to reduce the length of the meeting, so that the Labour broadcast lost part of its final interview, and the Conservative broadcast lost its filmed discussion between Selwyn Lloyd and the Prime Minister.[3] The Labour broadcast, which is described below, was almost indistinguishable from later Labour broadcasts. The Conservatives changed their television tactics completely after this first programme. This was not anticipated, but the broadcast used does usefully typify an alternative presentation.

The first Conservative Party election broadcast

The broadcast was a discussion between members of the Cabinet in Mr Macmillan's home. The atmosphere was informal, the conversation apparently unscripted, and there was a deliberate emphasis on the ease and friendliness of the occasion. There was little attempt at exhortation or direct address to the electorate or the viewer. The talk was confined to home affairs, and covered what had been achieved over the previous period of office of the Conservative Government. Most of the items mentioned were fairly specific, and in most cases the Minister responsible spoke about his own department. The social services and public building programmes took up most of the time. No use was made of filmed material to illustrate any point, and the Ministers as individuals were under close observation for the length of the broadcast. There was a certain amount of banter between the participants, and one or two confused moments. An impression of confidence and trust seemed to be the aim, since the speakers expressed no strong doubts about the success of the policies that had been pursued, or the continued success which could be expected. One or two speakers made qualifications about the problem of unemployment in some areas, about old people, and housing, but the general tenor of the broadcast was one of quiet confidence. There were no exaggerated claims, or any alarm at the difficulties encountered or likely to arise. There were almost no gratuitous attacks on the Labour Party or their policies; the Opposition was scarcely mentioned.

It has been observed that the Conservative Party hoped at first to keep the campaign a quiet one,[4] to avoid opening old wounds or arousing strong passions. This programme exemplifies this policy. It appears as an attempt to stand aside from normal electioneering. Stress was laid on the continuity of Government policy, on the fact that the Government was in the middle of a programme which would only be disrupted, to say the least, by an electoral reverse.

The first Labour Party election broadcast

In tone, this programme contrasts with the Conservative broadcast. It was intended to appear business-like and efficient – to show the Labour Party as a vigorous and alive organization. Techniques used in television for topical programmes and news presentation were adapted to stimulate interest in what was being said, and to make the right sort of impression. Mr Gaitskell spoke at the beginning of the programme about international negotiations and disarmament talks with Russia. The intention, it seemed, was more to show Mr Gaitskell in a favourable light as a statesman, and a possible national leader, than to state any particular policy, or departure from existing policy.

The opening Conservative Party election broadcast, showing (left to right) Mr Macmillan, Mr Butler, Mr Macleod, Mr Heathcoat Amory and Lord Hailsham

Mr Anthony Wedgwood Benn speaking in the opening Labour Party election broadcast (from a telerecording)

Studio scene during an election broadcast by Mr Gaitskell

Dry-run (rehearsal) with stand-in speakers for an 'Election Marathon' broadcast

To the Labour Party it was important to show the public that it had men equally capable of running affairs and representing the country abroad.

The programme continued with a series of interviews with a cross-section of Labour MPs, with comments on their careers and interests, as a demonstration of the greater representation of ordinary people in the Labour Party. The point was emphasized with a cartoon of Vicky's making fun of the uniformity of Conservative MPs despite the variety of labels they adopt.

The third section of the broadcast consisted of recorded interviews with old people, who explained the difficulty of living on the present old age pension. The emphasis was on the hardship involved, the difference between the standard of living of old people and those in work. The problem of old age was brought home in detail as a prelude to an explanation of the proposed superannuation scheme. The intention might also have been to ensure that even if the superannuation scheme was not understood, something of the concern for old people would be conveyed, along with the idea that an immediate increase in pensions would be granted. Before the end of the programme an animated cartoon was introduced guying the 'failure' of the Hawker Hunter aircraft, and the Government's 'wasteful' defence policy.

The broadcast attempted to present the Labour Party as being primarily concerned with social welfare, but also as being competent and go-ahead. Familiar television personalities (like Richard Crossman, Wedgwood Benn and Woodrow Wyatt) were used to establish rapport and perhaps to lull the suspicions of the uncommitted, and make the intrusion of politics into the home seem less alien.

The content of the broadcasts and how it was recalled

The content of each broadcast was first compared with the audience's recollection of it. The Conservative broadcast covered a wide field, giving an equal amount of time to a variety of subjects, and this diversity is reflected in the impressions of the audience. There is no correspondence between the amount of time devoted to a particular point, and the number of people who recall it afterwards. The two items most mentioned by the audience were 'old age pensions' and 'building hospitals and the social services', but neither of these things was given more than a passing reference. Two conclusions are suggested by the comparison: one is that people notice what they are interested in and concerned about – that wishful thinking to some extent determines a perception – and another that people find it much easier to remember specific than general remarks.[5] Pensions, even before the election, were thought by both Conservative and Labour voters to be second in importance only to the cost of living as an issue facing the political parties. People obviously were very interested in what was to be done for pensioners and it seems likely that this fact influenced what people noticed in the broadcast. A large number of people also singled out hospitals and hospital building, although relatively little time was devoted to the subject in the broadcast. Again it was something immediately relevant to a good many people, and it was also a concrete point, since it was said in the broadcast that the Government intended to double the existing programme of hospital building.

Confirmation of this explanation seems to come from the high proportion of people who noticed the mention of house-building, another popular issue, and who mentioned roads and road building. Road building had been given a good deal of publicity and was at the same time a popular and non-controversial policy.

There appears to be some difference between men and women, in their perception of what the broadcast was about, with a greater tendency for women to notice points associated with welfare and the social services – housing, education, health, and provision for the old. In fact, they tend to notice the things associated with the issues they consider most important.[6] Men, on the other hand, were more likely to notice items like road policy, or general topics like prosperity and building.

This evidence underlines what is always the case – that a broadcast does not mean the same thing to all of its audience and does not necessarily convey what it intends to the majority of it. The wide scope of the Conservative broadcast left a good deal of room for selectiveness on the part of the viewers. A concentration on one or two main items, as in the Labour Party broadcast, is likely to produce a more uniform impression on the viewer, but there may be compensating disadvantages in view of what is said in Chapter X about the elector looking for evidence of a complete policy.

A comparison between the content of the Labour television broadcast and the account given of it by the audience shows a much closer correspondence between the subject matter and what was recalled. Half the broadcast was devoted to the problem of old age, and almost everyone noted this. A third of the audience also recalled what Mr Gaitskell had been talking about in his relatively brief appearance at the start of the programme, even though he spoke in fairly general terms about international negotiations. In contrast to this, very few people noticed the point of the second section of the programme – where MPs were introduced to show the varied walks of life they represent. It may be that people noted in detail what was said by each MP, and that each as an individual made an impression, but the general notion of the diversity of talent was either too abstract to appreciate easily, or was simply difficult for many people to express in writing. On the whole the programme appears to have made the points it was intended to, and there is no apparent difference between Labour and Conservative supporters, or between men and women in their perception of what the programme was about. It does appear from this that a broadcast which is confined to making a limited number of points in detail is recalled more accurately than one which covers a wide range of subjects, and deals with them in general terms. Other effects may of course be produced by the latter sort of broadcast, but if the aim is to convey information economically, rather than to create a general impression, the Labour Party broadcast seems to have been more successful. We have only been able to test immediate recall, but this should be an indication of what will make the most lasting impression.

The impression made by the Conservative speakers

(a) *Mr Macmillan*

Two-thirds of the audience made some comment on Mr Macmillan, including a rather higher proportion of Conservative than Labour supporters. About a third of all comments were critical and they occurred both amongst the politically favourable and others. The majority of these criticisms were of the delivery, rather than of the politician, particularly the lack of clarity. This may in part be due to the quality of the recording, but the Prime Minister's habitual style of delivery is often hesitant and occasionally indistinct. Isolated comments described the Prime Minister variously as 'self-satisfied', 'insufficiently forceful', 'too old', 'too unsure', and even 'too modest'.

In the favourable comment, apart from generally approving remarks, Mr Macmillan's 'calm and gentleman-like manner' was most frequently mentioned. He is described as 'cool headed and sincere', 'a calm and clever leader', 'a perfect gentleman and Premier', 'quite a gentleman', 'a sensible gentleman', and 'very like a grandfather'.

The approving comment is on the whole consistent with the criticism. What some people will interpret as dignified and self-possessed, others may regard as self-satisfied or ineffectual. The interpretation does not depend entirely on political loyalty. Although political opponents are more critical, there is agreement on the nature of the criticism amongst all those who saw the broadcast.

(b) *The other Conservative speakers*
Although the broadcast consisted principally of a group discussion and not a series of speakers, and little use was made of close-ups, most of the actual speaking was done by Mr Macmillan and Mr Macleod, while Mr Butler and Lord Hailsham contributed almost nothing to the discussion. This does not seem to have affected the extent to which people were able to recall the speakers after the broadcast. The four speakers (other than Mr Macmillan) were each recalled by roughly the same number of people, Mr Macleod by rather fewer than the others, despite the larger part he took in the discussion.

Reactions to the other speakers (with Mr Macmillan) seemed to be very little affected by the viewer's partisanship, though this may only indicate an attempt to be as fair as possible for the purposes of the test, rather than the extent of tolerance normally given to a political speaker on television. Of the four speakers, Mr Macleod and Mr Amory were most favourably received. Mr Butler and Lord Hailsham were not strongly criticized; what was said by viewers expresses more a dissatisfaction with the diffuseness of some of their material. Mr Macleod, on the other hand, was described in consistently appreciative terms, both by Labour and Conservative supporters.[7] Conservative comment included such remarks as: 'came over with sincerity', 'the best of the younger set', 'definitely the type for TV', 'the best of the bunch'. Labour supporters agreed that he was most effective as a speaker, though some felt that he was too aggressive. His practical and forthright approach seemed to have had some appeal, and since most of the practical exposition in the broadcast was left to him, it may be significant that of the five Conservative speakers, only Mr

Macleod is not criticized for being indistinct. The lack of clarity, complained of so often, appears to be more the result of speaking in generalities than of physical inaudibility. Where what was being said could not easily be understood, the lack of comprehension tended to be blamed on the conditions of reception. Mr Amory was also liked, as a speaker, for being precise in what he said and modest in manner.

The impression made by the Labour speakers

(a) *Mr Gaitskell*

Only one in ten of the comments made were unfavourable, compared to over one-third of those made about Mr Macmillan's part in the Conservative broadcast.[8] The main appeal of Mr Gaitskell's appearance seemed to be what was regarded as his clarity, good sense, and sincerity. Conservative and Labour supporters had much the same impression. Typical comments were: 'very sincere and forceful', 'knew what he was talking about', 'a good speaker, and a good leader of men', 'sensible and I think genuine', 'put his points very clearly'. Conservative criticisms such as 'a little too charming' and 'too smooth' are consistent with this largely favourable reaction.

There is a significant agreement here not only on the general impression made, but on the particular reasons for this. The qualities in the speaker which the broadcast was designed to emphasize had been noticed by the audience and favourably commented on. The average audience is not by nature suspicious or highly critical of something which at its face value is sincere and reasonable.

(b) *The other Labour speakers*

The remaining Labour speakers did not inspire as detailed comment as the Conservative spokesmen had done, and the only ones recalled with any frequency were familiar public figures – Richard Crossman, Wedgwood Benn, and Mrs Braddock. The programme was not designed, as was the Conservative broadcast, to present the politician to the public, with the exception of the initial address by Mr Gaitskell. Interviewers and speakers appeared relatively briefly, and there was a good deal of film and other illustrative material. The aim was to give an overall impression of variety and efficiency and to convey a certain amount of information.

The impression made by the broadcasts as a whole

The audience was given a short list of ten opinions derived from the comment which had been made in the Press and by our own monitors, and asked to say whether the opinion applied to the broadcast or not. As the sample was small, the percentages in the Party supporter groups should be regarded as indications of possible trends rather than individual values.

(a) *The Conservative broadcast*

TABLE 20

Opinions of the Conservative broadcast

Opinion	Percentage agreeing		
	Whole sample %	Conservative only %	Labour only %
Likely to make a good impression	36	50	6
Friendly and informal	55	68	46
Too confused	24	18	42
More likely to put people off	16	8	25
Too strong	0	0	0
Not interesting at all	13	3	35
Too self-satisfied	38	21	62
Brisk and forceful	14	23	0
Too slick	10	0	25
Gives a good impression of present-day Britain	33	44	8

Allowing for the basic division of opinion according to party allegiance there is some agreement on certain criticisms and on certain merits of the broadcast. Its informality was allowed by both Labour and Conservative supporters but there was an accompanying charge of self-satisfaction, which a fifth of Conservative supporters agreed with. Conservatives were moderately satisfied that it made a good impression, but could not regard it as brisk and forceful.

In answer to open questions, over half of those who commented had something unfavourable to say. Objections fell into three categories. There were complaints about technical faults in presentation, about the lack of clarity of the speakers, and about the tone of the broadcast, which was felt to be over-complacent.[9]

The main technical point raised was the failure of the camera to show who was actually speaking and its slowness in moving from speaker to speaker. Several thought this form of filmed discussion unsuitable for television and the average audience is clearly used to much more sophisticated camera work and studio arrangement and notices such deficiencies.

Over a quarter of the audience complained of inaudibility in some of the speakers or confusion in the discussion itself. Specific mentions were made of the difficulty of following Mr Macmillan and of the disruption caused by one speaker interrupting another. Dislike of the obscurity of parts of the broadcast was expressed in such responses as: 'the Prime Minister's speech was indistinct, but Mr Macleod's was excellent'; 'rather tended to confuse one'; 'very confused, too many people spoke at once'; 'I prefer more direct speech into the microphone'.

The accusation of self-satisfaction was voiced largely by political opponents, although a number of Conservatives agreed that it was too smug. A number of other viewers, who had, on the whole, liked the broadcast, qualified their approval with remarks like 'this particular broadcast showed the Government were very self-satisfied,' or 'too much backslapping, far too many bouquets flung at each other'. Appreciative comment on the broadcast from half of those who had put forward an opinion stresses the informality and pleasantness of the occasion, partly a favourable interpretation of what others chose to regard as self-satisfaction.

There was a wide range of answers expressing much the same theme: 'I liked the friendly setting and the friendly atmosphere', 'I liked the informal way in which things were chewed over'. Some found the setting particularly attractive: 'Homely and interesting', 'I liked the way it was televised in Mr Macmillan's home'. In one or two cases it was compared favourably with the more professional Labour broadcast: 'It was not run like a military operation', and 'I liked the obvious lack of scripts. Everything seemed to come from the individual speakers' minds.'

There was, all the same, in answer to questions, no strong feeling that the programme would achieve any useful effect. People are naturally unwilling to admit that a television broadcast is going to make much difference to their views, but they might feel it would carry some weight with other voters, and a good many Conservatives in the audience were dubious about the electoral value of this broadcast.

One point generally appreciated about the broadcast was the absence of any attack on the Labour Party. A Liberal thought the broadcast might have some influence because the speakers seemed to speak sincerely, and did not try to ridicule members of the other party. There is some evidence that the average audience does not like strong criticism even of political opponents in a television political broadcast.

(b) *The Labour Party broadcast*

TABLE 21

Opinions of the Labour Party broadcast

Opinion	Percentage agreeing		
	Whole sample %	Conservative only %	Labour only %
Likely to make a good impression	42	29	54
Friendly and informal	45	35	75
Too confused	14	24	4
More likely to put people off	17	23	0
Too strong	5	6	0
Not interesting at all	10	17	0
Too self-satisfied	24	41	4
Brisk and forceful	22	17	25
Too slick	12	21	4
Gives a good impression of present-day Britain	23	24	34

There is almost no criticism at all of the broadcast by Labour supporters and a fair amount of agreement on its strong points between Labour and Conservative supporters. It was thought likely to make a good impression, to be informal, and, to a lesser extent, to be brisk and forceful. The main Conservative criticisms are that it was too self-satisfied, confused and too slick, but only the first of these was endorsed by more than a quarter of the Conservatives in the audience. Compared to the Conservative broadcast it was thought to be somewhat less informal, but more likely to make a good impression and also less confused and less self-satisfied. One in five of the Conservatives thought it 'too slick', and a similar proportion of Labour supporters said the same of the Conservative broadcast. The criticism can obviously have no common meaning for it is difficult to see how the term could possibly be applied to the Conservative broadcast. In the sample as a whole, despite the smaller number of Labour supporters, the Labour broadcast was more highly rated. If a score of $+1$ is given for each favourable item and -1 for each critical one, the Conservative broadcast scores 36 and the Labour broadcast 59. There is virtually no sign that the greater vigour of presentation or content in the Labour broadcast earned it any disfavour. This conclusion appears to be corroborated by the reports received by the BBC from their Audience Research panel.[10]

Amongst volunteered criticisms of the broadcast there are almost none by Labour supporters, whereas many Conservatives expressed disappointment with *their* party's contribution. Two main points in the Labour broadcast were singled out for criticism by Conservatives. One was the attack made on the Conservative Party; the other was the use made of old people to illustrate the case for a change in the pension scheme. Typical comments on the first of these points were: 'Disliked the un-British method of blacking the other party', 'I disliked the absence of the other party to answer back', and 'too many shots at the other party'.

Critics who complained about the presentation of old people were plainly made uncomfortable by the interviews with pensioners; they felt that it was unfair and perhaps dishonest. Typical responses were: 'I did not like the old people being dragged into the film', 'Did not like the use of old people to express the idea of poverty', and 'Disliked playing on the poverty of old people'.

Those – again mainly Conservatives – who volunteered favourable comments on the broadcast stressed four points: the efficiency and clarity of the presentation, the attention to everyday affairs, the depiction of typical members of the Labour Party, and Mr Gaitskell's personal appearance.

Several aspects of the production were praised: 'well presented with known TV personalities', 'put over in a workmanlike way' (Conservative), 'I liked the efficient production' (Conservative), and 'speed and speech excellent' (Conservative).

Several people praised the use of ordinary people and the concrete subject matter: 'they have got down to the ordinary level', 'effective use of man-in-the-street characters', 'got down to the root of life', 'I liked the way it dealt with everyday things'.

A few mentioned the way the careers and work of members of the Parliamentary Labour Party were depicted: 'I like to think that ordinary people appear in Parliament', 'a good idea to show MPs from every walk of life'. One Conservative reluctantly admitted that the 'depiction of Labour members might appeal to the uneducated', but there was no other Conservative criticism of this part of the broadcast and it seems that people found it interesting for its own sake.

Several people mentioned Mr Gaitskell personally as making a favourable impression and there was practically no criticism of his appearance.

In their answers to the question on the possible influence of the programme, viewers were more sure about the effectiveness of this broadcast than of the Conservative programme. Almost two-thirds of the audience thought the programme might influence people in their voting, and a number of these were themselves Conservative supporters. The more usual reasons were that it would influence people by the promise of higher old age pensions, and that the picture of the Labour Party put over in the broadcast would have an effect.

Some Conservative admissions of the possible influence of the broadcast were also critical: 'it would only influence people who do not think for themselves', 'it might influence those who read strip cartoons', and others said 'it might influence only those who want something for nothing'.

The comment taken as a whole is a fairly striking justification of the method used in the Labour Party broadcast, even if it does not throw light on the part actually played by such broadcasts in the complex pattern of persuasion and counter-persuasion in the election campaign.

How audience reaction compares with critical comment by the Press and professional critics

(a) *The Conservative broadcast*
It was unanimously agreed by the Press that the bulk of the first Conservative television broadcast (the recorded conversation in the Prime Minister's home) was inferior to the Labour broadcast. The reaction of the Conservative Central Office in revising their television plans suggests that they took the criticism seriously.

Inevitably, political comment in the Press is not impartial, but on this occasion the sharpest criticism came from the Conservative, and not the Opposition Press. The *Sunday Times* commented: 'The main fact has emerged . . . that none of the three Parties is competing on the basis of an agreed recipe for successful political television. . . . Though it is too early to assess the impact of these

TELEVISION ELECTIONEERING – THE VIEWERS' RESPONSE

rival methods, many people appear to have had second thoughts about the opening Conservative broadcast. . . . The fact that most of this programme was filmed as long ago as July 30 gave it a refrigerative look that could scarcely have appealed to the type of viewer who wants his political television "live" in every sense of the word. A number of blemishes – flattish production, a dragging script, Lord Hailsham not much seen or heard from – combined to make this broadcast something of a disappointment to those who had expected an opening flourish. One had the feeling that too many positive qualities had been sacrificed to dignity and restraint.'

Peter Forster in *The Spectator*, discussing the whole television contribution, wrote: 'The aim of any party telecast had surely to be either reinforcement or conversion. In the former case the faithful must be roused to such a pitch of agreement with themselves that they would duly turn out on the 8th. The first major Tory quarter-hour came in this category (whether intentionally or not), when the Prime Minister and principal ministers were found grouped like honest Burghers of Downing Street, Christian-naming each other in a careful-cordial staff-common room way, and rather languidly claiming to be full of beans.'

The *News Chronicle* also complained of the lack of spontaneity: 'People telling each other what they must know already is an unconvincing device at the best of times. Popping the result carefully into the deep-freeze for seven weeks makes it seem even less spontaneous, and all the Christian-names and votes of thanks couldn't retrieve the situation.'

These quotations fairly represent considered comment on the broadcast. It differs from the more articulate views expressed by the audience in our group study in underestimating the credit side of the broadcast, and in a too sophisticated approach. *The Spectator* did, however, qualify its criticism by remarking: 'The performance was easy enough to mock, but may well have reassured many. Indeed the strength of the Tory TV approach, possibly underrated by commentators, was the impression they sought to give of solid citizens handling our affairs, of men at the helm so clearly dependable that their actual showing on the screen, in terms of syntax and sentiment, mattered little. This may well have capitalized on the instinctive popular desire to be able to look up to the leaders.' Most commentators overestimated the critical awareness of the audience, and underestimated the rather more serious response which the audience is prepared to make to political television. There will be some who find politics a bore, and prefer to keep their screen free for quiz shows and westerns, but many are prepared, when called upon, to judge the content of a serious programme on its merits. Nor is the average audience over-critical of efforts to arouse stock responses. Much of television drama uses methods which are no less clumsy and obvious to a more sophisticated viewer, but which are not severely judged by an audience concerned mainly with the story or with the content of what it sees.

The reactions recorded during our study certainly suggest that hostile Press criticism was largely concerned with inessentials. The audience did not stop to think 'what is this programme trying to do to me?', but rather 'what have they got to say for themselves?' They tend to believe that Cabinet Ministers must be decent people, and are more put off by obscurity or evasion than by deficiencies of technique.

(b) *The Labour broadcast*

The production, with techniques allegedly borrowed from 'Tonight' along with its assistant producer, was allowed by nearly all critics to be excellent. After describing the content of the programme, *The Spectator* commented: 'Beyond doubt this was expert, shrewd propaganda.' The *News Chronicle* TV critic said 'It gives an air of urgency, of excitement and best of all, of involving the viewer.... It permits an easy inter-mixture of facts and figures, interviews, snippets of film and direct appeal.' The *Sunday Times* commented favourably on the efficient production, and singled out Mr Gaitskell's personal appearance for particular praise.

The main point made by many commentators was again, not the favourable impression made by the broadcast but the uncalculated effects, the danger of putting off the uncommitted voter, and offending political opponents. If the reactions noticed in our study are typical, these objections were very much overrated. 'Slick' was a word which cropped up repeatedly, even in comments ostensibly favourable. This suggestion of slickness was developed by the Conservative Press. The *Yorkshire Post's* critic wrote: 'Night after night this artful, artificial barrage has shown us what we do not wish to see – those who should hold our respect shedding it fast. Do they think we have not noticed the half-truth, the too-clever bit of mathematics, the terpsichorean posture? All made larger than life by the concentrated light, and the give-away close-up.' The *Daily Express* and the *Daily Sketch* echoed the tone of this comment.

It seems likely from opinions expressed by our groups that the average audience was less interested in the techniques than in the people they saw on the screen, and the points which were made. The techniques were taken largely for granted, and where they made the programme easier to follow and more interesting, they were welcomed, both by political opponents and supporters. Conservatives amongst the audience were prepared to take strong exception to what was said and perhaps to some of the methods used, but did not interpret the efficiency of the broadcast as a sign of meretriciousness.

The technical merits of the Labour Party broadcast may have served less to reinforce the image of an efficient go-ahead party, than to convey essential material clearly and vigorously.

Some tentative conclusions

Too much has perhaps been made by professional critics of the technical difficulties of the medium, and of the technical deficiencies and excesses of some of the party broadcasts. Judging by what local electors themselves say, the more important problem is to decide what the broadcast can hope to achieve and to concentrate on the *general* impression it is likely to give, remembering that ordinary people find concrete points easier to assimilate than abstract arguments. The audience has no particular interest in the way the medium is being used by the politician, but is concerned with what the programme is trying to say. As far as there is critical thinking it centres on the clarity and interest of the broadcast. The use of feature-type techniques is accepted as a matter of course, and a high standard of production is simply regarded as an aid to understanding.

The limitation of subject matter observed in the Labour broadcast has some advantages, and may produce a greater uniformity in the information conveyed. Where a wide range of subjects is treated, the audience may simply select familiar material, and not perceive, or easily forget, what is new. On the other hand, if, as is suggested in Chapter X, the electors are looking for a complete and coherent policy, a narrow selection of topics may seriously weaken a party's case. The Labour Party is particularly vulnerable because of the strong urge for a more coherent policy expressed in one feature of the party image among its own supporters.

One issue that arises is the wisdom of using polemic hostile to the other side. The parties no doubt want to rouse their more active supporters, without at the same time alienating the apathetic and the neutral. But this, television does not allow, because of its undifferentiated audience. It seems clear that outspoken political attack on another party is not welcomed by the average member of the audience and may even cause a certain amount of discomfort. This need not, however, apply to criticism of social injustice or even antisocial groups or individuals, where there is no danger of a large part of an audience identifying itself with the object of the attack.

The aversion to polemics is not only found in Party election broadcasts. A long standing favourite like 'Any Questions' will have adapted itself fairly closely to the audience's expectations. The mild banter and the restrained comments of its political speakers, like those of MPs in the 'Who Goes Home?' or candidates in the 'Hustings' programmes, are surely an indication of a general public attitude which is in sharp contrast to the behaviour tolerated at public political meetings. Granada's 'The Last Debate' seems to have been an exception to this rule, but the acrimony was directed by the audience to the speakers, and even then the candidates made their effect more by their restraint than by any sign of hostility. Furthermore, the scene closely simulated that of an indoor public meeting. The explanation must lie in the viewing situation in the home. It is partly that a fairly large section of the audience will be politically immature or indifferent, but probably the inhibiting effect of the family viewing situation is the main reason, and since this is unlikely to alter, politicians must come to terms with it.

CHAPTER VII

Changes of Allegiance during the 1959 Campaign

The ultimate aim of political propaganda is to influence voting behaviour by making converts, confirming wavering supporters, and informing new voters, and the relative success of one party's intensive campaigning should become apparent in a swing to the party concerned, a movement over the period of the campaign from voting intention to actual vote.

Since the concern of this study is the effect of television over a short period of time, it is important to know just what overall change did take place, and how the period of time compares in this respect with the four years between the elections, when changes in the electorate, in personal circumstances as well as in the national situation, must play a large part in shaping attitude and opinion.

The pro-Labour shift noted by the parties and opinion polls

The assessments made at the time and in retrospect by the party headquarters, and the published opinion polls, depicting the course of electoral fortunes at intervals during the campaign, tended to solidify into a semi-official view of the ebb and flow of 'battle' during the campaign. Party headquarters based their assessments of the changing situation on the reports of area and constituency agents and on their view, from the centre, of the progress of the national campaign; naturally the views made public during the campaign were coloured by the need to maintain the morale of party workers and supporters, and both parties were optimistic about their chances on the eve of the Poll.

There was a good deal of Labour optimism based on a belief in a steadily rising stream of support, while Conservatives remained confident that they had not materially lost any of their pre-election lead. Both these views owe a good deal to the evidence of the opinion polls, all of which agreed on the existence of a substantial Conservative advantage over Labour early in September and of a Labour revival which appeared to coincide with the opening of the election campaign.

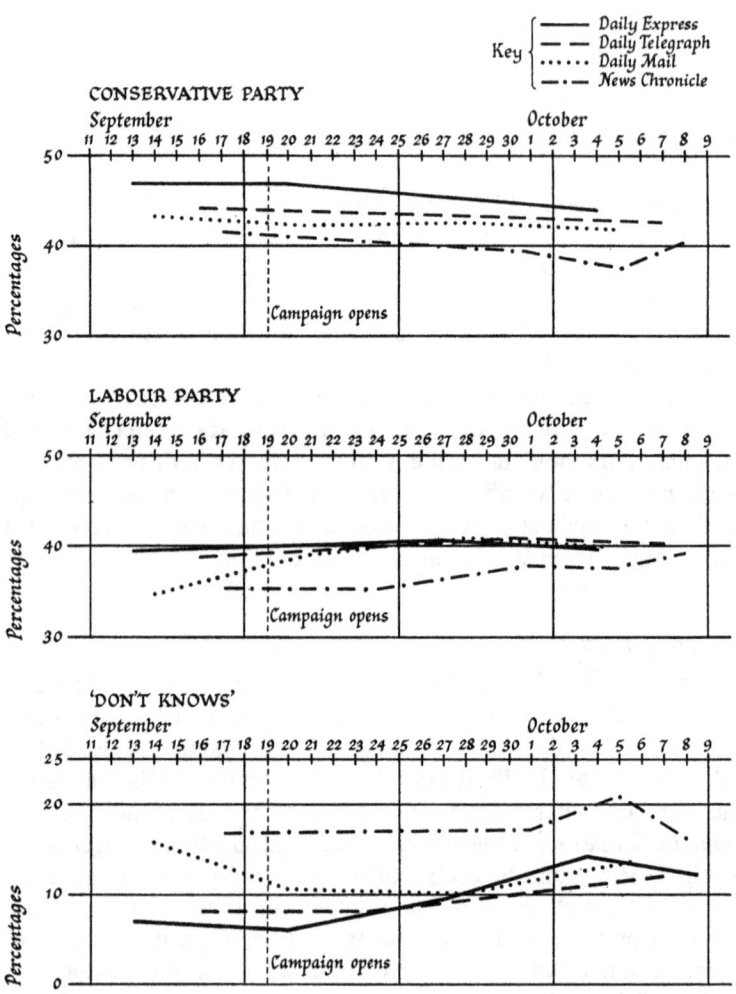

Fig. 4. – Public opinion poll estimates of voting intentions (excluding Liberals) over the four weeks preceding Polling Day, October 8, 1959.

There is a fair measure of agreement between the different polls on the main changes which took place during September and early October in the relative support for each of the political parties. The Labour Party made ground at the expense of the Conservative Party at the start of the period, and shortly before Polling Day itself the Conservative Party recovered slightly, producing a virtual stalemate. It is this view which many people appear in retrospect to have accepted, and it has been used as an indication of the success and failure of party tactics during the campaign.

In interviews with Mr D. E. Butler, which were recorded and broadcast,[1] Lord Hailsham and Mr Richard Crossman, MP, both partly responsible for the conduct of their own parties' campaigns, gave their views of what happened, and although Lord Hailsham claimed that he relied on the more favourable reports from the constituencies which he found in the end more accurate, what they have to say reinforces the evidence of the polls. Both seemed to agree that the first 'round' went to Labour, particularly after the admitted success of the first Labour television broadcast, and the generally unfavourable comment on the first Conservative one. They also agree that Labour suffered a reverse after the pledge not to increase taxation, made at the beginning of the second week of the campaign. Mr Crossman felt that a tactical error had been made, since the taxation pledges were meant primarily to anticipate criticism over the cost of Labour's programme. In fact he agreed that they were taken as proof of Labour's financial irresponsibility and used as a weapon by the Conservatives.

The picture that emerges is that the Labour Party made gains during the campaign, and then found its advance held by a Conservative counter-attack; it also involves the assumption that this brief period of in-fighting could still have gone the other way.

Such a view states a theory of the effectiveness of propaganda methods which is at variance with the evidence in this study, and it is so clearly dependent on interpretations of the opinion polls that it is worth looking in some detail at their findings.

Two very important qualifications must be made, which in no way impugn the reliability of the polls within their own limits. The first concerns the margins of error inherent in all sample estimates, and the second the intervals of time involved between actual interviewing and publication of the results. Both must be taken into account in assessing the degree of movement actually measured, and the extent to which the polls are agreed on the timing of this movement.

Figure 4 does in fact show remarkably little change in the relative position of the parties during the actual period of the election campaign. The four polls, with the exception of the *Daily Telegraph*, which confined its attention to fifty marginal seats, are similar in their methods and scope, and their results are comparable.

Conservative support is shown to fall during the early part of the campaign by three of the four newspaper polls – the *Daily Telegraph*, the *Daily Express* and the *News Chronicle*. The *Daily Mail* showed a fall of 0·5 per cent and a rise of 0·5 per cent bringing the position on September 27 apparently back to the position two weeks earlier. Their last poll, published on October 5, showed a fall of 1 per cent. This movement is small enough to lie within the range of expected sampling error, which on the National Opinion Poll[2] (*Daily Mail*) sample of 3,000 would be about 2 per cent, if the sample were a complete and random one. Between the start of the campaign on September 18 and the end of the month the biggest measured fall in Conservative support was that of the *Daily Express* poll, showing a drop of from 47 per cent to 43 per cent on October 4. Very small losses in Conservative support between the start of the campaign and October 8 were measured by Gallup Poll[3] in the *News Chronicle* and by the *Daily Telegraph*, though the former showed a slight Conservative rise of 1 per cent between October 1 and October 6.

Although the degree of consistency between these separate measures of Conservative support, and the corresponding rise in Labour support, strongly suggests a rallying to the Labour cause, the changes measured between adjacent intervals of polling are nearly all too small to be statistically significant.[4] Certain variations between polls, for example in estimates of the numbers of 'don't knows' are puzzling because they cannot be explained by sampling errors alone. Comparisons are made unnecessarily difficult because newspapers are reluctant to publish information about the size and location of samples: they appear to believe that the public would lose faith in estimates based on only a few thousand interviews or less.

Do the changes coincide with the campaign?

The timing of the changes measured is also vital if an attempt is being made to relate particular events in the campaign to change. In using the opinion polls for this purpose it is necessary to allow for the unavoidable delay between actual fieldwork and publication of results. In the case of the *Daily Mail*, for example, a poll result published on September 30 was based on interviewing carried out between September 20 and 23 and only the *Daily Express* dated its poll according to the date of the fieldwork. It follows that the timing of the move towards Labour must in the case of three of the polls shown in Figure 4 be shifted back several days. If this is done the dramatic rise in Labour support shown by the *Daily Mail* can be seen to have taken place well before the start of the campaign, and in each case we see that the narrowing of the gap between Labour and Conservative occurred before the opening of the official campaign, and certainly before the first television broadcasts. We are left with a picture of virtual stalemate over the period of official campaigning.

The figures are a tribute to the consistency of the polls, but they also suggest that they were measuring the same thing, but at intervals which were too short to allow any real shift in allegiance to have taken place. It would seem that sometime during the earlier part of September there was a rise in Labour support which came to a halt during the election campaign. Within these terms it can be said that the polls reliably predicted the result. But no explanation in terms of the effect of particular items of propaganda or particular means of reaching the electorate seems justified since the timing of the change rules out such an interpretation. It looks very much as if the need to come to a final decision had more to do with the change than anything else. In such a situation fundamental attitudes reassert themselves, and it is very probable that the announcement of the election served more to re-establish old ways of thought and habitual loyalties, than to set up any real changes. Since the trend in the year or two before the election had been away from rather than towards Labour, one would expect the pre-election adjustment to be pro-Labour, on the grounds that when it comes to choosing a Government (instead of giving a snap-judgment at a street interview) there would be a return to more fundamental attitudes. This, in fact, is what the opinion polls show.

The evidence from the present survey, within broad limits, helps to answer a number of questions about the detailed changes taking place over the period of the election. There are differences between the two constituencies covered, and the net movement which takes place between parties is made up of a complexity of smaller changes. The changes involved depend on the decisions made by the 'don't knows', the extent of abstention, and the amount of direct movement which takes place between parties. Information about such changes can only be obtained by questioning the same people a second time, which polls are not normally accustomed to do.

The overall swing between 1955 and 1959

A comparison between the reported voting in the two contituencies in 1955 and voting in 1959 shows a pronounced swing to the Conservative Party. If we accept the intention stated before the start of the 1959 election campaign as a true record of the state of opinion at that time, then the inter-election years become more important than the nineteen days of campaigning, however intensive, because the swing is almost entirely accounted for before the opening of the election campaign. The changes in voting over the longer period in these two constituencies are more fundamental and more permanent than those during the campaign and show a clear movement in one direction. (*'No vote'* in the tables below indicates abstention.)

TABLE 22

Voting change (in the combined constituencies)
1955 to 1959[5]

1955 vote	1959 vote				
	Conservative (304) %	Labour (242) %	Liberal (42) %	No vote (73) %	
Conservative (234)	87·2 +	2·6 +	3·4 +	6·8	= 100%
Labour (260)	11·9	75·8	3·8	8·5	
Liberal (39)	41·0	15·4	38·5	5·1	
No vote and Don't know (78)	35·9	21·8	7·7	34·6	
Too young (48)	43·8	35·5	6·2	14·5	

There is a very marked difference between the later behaviour of those who had voted Conservative in 1955 and those who had voted Labour: 87 per cent of Conservatives voted Conservative again, and only 76 per cent of previous Labour voters voted Labour in 1959, while both parties lost equally through abstentions. Of those who had not voted at all in 1955, because they were too young or for other reasons, a higher proportion voted Conservative than Labour in this election. Where Liberals changed, whether or not it was because they had no candidate, they also tended to favour the Conservatives. But the main source of movement to Conservatism consists of direct

CHANGES OF ALLEGIANCE DURING THE 1959 CAMPAIGN

moves from a Labour to a Conservative vote with very few compensating moves in the opposite direction.

This picture of a swing to the Right does not alter significantly if the comparison is made between 1955 and voting intention before the start of the 1959 campaign. The movement had already largely been accomplished, and any final adjustments made during the campaign merely cancelled each other out. The campaign period in fact represents a discontinuation of the pro-Conservative swing, and though it might be viewed as a stemming of the tide, in terms of voting behaviour, by successful Labour campaigning, it is more realistic to see the campaign as a rather special three weeks at the end of two hundred weeks of gradual change.

TABLE 23

Voting change (in the combined constituencies)
1955 to 1959 intention

1955 vote	1959 intention						
	Conservative (292) %	Labour (233) %	Liberal (50) %	Don't know (70) %	Will not vote (14) %		
Conservative (234)	93·6 +	0·4 +	1·7+	4·3 +	—	=	100%
Labour (260)	7·0	78·1	4·2	9·6	1·1		
Liberal (39)	12·8	5·1	71·8	7·7	2·6		
No vote, Don't know and Too young (126)	39·0	22·2	5·5	25·4	7·9		

Table 23 shows the extent of the swing from Labour which had already taken place before the opening of the 1959 campaign. Although change during the campaign itself equalled in volume the change which took place in the intervening years, it was of a different kind, consisting largely of a late decision to vote for a particular party or alternatively to abstain. The movements during the campaign cancel each other out while those in the intervening years significantly alter the balance between the major parties. The number of people involved in a change of decision between the previous election and the start of the 1959 campaign was not large, and many of these were simply undecided in September 1959, but the change to Conservatism which some had decided upon before the election campaign seems to be firm. Of the eighteen former Labour supporters who said they would vote Conservative at the coming election, fourteen actually did so, and only two of them moved back to Labour.

The swing in each constituency

A division of the sample into its component constituencies provides much the same picture. In Pudsey before the 1959 campaign opened, 91 per cent of those who had voted Conservative in 1955 still meant to vote Conservative, while the corresponding Labour proportion was only 77 per cent. In West Leeds 97 per cent of the Conservative vote was still loyal and only 79 per cent of the Labour vote. In this constituency Labour recovered some of its former supporters during the campaign, and the Conservatives suffered from abstentions more than was predictable from voting intentions, but the resultant swing to Labour in West Leeds was accompanied by a pro-Conservative swing in Pudsey. It seems likely that these small swings within constituencies are accounted for more by electoral conditions than by national movements in political allegiance.

Taking the population represented in the present sample, the movements can be described in terms of 'swing' between parties, though the concept is here of strictly limited use, and the figures are more useful as comparisons between two periods and between constituencies, than as absolute values.[6] Between the 1959 vote of the sample, and its vote at the 1955 election, there is a net swing to the Conservatives of 8·9 per cent. Up to the start of the 1959 campaign it stood at 8·6 per cent. The implication is that the campaign could have made only the slightest contribution to the overall shift of allegiance from election to election, and that the Labour Party did not make any real recovery of support between the dissolution of Parliament and Polling Day.

In West Leeds alone the swing, measured in the same terms, was of 6·6 per cent to Conservative from election to election, though at the start of the campaign it stood at 9·5 per cent. Labour recovered 2·9 per cent in the course of the campaign. In Pudsey a reverse situation is found; the swing between 1955 and 1959 continued during the campaign, to make a total movement to Conservative of 11·2 per cent, an increase of 3·3 per cent during the campaign. The small swing to Labour in West Leeds in terms of votes is not accompanied by a rise in pro-Labour attitudes, but Labour partisanship was already high (see Chapter VIII).

The apparent unimportance of the campaign swing compared with the inter-election swing is a necessary qualification to any hypothesis about the influence of propaganda, and the study of the Bristol election of 1955 provides some confirmatory evidence. Milne and Mackenzie found a pro-Conservative swing between elections, though a much smaller one than we have measured, but no swing at all during the campaign.[7]

The effect of sample bias

The sample had a Conservative bias in that we interviewed a larger proportion of Conservatives and fewer Labour voters than would be expected in a true sample of the electors who were eligible to vote on Polling Day. This could have come about by chance, since the sampling errors ($P = \cdot 05$) are around 4 per cent for proportions of the sort we are discussing, and our estimates of Conservative and Labour voters are about 4 per cent out in the Conservatives' favour. It is much more likely that the bias is produced by the sampling situation, in which the people whom our interviewers failed to reach were more likely than not to have been Labour voters, and by a further tendency, at least in the constituencies where there is not a strong Labour predominance, for some Labour voters to be reluctant to reveal their true voting behaviour.[8]

There is also a discrepancy between the sample estimate of 1955 voting and actual voting in the constituency, which is a separate consideration. The sample overestimates Labour's share of the votes in 1955 by $3 \cdot 5$ per cent, and this tends to exaggerate the pro-Conservative swing in the interval between elections. Too much reliance should not, however, be placed on the sample estimate of the 1955 vote, because a sample drawn on a register four years after the event cannot represent the electorate in the 1955 election. The large movement away from Labour between the two elections in the present sample can be taken to represent the general movement from Left to Right which voting figures in the two constituencies show, but accurate comparisons between the two sets of figures, the constituency vote and the sample, cannot be made.[9]

How the swing is made up

The large swing to the Conservative Party over the four-and-a-half years since 1955 is not simply the result of direct conversion of former Labour supporters, but is a product of different motivations and influences.

A distinction must be made between changes which involve uncertainty, abstention, or switching from one party to another. It has already been shown that important changes in allegiance had taken place before the opening of the 1959 campaign. Analysis of the change during the campaign involves answering questions about the former allegiance and eventual vote of those who were undecided in September 1959, and about the extent and effect of non-voting.

At the start of the campaign seventy voters in the sample, or 10·5 per cent, did not know how they would vote, and a further sixteen voters were 'not very certain' about the choice they had made.

TABLE 24

Previous allegiance of the Don't knows and uncertain voters

Total	Previous (1955) vote				
	Conservative	Labour	Liberal	Young voters	No vote and Don't know
86	13	34	3	12	24

There are almost three times as many previous Labour voters as Conservative among the undecided electors and it suggests a close relationship between actual conversion from one party to another and uncertainty. Support for the Labour Party in this sample appears to have weakened in proportion as complete movement away from the party has taken place, and confirms the view that the 'don't knows' are more likely to be genuinely half-way between the political parties than to be people who will not vote or do not care. This view is reinforced by a closer study of the political attitudes of the late-deciders vis-à-vis the main parties. (See Chapter XI.)

The actual voting of the 'don't knows' shows a very even distribution between the parties, in fact a distribution very similar to that of the electorate as a whole.

CHANGES OF ALLEGIANCE DURING THE 1959 CAMPAIGN

TABLE 25

Voting of the Don't knows and uncertain voters

Total	1959 vote			
	Conservative	Labour	Liberal	No vote
86	33	29	10	14

'Don't knows' are influenced by the local political situation

There is, however, an interesting difference between the two constituencies, which is highly significant.

TABLE 26

Voting of the Don't knows and uncertain voters in each constituency

	Total	Conservative	Labour	Liberal	No vote
WEST LEEDS	35	8	20	—	7
PUDSEY	51	25	9	10	7

In each constituency the 'don't knows' divided in the ratio 2:1 in favour of the dominant party. A coincidence can be ruled out[10] and other evidence suggests a more rational explanation in terms of the local situation, and in terms of the sort of pressures which bear on voting. Perhaps a contributory cause is the operation of what Lazarsfeld[11] calls a 'band-wagon effect', a wish to be on the winning side. A more likely explanation is that community and group pressures exert an influence leading to conformity with a behaviour norm, and this one would expect to result in a reinforcement of Labour strength in a more working class constituency, and a move to the Right in a Conservative constituency.[12]

If the uncertain element were constituted solely according to the strength of the local parties, one would expect the 'don't knows' in West Leeds to be predominantly Labour in origin, which they are. But we find that they are also predominantly Labour in origin in the Conservative constituency, which supports the view that they are the product of a general swing, although it is the local situation which decides how the uncertainty will be resolved.

It follows from the fact that the undecided were mainly former Labour voters, and that they eventually divided evenly between the parties, that a net loss to the Labour Party is involved. The Labour Party not only had more waverers to lose than did the Conservatives, but lost proportionately more than did the Conservatives. It failed to recover the allegiance of half of its former supporters who had become uncertain of their voting intention by September 1959, while practically all the Conservative waverers returned to the fold.

These movements amongst the 'don't knows' and especially the relation with local circumstances points to the existence of strong forces acting independently of the more superficial aspects of the campaign as it is conducted by the political parties. There are clearly influences on voting which overshadow the activities of national propagandists and the theoretical control which the party leaders exercise over party strategy and the propaganda machine.

Local factors also govern abstention

As a demonstration of the action of local influences, a breakdown of the sources of abstention produces much the same conclusions as the analysis of the voting history and behaviour of the 'don't knows'. In the sample as a whole the lack of any swing between the parties is reflected in the even incidence of abstention, which does not hit one party more than another.

TABLE 27

Voting intention of non-voters

	Intention (September 1959)				
Total	Conservative	Labour	Liberal	No vote	Don't know
73	26	25	3	8	11

Although 10·5 per cent of the sample said they had not voted, in the population as a whole 21 per cent of the listed electorate failed to vote. The under-representation is produced partly by the age of the register, which was compiled twelve months before the election,[13] and partly because non-voting is also associated with refusal to answer questionnaires. Those who refused to answer the second questionnaire or who could not vote share some of the characteristics associated with non-voting.[14] It is again the separation into constituencies which illustrates the effect of dominant loyalties on voting behaviour.

CHANGES OF ALLEGIANCE DURING THE 1959 CAMPAIGN

TABLE 28

Variation in abstention between constituencies

	Percentage of pre-campaign Labour intenders abstaining %	Percentage of pre-campaign Conservative intenders abstaining %
West Leeds abstentions	11	15
Pudsey abstentions	10	4

Where the constituency was predominantly Labour (West Leeds), Conservative abstentions were greater than Labour abstentions, and in Conservative Pudsey it was the Labour candidate who suffered most from non-voting.

It is sometimes argued that the elector intending to vote for the weaker party may feel that his vote will make very little difference to the situation in the constituency. Against this there are strong arguments. It seems unlikely that many people think in this way, even where a landslide victory is anticipated. Turnout is not consistently lower where the outcome cannot possibly be in doubt[15] nor are many electors sufficiently aware of the precise chances of their party even in their own constituency. A much more probable explanation of abstention and turnout is the one already proposed – the effect of community and political group pressure to conform to accepted behaviour, which plays a large part in determining fundamental beliefs and actions.

The third constituent of change during the campaign, movement from an intention to vote for one party to an actual vote for a different party, can most easily be described by comparing the voting of those with differing voting intentions.

TABLE 29

Voting of electors with Labour, Conservative and Liberal intentions

WEST LEEDS ONLY

Intention (pre-campaign)	1959 vote			
	Conservative %	Labour %	Liberal %	No vote %
Conservative (129)	80·0	5·4	—	14·6
Labour (136)	2·2	86·6	—	11·2
Liberal (22)	54·6	40·7	—	4·7

PUDSEY ONLY

Intention (*pre-campaign*)	Conservative %	Labour %	1959 vote Liberal %	No vote %
Conservative (163)	89·5	1·3	4·9	4·3
Labour (97)	6·2	82·0	1·5	10·3
Liberal (28)	10·9	—	82·0	7·1

Of the total sample of 661, 27 per cent made some sort of move during the campaign, either in coming to a final decision, deciding not to vote, or choosing a new party. Despite this, there was a large measure of solidarity. The dispersal of Liberal support in West Leeds is explained by the lack of a Liberal candidate which most electors were not aware of at the start of the campaign.[16] Apart from those who had no choice but to change from one party to another, only thirty-one, or under 5 per cent, actually switched parties during the campaign, and of these, nine moved from Labour to Conservative, and nine from Conservative to Labour.

Each constituency produced a small movement, to the Left in West Leeds, and to the Right in Pudsey. The bulk of the swing is accounted for by abstention, but the extent of desertion to the other side seems governed by the same factors as affect abstention. The Conservative gains from Labour are virtually confined to the Conservative constituency, and Labour gains to the Labour constituency. One must assume again that within each constituency there are pressures exerted by the dominant party, and by the whole ethos associated with that party.

Social influences on voting

The effects of social, biological and environmental factors on voting have been noticed in the past, and attempts have been made to estimate their importance. Associations between these factors and party allegiance can be seen in the sample used in this survey; they are an influence which may act independently of party propaganda, but have some bearing on how and which propaganda is received. For any individual they are permanent characteristics and in so far as political parties are strongly identified with certain social groupings they will be long-term determinants of political behaviour, and their effect should be most visible in correlations between movements of social change and political change, whether the latter is shown in a shifting balance of power between parties, or in a revision of policies and programmes. During a brief campaign, permanent social characteristics appear to act as a pull on the voter, drawing him towards a position consistent with the political expectations of his social group.

The main factors considered in connection with political studies have been age, sex, and social class, however this last is defined. Because assessment of social class is so subjective, especially when left to the imagination of a number of different interviewers, no attempt has been made to use it, and the only index of class which we have used is occupation, itself the most important determinant of class.

Occupation was graded on a six-point scale, according to the amount of skill and training required and the degree of responsibility assumed. It was originally devised as a means of gauging intelligence by correlating grades of skill with intelligence test scores. It is therefore a more useful classification of ability than, say, an educational rating and has the advantage of reducing subjective interpretation on the part of the assessor to a minimum.[17]

The main differences in social characteristics can be summarized: Conservative voters are in more skilled occupational groups, and are slightly older. Labour voters are in less skilled occupational groups, are younger[18] and over-represent women. There are too few Liberal voters in the sample to provide much information, but they tend to be as high occupationally as Conservative voters and include more women than men. The differences are expected ones and they represent trends rather than immutable laws.

Age and party allegiance

TABLE 30

Voting of younger and older electors

	Whole sample	Conservative	1959 vote Labour	Liberal	Non-voters
	(661) %	(304) %	(242) %	(42) %	(73) %
Age 21-44	45	42	49	50	42
Age 45 & over	55	58	51	50	58
	100				

Although the Labour vote is significantly younger than the Conservative vote it seems that the difference is accounted for almost entirely amongst voters in their thirties and forties. The Labour Party has not received as much support as it might have expected from those who were voting for the first or second time,[19] and although the numbers involved are rather small for firm conclusions, this finding is confirmed by the Gallup Poll,[20] which shows that between 1955 and 1959 there had been a fall in Labour support amongst the under-thirties. Our sample also shows that a high proportion of young Labour voters are now women, and there is some indication from other parts of the survey that the movement away from the Labour Party, during the 1959 election campaign at least, was more noticeable amongst men than amongst women.

It may be significant that, although the Labour Party has no predominant appeal to new electors, it has retained the loyalty of the young generation of the war and immediate post-war years who could have combined some experience of pre-war England with war service, and who were affected by the spirit which brought Labour to power in 1945. It is in the first years of adult experience of politics that loyalties are formed and habits established which are not easily broken. The uncertainty of young voters may be a prelude to decision making of this kind, but since, for most people, a political decision is not altogether a conscious process, one suspects that the present uncertainty in the young is due to lack of pressure in one direction or another, and some confusion about the relevance of what the political parties are offering.

There are only forty-eight first voters in the sample, but they differ from the sample as a whole in their greater political uncertainty and their tendency to change. Only half of them named a party three weeks before the election and also voted for it on Polling Day.

TABLE 31

Intentions and voting of First voters

Intention (pre-campaign)	1959 vote			
	Conservative (21)	Labour (17)	Liberal (3)	No vote (7)
Conservative (22)	15	2	2	3
Labour (14)	2	9	—	3
Liberal (—)	—	—	—	—
Don't know (11)	4	6	1	—
No vote (1)	—	—	—	1

CHANGES OF ALLEGIANCE DURING THE 1959 CAMPAIGN

The same ambivalence is reflected in the attitude scores of these first voters before and after the campaign. We find that they are less partisan in their views, and presumably more open to influence as a result:

TABLE 32

(a) *Labour Party attitude scores of First voters*
(before and after campaign)

First voters voting Labour		All Labour voters	
Before	After	Before	After
2·18	2·55	2·68	2·65

(b) *Conservative Party attitude scores of First voters*
(before and after campaign)

First voters voting Conservative		All Conservative voters	
Before	After	Before	After
2·30	3·10	3·12	3·84

These young voters are less favourable to their own party than older voters and also less critical of their opponents.

They cannot easily be distinguished in other ways; their interest in political information and propaganda is neither below nor above average, and the same is true of their knowledge of what the parties stand for. Their view of the relative importance of national issues does not coincide with that of the electorate as a whole. At the start of the election they place the control of nuclear weapons as the most vital issue, though with the electorate as a whole it only takes fifth place. It may not be a tribute to the political campaigners that at the end of the campaign it had been replaced by 'the cost of living' as the first voters' estimate of the most vital issue facing any Government.

Sex and party allegiance

TABLE 33

Voting of men and women

	Whole sample	1959 vote Conservative	Labour	Liberal	Non-voters
	(661)	(304)	(242)	(42)	(73)
	%	%	%	%	%
Men	46	49	45	38	37
Women	54	51	55	62	63
	100				

The electorate, which has rather more women than men, is correctly represented by the sample. The sex differences between the two parties, and between both and the sample as a whole, are not large enough to be statistically significant, but the higher representation of women in the Labour vote is consistent with other evidence in the present survey that women are more favourable than men in their attitudes to the Labour Party. Past voting studies have shown women to be more Conservative,[21] and the Gallup Poll[22] on the basis of a large number of post-election interviews give the 1959 Conservative vote in the country as 55 per cent female and 45 per cent male, and the Labour vote as 49 per cent female and 51 per cent male. Although they find this to be an increase in the proportion of women who voted Labour over 1955, it differs sufficiently from the survey evidence to suggest that a local factor, perhaps the extensive employment of women in the textile industry, here produces an above-average Labour vote amongst women. What evidence there is of change during the campaign[23] suggests that movement away from Labour is more marked among men than among women, and the same may be true of change during the years between elections. Certainly a swing from Labour occurred over that period, and the explanation of Labour's support amongst women, and of the slight movement measured by the Gallup Poll may be a greater solidarity among women supporters, a reluctance to abandon a former allegiance, rather than a positive pro-Labour movement. In a time of movement away from the Left, women's traditional conservatism may in fact not operate in favour of the Conservative Party.

Occupation and party allegiance

TABLE 34

Voting and levels of occupation

1959 vote

	Whole sample	Conservative	Labour	Liberal	Non-voters
	(661) %	(304) %	(242) %	(42) %	(73) %
Highly skilled and skilled	47	61	32	62	33
Semi-skilled and unskilled	53	39	68	38	67
	100				

CHANGES OF ALLEGIANCE DURING THE 1959 CAMPAIGN

The principal difference between the Labour and Conservative vote is the high representation of the more skilled occupational groups amongst Conservatives. A wide range of occupations is in fact covered by this category – the majority of office and white-collar jobs, a number of highly skilled trades, as well as supervisory jobs. Many of these jobs would not be regarded as middle-class occupations. It is also evident that a large measure of Conservative electoral support comes from those in less skilled and less responsible occupations, but it is not at all clear that this represents any new tendency for the working class to become more Conservative.[24]

CHAPTER VIII

Changes in Political Attitudes

We have seen that, in these two Northern constituencies taken together, the balance of political allegiance remained almost unchanged over the course of the General Election campaign, though there were slight movements in the separate constituencies. The analysis of political images showed how strongly the attitude scales are tied to traditional-vs.-radical positions and how closely they are related to voting behaviour. Each elector recorded an attitude score towards the two major parties, and his voting decision was almost invariably in the direction of the party obtaining the higher score.

Our purpose in constructing the scales was also to have some means of gauging movements in attitudes towards several features of the party and party leader images over the course of the campaign which would not perhaps be expressed in voting changes. It might be supposed, for instance, that particular policies put forward by a party, or criticisms levelled against it by another, would 'dint the image'. The politician generally works on the assumption that something of that sort does happen. What we now propose to do is to see whether, below the unresponsive level of voting decisions, we can trace currents of political attitude – not necessarily expressing themselves as changes of allegiance – and in Chapter X, whether they can be attributed to certain aspects of the campaign.

We should first ask where attitudes stand in relation to voting behaviour and to conscious perceptions of political events. As we shall find later, what an elector sees of the parties' propaganda has virtually no direct effect on the way he votes or on his attitudes. Yet both attitudes and voting decisions do change and are connected. We infer that attitude movements precede voting changes. When Labour supporters suffer a loss in attitude strength in relation to the Conservatives, some of them change their allegiance but some of them continue to vote for the Labour Party although their attitudes already incline them the other way. One would therefore expect their voting behaviour to fall into line at some later date unless something happens to redress the balance.

CHANGES IN POLITICAL ATTITUDES

Attitudes are projected in the form of a composite image of a party. They are not easily affected by outside events. The Suez crisis defections do not appear to have done any permanent damage to the Conservative Party image. They are, as a rule, modified only slowly, though we shall see that during an election there are widespread general changes in attitude strength and, occasionally, abrupt changes in direction.

What is it, then, that governs attitudes? We know that attitudes vary as between people, in direction and strength of expression, and also in depth. In some, a political attitude is rooted in a lifetime of rich experience and seems to be part of the very fabric of the person. In others, it is lightly held and equally lightly changed. Many factors must be at work – personality traits, social background, combinations of experiences, political interest, intellectual capacity. When we talk of attitudes we speak in parables, and indeed we can still add little to the commonly accepted interpretation of the parable of the sower. We might in this study have confined our measurements of attitude to the traditional-vs.-radical element, which was our first intention, but the further components of political images were too interesting to be neglected. They have led us to the edge of what is known in this field and we must wait for more ambitious, clinical studies to explore their determinants.

A note on the attitude scales

The attitude scale has been used in several different ways in this study, which we shall need to distinguish.

1. The party and leader images are derived from an analysis of far more statements of opinion than were used in the scales reproduced in this chapter. The images are composites of groups of opinions having common underlying features.

2. The scale referred to in this chapter is a reduced list of items drawn from the image analyses. As the general traditional-vs.-radical position of an elector is the basic index of political attitude, the scale *as a whole* was intended to measure this, and a score was obtained by summing the values of the items endorsed. The score represented a person's position along that dimension.

3. Each elector expressed his attitude to both main parties. By comparing his total score for each and measuring the lead of one above the other, we get a valid indicator of political morale and of

voting intention. We call this index 'partisanship'. It proved to be a more reliable measure than the single score towards any one party because we have no datum line on the single scales from which to decide whether any given elector is 'pro' or 'anti'. A person may, for example, have a low attitude score towards both parties but the chances are that he will vote for the party towards which his attitude score is less low. To illustrate the way the attitude scores are obtained, we may take the case of a Conservative voter who endorsed four out five favourable items towards the Conservative Party, and one out of four unfavourable items. His Conservative Party attitude score would then be $+4-1=+3$. In the same way, his attitude to the Labour Party score proved to be $+1-3=-2$. His 'partisanship' score is then the difference between these two scores ($+3$ and -2), which is $+5$.

4. The more prominent features of the party and leader images are represented in the scales by groups of items, not necessarily adjacent, and we shall discuss some attitude movements in terms of these separate image features.

5. Although most of the items of the scale are triggers for the images, a few have a specific meaning for most people. These may indicate changes in opinions of the parties.

Overall movements in attitudes to the parties

The percentages of electors endorsing the individual items in the attitude scales before and after the campaign are shown in the table below.

The proportions of endorsements before and after the campaign in Table 35 do not show how many of the *same* people are included on both occasions. On average, about three out of every four people endorsing an item before also endorse it after. This factor has been taken into account in working out tests of significance.

Sampling errors apply with as much force to attitude scales as to any other population statistics. The panel technique of questioning the same people before and after the campaign adds considerably to the confidence one can place upon any changes recorded, but surveys of opinions never have the precision of measurements in the natural sciences and no amount of statistical qualification can increase their accuracy. Wherever differences between attitude values are discussed, the expected margins of error have been calculated and taken into

CHANGES IN POLITICAL ATTITUDES

TABLE 35

Endorsement of attitude items to the Conservative and Labour Parties before and after the campaign by all electors (sample of 661)

		Conservative Party		Labour Party	
		Before %	After %	Before %	After %
1.	Talks too much	48	50	63	70**
2.	Would get things done in a forthright way	56	67**	48	45
3.	Out for the nation as a whole	67	74**	53	52
4.	Out to raise the standard of living for the ordinary man in the street	48	54*	77	78
5.	Don't keep to their promises	39	38	45	55**
6.	Fair treatment for all races and creeds	58	62	65	69
7.	Has no clear policy	24	18*	35	46**
8.	Would be too free with public money	28	21**	61	69**
9.	Would make the country more prosperous	64	77**	35	34

* Difference between before and after figures significant at $P = \cdot 05$ level.
** Significant at $P = \cdot 01$ level.

account but we have felt it necessary to add to these normal limits before drawing any firm conclusions.

Attitudes of the Liberals

This study has been less than fair to the Liberals. It was not possible without unduly prolonging the interviews to include separate scales of attitudes towards the Liberal Party. But we have isolated attitudes towards the two major parties among those who voted Liberal. They take up a midway position between the views of the Labour and Conservative voters on every item of the attitude scales. Where one is high and the other low, as is normal, they stand midway. But where both are high, they are high, and where both are low, they are low. They take up the same intermediate position before and after the election. Two conclusions seem to follow. The Liberals are a compromise party in terms of the Conservative-Labour division, and this is, in part, their image. They become involved in the struggle between the major parties and their attitudes reflect changes in the relative positions of those parties. They may also have a characteristic image of their own which we have not been able to pursue in this study.

Political attitudes are stable

If we look at the proportions of the population, before and after the campaign, endorsing the attitude statements about each of the two major parties (see Table 35), we are struck by the resemblance between the two columns of figures for each party. In other words, the stability is much more significant than the change. If we take the scores for the attitude test as a whole, and compare the scores gained by each elector before and after the campaign, the resemblance is even closer. And if we use the tests as indicators of allegiance, by reckoning the 'partisanship', or the extent by which a person's score for the most favoured party exceeds his score for the other party, comparing the 'partisanship' scores before and after the campaign, then the correspondence is extremely close.

Some confirmation of the stability of these attitude items is suggested by the results of a survey involving 724 electors in fifty constituencies drawn at random from the whole list for Great Britain undertaken by Dr Mark Abrams three months after the election. He used a number of the statements obtained from our attitude scales. Nine item endorsements on the Macmillan scale averaged 69·7 per cent in the Abrams' survey and 69·2 per cent in ours; nine on the Gaitskell scale averaged 58·4 per cent in the Abrams' results and 58·4 per cent in ours; four items on the Labour Party scale averaged 76·2 per cent against 82·8 per cent in ours; and four in the Conservative Party scale averaged 47·7 per cent and 43·7 per cent respectively. The figures quoted above from our survey showed a greater change over the short period of the election campaign than in the three months that followed it.[1] Tests of significance were made on twenty-six comparable pairs of figures, and in only five cases were there significant differences; in other words only a very small degree of change in attitude can be established. Even this may be due to differences of method or variation between the samples.

Of the whole body of consistent Conservative voters, only thirty-three were slightly less strongly aligned to their own party than to the Labour Party. By the end of the campaign all but two of these thirty-three voters had changed their attitudes so that their views of the party they voted for were dominant. In the case of the consistent

CHANGES IN POLITICAL ATTITUDES

Labour Party following, twenty-seven rated their own party below that of the other, at the beginning of the campaign, and by Polling Day all had moved into line with the other voters, though nineteen others had lost faith, and although still voting Labour, had a more favourable attitude towards the Conservatives than to their own party. So we see that where, despite their general stability, attitudes do change they carry voting behaviour with them.

Stability of attitudes is so common a finding of political studies that it must be accepted as a general principle. Lazarsfeld, Berelson and Gaudet[2] found that 'fully 77 per cent of the panel members said that their parents and grandparents had voted consistently for one or the other of the major political parties, and they maintained these family traditions in the 1940 election'. In our sample only 13 per cent of those who voted in 1955 voted for a different party in 1959.

Benney, Gray and Pear,[3] in the Greenwich study, find that 'the most important fact about political allegiances is that the large majority of people do not change'. They found 77 per cent voting for the party they had named seven weeks before. Milne and Mackenzie[4] say that 'stability is still the predominant feature of voting behaviour even amongst the group who are subjected to these cross-pressures'.

Political attitudes, like those towards religious and social situations, are the cement that holds society together. If they were not stable the social order would disintegrate; parties could lose their allegiance overnight and electors would fall prey to the most convincing mountebank.

The inference in earlier political studies like Lazarsfeld's is that the individual sets up resistances which largely, though not entirely, enclose and preserve his attitude against direct attack or encroaching doubts. He is quick to recognize any alien opinion. He describes as propaganda any view that challenges his entrenched position. He tends to select his reading, listening and viewing on any controversial matter, according to what he thinks is 'true' or comes from a generally trustworthy source. Hence, with certain exceptions, he reads the newspaper he feels he can trust, unless he regards the editorial bias as innocuous or his own resistance as particularly strong, which is possibly the case with many readers of the *Daily Express* and the *Daily Mirror*. One would expect the selection to become even more rigorous during elections, and the defences to become even stronger. Writing of the 1940s, Lazarsfeld, etc.[5] say that, 'despite the flood of propaganda and counter-propaganda available to the prospective voter, he is reached by very little of it'.

They found that the people exposed to one medium of communication were also, on the whole, those who were reached by another, and that they were the more interested, better-educated, better-off members of the community. Nearly two-thirds of their sample confined their attentions to propaganda which supported the views they already held.

Television introduces a new situation. Viewing is as yet a less selective business than listening to the wireless or even reading the newspaper. Though newspaper reading cuts across political affiliations there is a good deal of selection in what an elector reads in his newspaper. Only 22 per cent of the voters in West Leeds and Pudsey read a morning paper the political leaning of which was opposed to their own loyalty, and only about half of these read much of the political news. The television public, with its massive viewing of at least two hours per person every day, must often see items that offend and even challenge privileged attitudes. This is no less true at election times. A fifth of the adult population saw each Party election broadcast and 57 per cent of our informants saw some. These viewers included almost equal numbers of supporters of the two major parties, whatever the broadcast. Some of them would view only because they were reluctant to switch the set off, but an estimate based on the numbers who saw the political news bulletins during the election campaign, when non-political items were always available on the other network, suggests that more than half of this large audience must have been viewing each Party election broadcast by choice. Milne and Mackenzie[6] noted in the 1955 election that 'for radio, television, party literature and reading politics in papers seen regularly, there is relatively little partisanship in exposure'. Without the long tradition of impartiality and political integrity in British broadcasting it is difficult to see how so large a part of the electorate could have been in a position where, either by choice or accident, they would hear so much of both sides of the debate. It is perhaps not too much to suggest that a habit has begotten a tradition and that very many electors now take it for granted that they will see something of all the evidence.

Some degree of tolerance towards the opposing party and of criticism of one's own is a characteristic of political attitudes. It is more marked among Labour supporters than with Conservatives, but we find that at the end of the campaign each Conservative endorsed one-and-a-half favourable statements, on average, about the Labour Party and half a critical statement, on average, concerning his own party. The average Labour supporter endorsed two favourable items about the Conservative Party, and one-and-a-half critical of his own, on average. It would, however, be easy to exaggerate this tolerance which does not much affect basic loyalties. That is one reason why the whole propaganda of the campaign appears to have brought about so few conversions by direct effect (see Chapter X).

The process of re-appraisal

Stability in attitudes is by no means the whole story. Political belief is viable to the extent that it conforms to the changing conditions of the times. New situations constantly arise, policies have to be re-examined: Conservatives find themselves operating a welfare state, and introducing socialist-inspired legislation; the Labour Party has to come to terms with capitalist prosperity.

During a General Election campaign, some of these re-orientations are forced on the attention of individual voters. A process of fermentation of political ideas is set up even within the body of loyal party supporters. There is a general changing of attitude patterns. The extremists become less extreme; the lukewarm are warmed up. And some of the moderate supporters move to the extremes. This is similar to a regression variation, which is a common phenomenon, first noticed by Sir Francis Galton when measuring the heights of the population in 1883.

The particular item on which the Conservative attitudes to their own party strengthened most was 'would make the country more prosperous', the endorsement rising from 79 per cent to 94 per cent. On two points the Conservatives rate their party rather less highly than socialists rate the Labour Party: item 4 ('out to raise the standard of living for the ordinary man in the street') is endorsed by 73 per cent of Conservatives but by 91 per cent of Labour supporters about their own parties. On item 6 ('fair treatment for all races and creeds') the difference, 6 per cent, between the parties is less marked. Among both Conservative and Labour voters this item received added support over the period of the campaign, rising by 7 per cent in each case to 81 per cent and 87 per cent respectively.

The most significant movement in Labour supporters' views of their own party was the rise in the proportion endorsing item 1 ('talks too much') from 39 per cent to 47 per cent. Their conviction of the party's intention of raising the living standards for the average man remained extremely strong at 94 per cent endorsement. Most of these changes of endorsement represent shifts within the image of the parties and are described in greater detail below. The items quoted above are mostly those with most specific meaning.

Lazarsfeld, Berelson and Gaudet[7] define this period of re-appraisal as 'reinforcement' and describe the process as one of finding reasons for being partisan and of partisans protecting themselves from doubt by finding, through the media of communication, new arguments which at the same time provide 'orientation, reassurance, integration'. The theory does not fit the facts as we find them in these British constituencies. The ordinary voter here appears to be more sceptical and also more tolerant than the somewhat bigoted person described in 'The People's Choice'. He has some freedom of action and he does reach decisions with a certain amount of independence. But he is a good deal swayed by group loyalties and also deep party loyalties. His loyalty to his party is not entirely a blind supporting force; it has several and distinct elements, and, as we shall see below, these sometimes push him in different directions. In so far as his opinions move with the tide of general party support, as in most cases they do, he may be said to play some part in the conflict between the contending parties.

Attitudes reflect the struggle for power

The General Election campaign is a conflict of ideas. Lord Hailsham[8] said 'you can cast yourself in the rôle of a prophet or you cast yourself in the rôle of an advocate or a general, or anyone else who's actually fighting a battle, but you musn't try to do both or you'll do neither'. This struggle is not only waged between two (or three) parties, but to some extent between different classes of the community, and between rival political philosophies each deeply rooted for many if not all its followers in social attitudes and traditions. Each party exerts its utmost pressure against the other. The positions of the contending parties may be gauged by the strength of their support in the community. It is not just a question of appropriate slogans, or of putting forward specific programmes which will appeal to a larger section of the public, or of demolishing the arguments of one's opponents. Seen through the eyes of the ordinary elector, as we find him in this study, the party is being judged *as a whole*, as a potential government, as embodying those qualities of statesmanship, skill and humanity which will entitle it to the final vote of confidence on Polling Day. This we find expressed in many ways, in the general movements over the whole attitude scale, in electors' own opinions and our own observations of their reactions.

The losses and gains in this conflict are reflected in the attitudes of the voters. It is not just that a few conversions are made on the periphery of the body of party supporters. Where there is advance or retreat it is reflected in the attitude scores of most supporters. The whole distribution has moved up nearly a whole point, in the Conservative group, and down the scale by half a point in the Labour group. These changes are highly significant. An average loss of even half a point is a considerable movement. It means that every second Labour voter can no longer accept one favourable aspect of the party image which he did accept before the campaign. Both groups continue to vote for the parties they have long supported. The level of morale has shifted.[9] In the Labour group, the average *partisanship* score was 3·5 before, and 3·0 after the campaign. The Conservative voters scores, on average, rose from 4·74 to 5·7.

A clue to the significance of these broad movements is provided by two items in the party attitude scales which are least loaded with the party image factors. The largest changes in opinion over the whole sample are expressed in these two particular items, which are number 9, the prosperity item, associated with the Conservative Party, and number 7, 'no clear policy' associated with the Labour Party. To a large extent these items may be taken as meaning what they say and changes in response can therefore be related to that meaning.

These general shifts in attitude operated as strongly in the constituency where the losing national party was still in the majority (West Leeds) as in Pudsey where the Conservative already held the seat. In fact the Labour partisanship in West Leeds was lower than in Pudsey to start with (3·2 cf. 4·0) but it dropped less (0·4 cf. 0·9).

The West Leeds situation is indeed a curious one. Labour recovered some ground and gained a number of doubtful voters, representing a movement of 3 per cent. Yet the majority of consistent Labour supporters suffered a slight set-back in attitude. It is relevant that the Labour Party attitude score was very high in West Leeds (as was the Labour attitude to the Conservatives, a factor which reduced the partisanship mentioned above). And the attitude level dropped less in West Leeds than in Pudsey.

Within the ranks of the party supporters a movement of another kind has taken place. This is additional to the regression variation, which despite appearances to the contrary does not in itself produce any change in the variability of the group as a whole. Variability within the group is measured by the standard deviation and when we compared the standard deviations of attitude scores, before and after the campaign, an interesting difference between Labour and Conservative attitudes was seen:

TABLE 36

Standard deviations of attitude scores
(partisanship scores)

	Before campaign	After campaign
Conservative voters	2·72	2·21
Labour voters	2·89	3·07

What has happened is that Conservative attitudes have consolidated. Their attitude scores increased. Some part of the bunching effect can be accounted for by the fact that a number of Conservative voters were already near the top of the scale and could not move much higher. So there is a slight piling up of scores at the upper limit. But over and above this effect there is a slight concentration of attitudes. The Labour voters' situation is the opposite. They have lost a little ground but their individual attitudes have become more dispersed. Here there is virtually no piling up effect. So we find, on this occasion, a tendency for cohesion as the *general* level of attitude rises, and a suggested tendency for dispersion as the general level falls.

The effects of local and group pressures

This general rise and fall in morale among the ranks of the party supporters must be affected by propaganda. But it is not a direct effect of persuasion acting on a passive electorate. As will be seen in a later chapter, almost no direct causation effects can be traced. It is largely that groups and individuals are using propaganda for their own purposes, not the propagandists'. What happens is that the propaganda stimulates interest and provides the material with which electors weigh up and reconsider the rival claims. The basic drive in the elector may be towards a reinforcement of existing attitudes, but the situation of public debate and the marginal tolerance of the average elector combine to bring about a reappraisal even of firmly held beliefs.

The individuals within the group of party supporters change their attitudes at different rates. Indeed the group is far from homogeneous. Men and women, old and young, husbands and wives, employers and employees and different social classes have some political characteristics peculiar to themselves. Any individual may belong to several of these categories and so feel the pull of conflicting loyalties upon him. Social pressures operate directly on the individual voter through his workmates, or friends or members of his or her family, or even in the crop of party posters of one colour that may surround his house. At such times it is, presumably, more difficult for the unorthodox elector to stand outside his group. We have seen in Chapter VII how these local pressures were probably felt by the 'don't knows' who divided in each constituency in the ratio of over 2:1 in favour of the dominant party. Such conflict, in a time of stress, between a person's subjective identification and his objective affiliation to groups that, as a whole, vote the other way, is described as the effect of 'cross-pressures' by Lazarsfeld, Berelson and Gaudet. Milne and Mackenzie (*Marginal Seat* p. 91) find cross-pressures operating in friends versus families, trade union loyalties versus family loyalties, 'and where social class conflicted with the political attitude of immediate friends and workmates'. An example of this sort of effect in the 1959 General Election was the tendency for Labour voters in the upper (more skilled) occupation groups to lose faith in the party, whereas those in the less skilled jobs slightly strengthened their attitudes. The higher grades of occupation are strongly identified with Conservatism; as was seen in Chapter VII they outnumber the less skilled by roughly two to one among Conservative supporters whereas among Labour voters the ratio is one to two.

The situation both before the campaign and as a result of it, can only be understood if we hold the grade of job constant and look at the differences between men and women within the grades. We then see that it is the men in the higher grade jobs who are most strongly pro-Labour before the campaign. The women in similar grades or whose husbands are working in these grades are below average in political morale. At the lower levels of job there is no appreciable difference between men and women. The effect of the campaign was to reduce the confidence of the men in higher grade employment; in fact they are the only group to lose ground. The other three gain a little.

TABLE 37

Attitudes to the Labour Party among Labour voters before and after campaign (mean scores)

	In more skilled jobs		In less skilled jobs	
	Men	Women	Men	Women
Before campaign	3·20	2·25	2·65	2·60
After campaign	2·37	2·37	2·70	2·80

Most men in higher levels of employment are Conservative and the minority who are Labour supporters may well have been affected by the people they work with. It is often suggested that the better-off sections of the working class, especially those living in the new housing areas, are developing social status expectations which would associate them with Conservative values, somehow as a result of an improved standard of living or of a new environment. An analysis of the particular occupations of the more skilled Labour voters did not provide any evidence to support such a case. Nor did a similar analysis of the occupations of Labour supporters whose attitudes towards the Labour Party were strongly critical (see Chapter III, p. 47)[10]

Occupational differences also come out in one of the issues chosen as important (making a new approach to old age questions) which formed a main plank in the Labour platform. People in upper grade jobs were rather less impressed by this issue after the campaign (72 per cent chose it before and 60 per cent after the campaign). People in lower grade jobs reversed the order (58 per cent before and 69 per cent after).

Differences of age are not an important factor in Labour supporters' attitudes.

There is rather less group variation among Conservative Party supporters. They are more partisan, less self-critical, more unanimous in their approach. As with the Labour following, it is the men in the

CHANGES IN POLITICAL ATTITUDES

higher levels of job who are the most enthusiastic politically. Before the campaign, the men are on the whole keener than the women, and the people in better grade jobs keener than those in lower grades. Looking at the attitudes, in Table 38 below, we see that there is a general rise over the campaign, but that the men in lower grade jobs lag behind. This is the inverse of the situation in the Labour following. Since the majority of men working in the lower grades of occupation are Labour supporters, the pressure of the working group at election time would drag on the political loyalties of members who vote differently. The women, mostly wives of men in this level of work, naturally do not feel the same effect. So we find the *less* skilled Conservatives being pulled towards Labour, and the *more* skilled Labour supporters being pulled towards the Conservatives.

TABLE 38

Attitudes to the Conservative Party among Conservative voters before and after campaign (mean scores)

	In more skilled jobs		In less skilled jobs	
	Men	Women	Men	Women
Before campaign	3·50	3·07	2·94	2·76
After campaign	3·97	3·83	3·36	4·04

No significant difference was found between the attitudes of different age groups within the Conservative following.

Changing features of the Labour Party image

We saw in Chapter III that the party image is not a simple whole and that several components are contained in it. As we look more deeply into the campaign changes, we find that the various components are affected in different ways – sometimes in apparent contradiction.

Taken as a whole, Labour supporters' attitudes to their own party did not strengthen over the course of the election campaign. In fact, there was a reduction in the gap between their confidence in the Labour Party and their lack of confidence in the rival party (i.e. their partisanship). Yet in each constituency, as Figure 5 shows, the stronger, favourable feature of the party image, identifying the Labour Party with the cause of the man in the street, improved its position among Labour voters. At the same time, the critical element also increased, more than cancelling out any effect of the other.

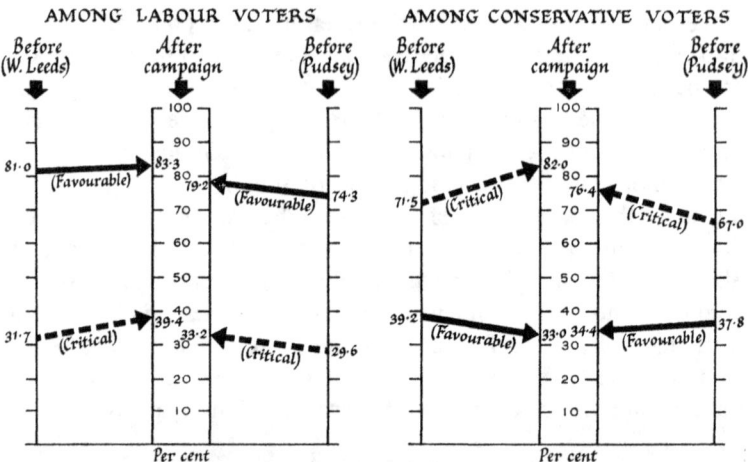

Fig. 5. – Attitudes to the Labour Party before and after the campaign, as average endorsements of favourable and unfavourable items.

Comparing the two constituencies, one sees that in West Leeds – the Labour constituency, the favourable feature of the Labour Party image is more favourable but the critical feature is more critical than in Pudsey. Movements in the two constituencies are similar, as the gradient of the arrows shows, but they operate at slightly different levels, a tendency which is expressed in each individual item composing the scale. But as the next diagram shows, stronger Labour attitudes in West Leeds are accompanied by milder attitudes to the Conservative Party on the part of Labour voters.

The Conservative inverse image of the Labour Party is consistent. After the campaign, the favourable aspect is reduced and the critical enlarged (taking for comparison the same items as in the two elements of Labour supporters' image). In West Leeds, the Labour stronghold, Conservative attitudes are sharper. Conservatives there are more critical of the Labour Party and more appreciative of their own party, than are their fellow-supporters over the constituency boundary.

Changes in the Conservative Party image

All the features of the Conservatives' image of their own party strengthen over the campaign, as they are represented in the attitude items (there is no point in separating them in the diagram). The rise in

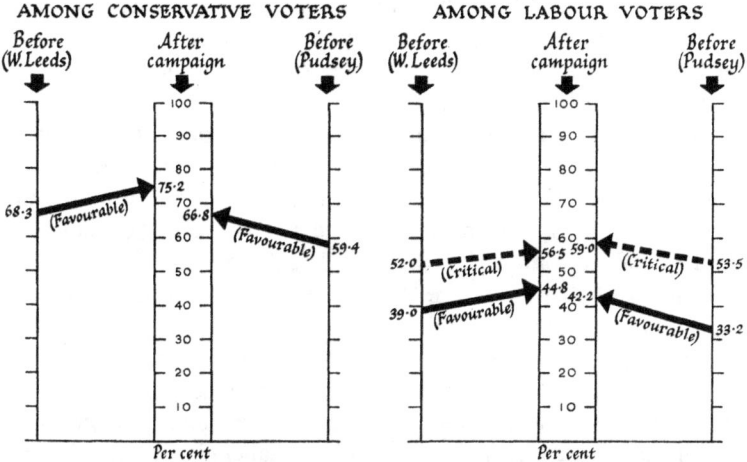

Fig. 6. – Attitudes to the Conservative Party before and after the campaign, as average endorsements of favourable and unfavourable items.

morale is steeper in Pudsey, the Conservative constituency, though the level remains below that of West Leeds.

The Conservative Party's inverse image among Labour voters is here divided into two components (by combining two of the favourable elements for convenience and contrasting them with the critical element). One expresses the idea of a national party and identifies it with increased prosperity. The other is critical of the Conservative Party, regarding it as an instrument of an upper class. But this criticism is not so sharp as the corresponding Conservative hostility towards Labour; and the favourable element is stronger than any appreciation expressed by Conservatives.

The remarkable feature of these two sets of responses is the way the Labour supporters' criticisms increase with their appreciation. This is as true of their attitudes towards the opposing party as to their own. One would have expected the critical aspect to diminish as the favourable increased. One can only put forward a few speculations by way of explanation. It may be a characteristic of Labour attitudes to temper praise with criticism, though this does not happen with the Conservative Party. Or possibly the Labour voter may have genuine grounds for dissatisfaction with his party's apparent lack of unity, and for criticism of the Conservatives. Or the critical feature in his own party image may represent the points at which the Labour supporter is vulnerable to attack, not only from the opposing party but from pressures deeply rooted in society. Like the American voter described by Lazarsfeld as suffering from 'cross-pressures', he has a foot in each camp. He is subject to the social aspirations, the prestige values of the whole social structure with its distinctions of class, rank and responsibility, and to the immense attraction of the whole cultural life of the community. It is not that these influences are in fact identified with Conservatism, but the elector feels that the Conservative Party is somehow identified with those values and to some extent represents them. He is therefore tolerant towards those elements within the Conservative Party image in which he recognizes the values he respects. And he is vulnerable to attack on those same grounds, e.g. of disrupting national unity, and of challenging accepted traditions. In projecting such criticisms on to the Labour Party he may merely be formulating ideas that arise from his own affinity with society. Such criticisms would be reinforced by the historical emphasis on unity and organizational strength in trade union life. The foundation on which the Labour Party's own image rests, as we saw from the earlier analysis, is its 'alterationism', its challenge to the order of things represented by the Conservative Party. This radical position is opposed to the concept of social and political continuity. The Labour supporter, being a member of society is attracted by both poles of the political magnet. The dilemma in which the Labour Party is perhaps finding itself is that it cannot weaken this radical foundation without destroying the only positive source of strength available to it.

The party leaders

If there were strong authoritarian tendencies in political attitudes one would expect to find the leader of a party playing an important rôle in the party image. Qualities which are more properly identified with the party would be projected on to him. There is some suggestion of this in the Macmillan image. Its strength feature matches a corresponding element in the party image; the 'cultural' feature in the Conservative leader image also parallels the national element in the party image in several particulars, as, for example, is seen in the following items which are prominent in the Conservative Party and Macmillan image components:

CHANGES IN POLITICAL ATTITUDES

Party image items	*Leader image items*
'Out for the nation as a whole'	'Tries to restore Britain's greatness'
'Would extend the welfare services'	'Interested in the welfare of the people'
'Fair treatment for all races, etc.'	'Humane and kindly'
'For the working class'	'Concerned rich and poor alike'

When one looks at the list of qualities so widely and readily endorsed by people for whom Mr Macmillan is little more than a name, and compares them with qualities desirable in any party leader suggested by the groups of electors who took part in the preliminary studies, one cannot help feeling that these images are descriptions, not of a man, but of an abstraction. When the man fits the myth, then things are easier for all concerned.

The analysis of political images (Chapter III) disclosed a strong traditional-versus-radical substructure in the leader images, strong enough to enable one to predict a person's voting direction from his score on the leader attitude scale. To this extent the party supporter sees the leader figure as an index of tradition or radicalism. No doubt, too, there is a broad concensus of opinion as to what a political leader should be like, for a comparison of the percentages of our samples endorsing corresponding attitude statements for each leader (Appendix G) reveals a general resemblance.

But one cannot press the analogy too far, for there are critical features in the leader images which are not matched in attitudes towards the parties. These criticisms may also represent latent objections to authority, but they were confined to minorities within the party supporters and could be simply what they seem – personal animosities.

There is one simple way of measuring the extent of the common ground between the party and leader images, and that is by correlating the total party score and the corresponding leader score for each individual. Attitudes to both major parties and both leaders were recorded for each elector, so that we can make an exact comparison between Conservative and Labour leader-party relationships, since both sets of comparisons will be drawn from the same sample. The result of this calculation shows a correlation of ·50 between attitudes to Mr Macmillan and to the Conservative Party, and ·41 between attitudes to Mr Gaitskell and to the Labour Party. This shows that, although the attitudes to parties and their leaders are fairly closely related, there are distinct leader images. What the correlation has done is to estimate the common traditional-versus-radical element in the two attitudes. And in fact the figures agree very well with the degree of variation measured by the traditional-versus-radical factor in the original leader image analysis (·48 for Mr Macmillan and ·42 for Mr Gaitskell). If one wanted to partial out the influence of the several factors, one might roughly estimate that the leader image is compounded of nearly one-half traditional-versus-radical feelings, about a quarter projections of other elements in the party image, and about a quarter personal attributes. These proportions are necessarily reduced by any unreliability in the tests.

What does this analysis mean in practical terms? First, that a leader's real contribution to his party in the way of popular support is a great deal less than his reputation might lead one to believe. Leaders can be changed without necessarily disrupting party morale. Mr Macmillan was a newcomer to the full glare of the limelight yet he had the settled image of a fully accepted political leader. Secondly, as the potential head of the Government, the leader should roughly conform to certain general public expectations. He must give some general impression of strength, of a cultured mind, and of a considerate outlook towards the general public. Thirdly, his character and personal attributes may also be appreciated but they cannot add much to the general attitude. The leader has a function to perform and it is difficult to see how a major political party could do without one. He is not expected to transcend the party and he is not indispensable. If, as we are suggesting here, the leader is to a large extent the embodiment of general political attitudes, one cannot expect his image to be much modified by television appearances, unless the disparity between the fiction and the man is very great. For the viewer tends to see what he is looking for, particularly where his vision is directed by strongly held prepossessions.

There are some significant differences between attitudes to the two leaders among their own supporters, and some broad changes were brought about by the campaign. They can be best seen by looking at the proportions of party supporters endorsing the items in the attitude scale:

TABLE 39

Endorsement of attitude items towards the party leaders by party supporters before and after the campaign

Attitude item	Mr Macmillan by Conservative voters		Mr Gaitskell by Labour voters	
	Before %	*After* %	*Before* %	*After* %
Interested in the welfare of the people	86	94*	87	92
Not vigorous enough	24	15*	28	35*
Strong willed and firm	71	84**	64	67
Straightforward and frank	82	89*	77	76
Not a pleasing personality	10	6	17	11*
Fairminded and unbiased	75	81*	62	73*
Humane and kindly	80	90**	74	85**
Too full of his own importance	10	6*	20	14*
Not always sincere	14	10	22	21
Really honest	77	85*	66	75*
Concerned with rich and poor alike	70	78*	63	71*
Out of touch with the needs of ordinary working people	28	19**	9	11
Tries to restore Britain's greatness	83	93**	70	75
Relies too much on those around him	12	9	25	26

* Difference between before and after figures significant at $P = \cdot 05$ level.
** Significant at $P = \cdot 01$ level.

The most striking feature of this table is not the differences between electors' estimates of the two leaders, but the close overall resemblance between the two sets of endorsements. Here we are dealing with two separate sets of people – Conservative voters and Labour voters – so that people's impressions of their party leaders seem to be much the same for either party. This similarity is all the more impressive when one compares it with the wide disparity in the views of the two groups of electors towards the opposing leaders. Perhaps a more candid view is obtained from such sidelong glances, though the analysis of images brought out almost as many common features as in the party images. Looking at some of the opinions at the end of the campaign, we find:

TABLE 40

Some attitudes to the party leaders

Item	Conservatives' view of Mr Gaitskell %	Labour view of Mr Macmillan %
Interested in the welfare of the people	67	54
Not vigorous enough	46	37
Out of touch with the needs of ordinary working people	21	70
Fairminded and unbiased	28	40

In general, towards their own party leaders, about 80 per cent endorse each of the favourable items and about 20 per cent each of the critical items. There is therefore not a great deal of room for improvement, though much for loss.

What Conservatives thought of Mr Macmillan

We see in Table 39 that the campaign served to strengthen Mr Macmillan's image among his own supporters. Those items in the scale representing the strength of leadership go up by an average of 8 per cent. The idea of Mr Macmillan as a statesman of broad and cultured outlook is also shared by 8 per cent more of the Conservative following. The critical element, which had previously extended in some degree to just under a third of the Conservatives, is reduced by 5 per cent as a result of the campaign. Here, then, is an all-round improvement much the same as the improvement in the Conservative Party image.

What Labour voters thought of Mr Macmillan

When we turn to the Labour voters and their view of the Prime Minister we find a different situation. Towards the Conservative Party they had actually become more appreciative over some features, though more critical towards others. Only in respect of his strength as a leader does Mr Macmillan gain ground with Labour voters. The proportion criticizing him for not being vigorous enough fell from 47 per cent to 37 per cent, a significant change. This regard for strength of leadership is in line with the Labour respect for unity and firmness which came out so clearly in the party image. On all other aspects they were slightly more critical – a decline in appreciation of about 3·5 per cent over all items. The consistency of the changes in all personal and policy items underlines the significance of these movements.

What Conservatives thought of Mr Gaitskell

The stronger element in the Conservative image of Mr Gaitskell is a critical one – he was felt to lack strength and resolution and this criticism becomes stronger by about 4 per cent – not a large margin but one that is consistent in all items.

The other component, which is favourable and is mostly concerned with the Labour leader's personal qualities, shows a consistent improvement by about 6 per cent. The percentage of Conservatives describing him as humane and kindly goes up from 50 per cent to 67 per cent. This change stands in contrast to the Conservative attitude to the Labour Party which became sharply more hostile in the course of the campaign.

What Labour voters thought of Mr Gaitskell

Among the Labour electors, Mr Gaitskell's image is also seen to have changed. Regard for his personal qualities improved by 8 per cent. Labour supporters, as we saw in Chapter III, are characteristically cautious in their assessments. This change is therefore a significant achievement, perhaps the most important of all campaign effects on images of the leaders. On his attitude to the electorate, Mr Gaitskell also gains in appreciation, by 4 per cent. He loses ground somewhat on strength of leadership, not so much because of any infirmity of intention, but for being 'not vigorous enough', the endorsement of which went up to 34 per cent. Was this change the result of what people saw of Mr Gaitskell, especially on television? We could find no connection whatsoever between seeing the Labour Party's broadcasts and this added criticism. There is a parallel between the strictures on Mr Gaitskell's strength of leadership and Labour criticisms of lack of resolution and coherence in their party, but whether what is going on in the minds of voters is a belief that he is responsible for the weakness of his party, or whether they have separate criticisms of him on this score, it is impossible to say.

It follows from our findings that electors put forward quite different sets of expectations towards different functions in their leaders. First, as a national leader, they have expectations of strength and culture which are quite independent of the others, so that no amount of time spent in projecting his more personable qualities can add an ell to his stature as a *leader*. Next, they judge him as a person, looking for certain moral qualities of integrity and humility, and, incidentally, the order in which these qualities are assessed is identical among both Conservative and Labour voters. Finally, they look to the leader's own attitude towards the electorate, requiring a compassionate concern with all sections of the community and especially for those in most need.

CHAPTER IX

The Electors' Knowledge of Party Policies and National Issues

1. POLICIES

Is a political campaign designed more to inform than to persuade the electorate? The intention appears to have been persuasion, but the effect was merely that the electorate came to know more of the proposals of the politicians.[1]

In order to establish some measure of political knowledge, a list of policies was selected from recent party documents, and informants were asked to identify the party of origin in each one.[2] When the survey was designed, it was assumed that the informational function of a campaign was more peripheral than it turned out to be, and that television might have a less distinctive contribution to make to this than it has to the voter's assessment of the parties and their leaders. Because of a necessary economy of interviewing time, the scale used is cruder than it might have been, and because the election manifestoes were not available until after the dissolution of Parliament some of the items used in the scale do not satisfactorily reflect the content of the campaign. It was difficult, for example, to summarize adequately the future policy of the Conservative Party, since its more definable aims had been achieved after eight years in office, and in expressing their policies we were forced to use generalizations which are slightly obscure by comparison with known Labour policies. The scale is in fact less a measure of knowledge of specific policies than a general index of awareness of what the parties stand for.

We found that the extent of knowledge before the campaign was quite considerable, and the increased knowledge during the campaign was significant. The average informant could correctly attribute four of the eight policies to the parties originating them. The average proportion of people correctly identifying each item increased from 51 per cent to 58 per cent over the three weeks of the campaign.

All the movements show an increased awareness of what the parties stand for, and items 1, 4, 5, 6, 7 and 8 show individual movements

TABLE 41

Correct identification of party policies before and after the campaign

Policy	Party responsible	Before %	After %
1. Provide for more people to buy their own houses	Labour and Conservative	72·5	78·1*
2. Stop the spread of H-bombs to other countries	Labour	57·5	60·5
3. Give more freedom to individual enterprise in business	Conservative	58·6	62·5
4. Stress the greatness and unity of Britain	Conservative	49·0	59·5*
5. Immediately increase Old Age Pensions	Labour	73·5	80·5*
6. Abolish the 11-plus exam	Labour	42·0	60·0**
7. Wait until the colonies are fully ready for self-government before giving it to them	Conservative	45·4	50·2*
8. Introduce schemes to enable workers to share in the profits of their own firms	Liberal	7·7	13·5*

* Difference between before and after figures significant at P = ·05 level.
** Significant at P = ·01 level.

which are significant by themselves.[3] The largest change is an increase of 18 per cent in the proportion of people knowing that the Labour Party proposed to abolish the 11-plus examination. The size of the increase is probably due partly to the fact that it was the least known Labour policy before the election, and partly because it is a very specific point, easily understood and easy to recall.

There is a marked correspondence in fact between the time devoted to particular policies on television and the changes noted, and this parallels the evidence of a strong association between viewing television and improved knowledge of party policies. A comparison, item by item, of television time and changes recorded is not easy to make, because a number of the statements used are of a general nature, and a good deal of material in party propaganda could have a bearing on them, without being explicitly concerned with them. Despite the difficulty of pursuing such a comparison far, it is significant that the amount of measurable space given in political television to one specific policy like the Labour promise to abolish the 11-plus

THE ELECTORS' KNOWLEDGE OF PARTY POLICIES

examination was twenty times greater than that given to the policy of the non-nuclear club, and the change noticed in the electorate's knowledge of the former item is much greater than the change in the latter.

Because of the difficulty of anticipating specific Conservative proposals in devising the scale it is not possible to make a direct comparison between the relative success or failure of the Labour and Conservative Parties in informing the electorate, nor can one assume that both parties felt the same urgency about conveying information.

Electors find it easier to identify the policies of their own party, although Conservative voters know rather more about the policies of the Labour Party than Labour voters know of Conservative policies. This may simply be a function of the scale which included as Conservative policies rather more abstract statements, which may either have seemed ambiguous, or general enough for Labour voters to feel they applied equally to their own party. The scale is too crude for us to be certain on this point, and the possibility remains that Conservative voters are better-informed in general than Labour voters.[4] Liberal voters in almost every case occupy an intermediate position. For example, before the election 50 per cent of Labour voters correctly associated the statement 'give more freedom to individual enterprise' with the Conservative Party; 62 per cent of Liberals did so, and 69·5 per cent of Conservatives also did so. Non-voters, on the other hand, knew consistently less about all policies than voters for any of the three parties.

TABLE 42

Average correct endorsement by sub-groups of the list of eight policies

	Before campaign %	After campaign %
(Entire sample)	(50·8)	(58·1)
Men	61·0	65·6
Women	42·3	52·0
Conservatives	55·5	62·5
Labour	49·5	56·5
Liberal	49·0	54·7
Non-voters	41·3	52·3

When the sample is broken down according to party allegiance, the significant changes occurring within each sub-sample show very little evidence of the operation of party loyalties on change. Where an increase in knowledge occurs it operates impartially, and it is possible to detect no sign of resistance to simple information about the programme of one's political opponents. Taking the most significant change as an illustration – the increase in the number of people attributing the 11-plus examination policy to Labour – the proportion of Labour voters recognizing it increased from 43 per cent to 60 per cent, and of Conservative voters from 45 per cent to 65 per cent. Non-voters showed the largest gains in information, but were more ill-informed than the rest of the sample to begin with; despite their large gains they remained less well-informed after the election than the average voter. The association between lack of information and non-voting is interesting, but both may be the result of the social characteristics which distinguish non-voters – greater age, lower political interest, and a greater representation of women.[5]

How the absence of communication affects the elector's knowledge of policies

A direct comparison between those who received very little or no political material[6] from any source during the campaign, and the remainder of the sample, underlines the important rôle played by the communication media, both during the campaign and at normal times. Table 43 gives a comparison between the sub-sample of those least open to information, and the remainder of the sample.

Despite the inadequacy of the list, the comparison brings out three points: (1) the absolute difference in knowledge before and after the campaign between those who are accessible to the parties and those who are not; (2) the overall difference in increment between the two sub-samples; and (3) the similarity between the two groups in their relative acquaintance with each item.

Before the campaign opened there was an average difference of 19 per cent between the two sub-samples in the proportions correctly placing each item. After the campaign the difference had widened to 23 per cent. Although, with the exception of item 6, none of the increases recorded amongst the minority group is statistically significant, there is a general improvement which shows that some knowledge cannot help finding its way even to those who do not look for it.

THE ELECTORS' KNOWLEDGE OF PARTY POLICIES

TABLE 43

Correct identification of party policies by those least exposed to communication during the campaign, and by the remainder of the sample

Policy	Less exposed (141)		More exposed (520)	
	Before campaign %	After campaign %	Before campaign %	After campaign %
1. Provide for more people to buy their own houses	53	60	78	83
2. Stop spread of H-bomb to other countries	43	45	61	68
3. Give more freedom to individual enterprise in business	42	45	63	67
4. Stress the greatness and unity of Britain	38	45	52	64
5. Immediately increase old age pensions	66	68	75	84
6. Abolish the 11-plus exam	24	38	50	66
7. Wait until the colonies are fully ready for self-government before giving it to them	29	27	50	57
8. Introduce schemes to enable workers to share in the profits of their own firms	1	1	10	16
Av. correct endorsement	35·9	41·0	54·9	64·0

Comparing the percentage endorsements before the campaign of the less exposed and the more exposed groups, the differences on all eight policies are statistically significant. This suggests also that although they may not consciously avoid politics at the opening of a political campaign, there is at any one time a sizeable section of the electorate, in this case about a fifth, who for a variety of reasons are less well-informed, less interested, and less inclined or circumstanced to receive new information. It appears too, that despite inroads made into this minority during a campaign, its level of knowledge remains far below the rest. The point is underlined that the electorate is not equally placed when it comes to making a political choice. There are people who, because of greater age, lack of education, or greater isolation are unable to make a reasonably informed or considered assessment of what is involved in voting for one party or another.

It is possible that only a very small minority do rely directly on such an assessment for their motives in voting. There is nevertheless, behind the habitual allegiance, an awareness of a distinction between the political parties, and voting behaviour is consistent with attitudes to the parties and their leaders. Although we can see virtually nothing of the process which actually modifies attitudes, or of the way attitudes affect behaviour, somewhere in the process experience and information will have a part to play.

The comparison we have made reinforces the view of the election campaign as an instrument for informing the community, but at the same time increasing the isolation of the minority not open to influence through the public means of communication. Of this minority, 18·5 per cent did not eventually vote, as against 8·5 per cent of the remaining electors. We know that the same combination of personal circumstances and predispositions is associated with non-voting as with a lack of interest in political communication, but no beginning can be found to this circular process. There is insufficient evidence for firmly concluding that isolation from the normal channels of communication produces a serious inability to share in the political life of the nation, though this view is suggested by the importance which people obviously attach to the political decision.

Women gain most in knowledge from the campaign

Before the campaign men are politically better informed than women. There is an average difference of 19 per cent in the degree of knowledge between men and women (women correctly recognize 42 per cent of policies, men 61 per cent). This gap is as large as that between those least exposed to communication and the remainder of the sample. The explanation is presumably that women, most of whom are housewives, are less personally involved in politics or political decisions, less likely to engage in political discussion or to read political material in newspapers – factors which also incline women electors to be uncertain and not to vote.

This, however, is the limit of the comparison between women voters as a sub-group, and those who do not lay themselves open to information during the campaign itself. In the case of the latter, their increase in knowledge of the party policies is only half that of the informed elector. Women, on the other hand, whose initial level of information is only a little above that of the other sub-group show

THE ELECTORS' KNOWLEDGE OF PARTY POLICIES

an increment over the campaign period *double* that of men voters. The inference is that intense political campaigning can go a long way towards informing those sections of the community who are normally most isolated from information, the only condition being that it must be able to reach them directly, through public means of communication.

As a group, women voters were only slightly less exposed to propaganda and news during the campaign than men, and it was probably their normal lack of contact or interest which had given them a temporary disadvantage. Despite the campaign, some differences in knowledge did remain between men and women, and the higher incidence of abstention among women electors may have some relation to their inability to make a choice between parties.

Women who voted Conservative were more knowledgeable than those voting Labour; each item was correctly endorsed on average by 44 per cent of Conservative as against 36 per cent of Labour women voters. This is largely accounted for by the higher status and education of most Conservative women. Because women in general, and Labour women in particular normally have less access than men to sources of information, they may also tend to be cut off from the sources of *persuasion*. This could account for their apparent reluctance to change their political loyalty. It is noted in Chapter VIII that women's attitudes to the Labour Party were less affected than men's by the swing to Conservative, and in Chapter XI that those who changed directly from one party to another were more likely to be men than women. No doubt the social situation of women plays a part in making them less responsive to changed political and social circumstances, as well as in insulating them from direct sources of political information.

2. THE ELECTORS' OPINIONS ON NATIONAL ISSUES

It was assumed that certain broad questions are of concern to the electorate as a whole, and that a person is influenced in his choice of party, as far as any conscious choice is made, by his views on the relative importance of different issues.

The general hypothesis followed in the survey is that the relative emphasis placed by the parties on the issues during the campaign will be reflected in what the electors consider to be important. The basis for any conclusion about the part played in the process by television and the other media is a comparison between the treatment of particular issues in party propaganda and any changes recorded in the before-and-after study of electors' opinions. We have distinguished between 'issue' and 'policy' and taken an issue to mean a question of general importance, recognized as such by all parties and which they normally have different specific policies for dealing with. In the 1959 election, for example, provision for old age was regarded by both parties as a question of national importance, but while the Labour Party chose to emphasize the need for a more comprehensive state system of superannuation as well as an immediate increase in pensions, the Conservative Party argued that stability of prices and an extension of private provision would be a better solution.

It is fairly clear that the political parties like to choose certain issues and concentrate on them, and the choice of issues is the result of the traditions of the party, and a changing assessment of the needs and wishes of the supporters of the party. Neither party can afford to abandon a whole field to the other side, but each may reckon to be more successful in some than others.

There are obvious implications for political propaganda, since a voter will make a broad differentiation between parties in terms of issues. A party must be aware of the particular issues which at any moment concern the electorate, produce policies to deal with them, and persuade the elector that the policies are sound. The thinking of a party, and its policy-making will itself contribute to opinion on issues, and to some extent it is the function and duty of the parties, certainly of Parliamentary representatives, to bring issues before the public. There may even be a choice to be made between exploiting existing feeling and leading opinion and the advantage may seem to lie with the former.

The method employed in the survey was to ask each informant, before the campaign opened, which issues he or she considered most important, to ask the same question after the campaign, and to compare the responses. Changes in the importance allotted to particular issues over the campaign should reflect the influence of political communication, as well as the failure or success of either major party in turning attention to the questions it claimed most capable of dealing with.

The list of fifteen issues which is given below was presented to each informant, who was asked to select the four which seemed most important for any Government to tackle. In compiling the list it was hoped to anticipate the main planks on which the election was fought, and it largely agrees with the finding of opinion polls taken nearer the election and on the basis of volunteered information.[7] Three of the fifteen items used were concerned with topics which had appeared in the Press near to the time of the election, and which were not regarded as matters of first importance. The purpose of their inclusion was partly to establish whether there was a distinction in the public mind between national issues and current news items. It appears from the low endorsements that such a distinction exists. A further single item – 'Look into the powers of local councils' – was included as a matter of local importance, to see if recent events involving the Leeds City Council had justified its ranking with other national concerns; in the event this proved not to be so. (See Table 44.)

The remarkable thing shown by the table is the stability of opinion on these issues, and the lack of any widespread reaction in the population as a whole to the mass of relevant material to which they were exposed during the election campaign.[18] There is a certain amount of fluctuation concealed by the absolute percentages, but the only items which show statistically significant changes are: the 'cost of living', which gained in the importance attached to it by the electorate, and two other items which showed a decline in importance, 'spend more money on education', and 'deal with juvenile crime'. Even allowing for the fact that the wording of the items may in some cases have given them a very specific meaning, and made them appear less general questions than was intended, the agreement before and after the election is very close. The same issues are chosen, and in exactly the same order of importance – cost of living, old age problem, peace, employment and nuclear arms control – regardless of exposure.

The relation between the content of election propaganda and the issues chosen

Table 44 also includes a broad comparison between the electors' views on the issues facing the Government, and the information or persuasion they may have been subjected to during the election. The comparison provides a basis for assessing the reactions of the electorate to the views pressed on them by the persuaders. The most obvious conclusion to be drawn is the close correspondence between what the electorate considered important at the start of the campaign,

TABLE 44

Percentages of electors selecting issues as important before and after the election, with the proportions of TV Election broadcast time and newspaper space devoted to each issue
(Sample of 661)

Issue	Before %	After %	TV time[9] %	Press space[10] %
1. Keep the cost of living down	67·0	74·8**	7·4	8·1
2. Make a new approach to the problem of old age	53·6	53·1	12·8	11·8
3. Get a permanent peaceful settlement among the great powers	44·9	46·2	16·6	11·1
4. See there is no return of unemployment	40·8	44·1	8·0	6·2
5. Control H-bomb production and testing	35·9	38·9	—	—
6. Deal with juvenile crime	30·7	23·1**	—	—
7. Provide more houses quickly and ensure fair rents	28·8	28·7	7·8	8·5
8. Spend more money on education	18·3	13·9*	—	—
9. Ensure greater productivity in Britain	17·2	19·4	11·4	11·1
10. Improve the health and other social services	15·6	14·8	3·1	0·8
11. Help the peoples of the poorer Commonwealth countries	10·6	9·1	—	—
12. Investigate the nationalized industries	10·1	11·0	—	—
13. Look into the powers of local councils	9·1	6·1	—	—
14. Improve the police forces	8·2	8·8	—	—
15. Modernize the laws on gambling	6·2	4·5	—	—

* Difference between before and after figures significant at $P = ·05$ level.
** Significant at $P = ·01$ level.

The four items not regarded as important national issues are Nos. 6, 13, 14, 15. Item 13 was intended as a local issue, the others as blinds. A lot of people did in fact regard juvenile crime as very important, though it lost in support during the campaign.

and what the parties decided to concentrate on in the campaign. Although the measures of television time and newspaper space include material directly emanating from the parties as well as news-

THE ELECTORS' KNOWLEDGE OF PARTY POLICIES

reporting and comment on the election, the order of priorities does not vary a great deal from one type of communication to another. The electorate emphasized the cost of living, pensions, peace and disarmament, and employment, as the vital issues, and the same issues are prominent in the communicated political material. With the exception of juvenile crime and the H-bomb, there is no item prominent in voters' minds which was neglected by the parties during the campaign. The four items not regarded as national issues which were not raised during the campaign all showed a decline in importance in the view of the electorate.

As an issue, the control of nuclear weapons provides an exception to the general rule: despite its neglect by politicians of either major party, and by the Press, there is an increase in the number of people mentioning the item as important. Although this might be taken as a sign of independent thinking on the part of the electorate, there is evidence that the increased endorsement is confined to those people least exposed to the public sources of communication, and that in the rest of the electorate a decline consistent with the playing-down by official party sources does in fact take place.

The closeness between the principal issues in the minds of the electorate, and those on which the parties based their campaign indicates either an awareness on the part of voters of current national concerns, or an attempt by the parties themselves to confine themselves to familiar themes. An election campaign is not generally regarded as a propitious time for innovations of policy or novel appeals. The political campaigner has his eye on votes, and as far as possible, policies have to be reduced to their most appealing and most readily-understandable minimum. Neither party cared to risk its chances by relying too strongly on an altruistic appeal. Probably neither party machine could have carried out a campaign on any other lines than those followed.

It is difficult at first sight to understand why, in response to such a barrage of material, change should have been so slight; why, for example, the vast amount of time and effort expended by the Labour Party on its proposed pension scheme should have produced no movement of opinion attaching greater importance to the whole question of old age pensions. The answer seems to lie first of all in the stability of existing opinion, and secondly in the conflicting and contradictory nature of political communication which is a feature of any general election. The majority of the electorate has in fact a fairly soundly based and well-informed view of what at any particular moment are the main problems facing society. This is partly because most people are directly or indirectly in touch with newas nd information during normal times, more perhaps because of their reading and listening and viewing than through their own experience. During an election it appears that, for the relatively well-informed majority, little of the argument and counter-argument can be novel and it is not in any case consistent.

There are issues which one party will emphasize more than another, and a certain amount of propaganda time is devoted by both parties to undermining the basis of the other party's argument. The table below compares the views of Labour and of Conservative supporters, and the attention devoted to each issue in the election broadcasts of each party.

Again one notices the lack of movement during the campaign, and the close correspondence between the views of party supporters and the priorities observed by the parties themselves. There is also a good deal of agreement between Labour and Conservative voters on what the important issues are. They both include the same issues in the first five of their choice. The Conservative order of preference attached to these five issues, over the campaign, remains unaltered. Amongst Labour voters the only important alteration of priorities is a tendency to relegate international agreement and to regard housing as rather more important, for reasons suggested later.

One rather obvious conclusion to be drawn from the comparison between propaganda emphasis and change, is that there is no relation between the emphasis placed by the party on a particular item, and the number of its supporters who regard it as any more important after the campaign than before.

If we consider the emphasis placed on issues by supporters of each party, we see that certain issues are more Conservative than others, and some are more Labour. The issues more favoured[11] by Conservatives are: investigation of nationalization, international negotiation, productivity. Those favoured by Labour voters are: employment, provision for old age and the social services. This is the situation at the start of the campaign, and it is unaltered after it, with the exception that housing becomes a predominantly Labour issue.

It is not surprising that the supporters of a party whose main

THE ELECTORS' KNOWLEDGE OF PARTY POLICIES

TABLE 45

Percentages of electors selecting issues as important before and after the campaign, with the order of importance attached to the issues in the election broadcasts of each party

Issue	Labour voters (242)			Conservative voters (304)		
	Before	After	Labour TV	Before	After	Conservative TV
	%	%		%	%	
1. Keep cost of living down	69·4	77·3*		65·1	70·6*	
2. Make a new approach to the problem of old age	60·4	60·0	I	48·6	41·5*	II
3. Get a permanent peaceful settlement among the great powers	37·6	32·3	IV	51·6	54·2	I
4. See there is no return of unemployment	53·0	53·8		34·6	36·2	IV
5. Control H-bomb production and testing	39·3	40·1		33·8	36·2	
6. Provide more houses quickly and ensure fair rents	27·7	36·4*	V	23·7	21·7	V
7. Spend more money on education	17·0	14·1	III	18·8	13·8	III
8. Ensure greater productivity in Britain	9·9	9·1	II	25·0	29·0	
9. Improve the health and other social services	19·8	19·0		12·2	11·2	
10. Help the people of the poorer Commonwealth countries	12·0	10·3		12·2	9·8	
11. Investigate the nationalized industries	4·6	5·0		14·5	15·8	

* Differences between the before and after figures significant at ·05 level.

raison d'etre is still a concern for social welfare, should have a predominant interest in matters which bear on it – the social services, employment and unemployment. It is fairly clear that despite the elaborate economic argument of the Labour Party about investment and expansion, the majority of its own supporters as well as Conservatives, interpret 'increased productivity', as meaning simply 'working harder'. It is perhaps for this reason that it is more eagerly endorsed by those in higher grade jobs, than by those who regard themselves as likely to have to implement it.

Electors reject the appeals of the opposing party

We have noted that the changes taking place over the campaign do not reflect the impact of either party's propaganda on its own supporters. Electors do, however, show some reaction to the propaganda of the other side.[12] The issue most emphasized in Conservative election material, at least in their television broadcasts, was the need to achieve a permanent international settlement, and this issue is thereupon seen to decline in importance with Labour supporters. The percentage endorsing it falls from 37·6 per cent to 32·3 per cent, although it becomes more important to Conservative voters. Correspondingly, the only item which Conservatives endorse significantly less after the campaign is the old age pensions issue which formed the main policy proposal in Labour's campaign. The decline is from 49 per cent to 41 per cent. Although a fair amount of Conservative time was devoted to the pensions issue, much of this was an answer to Labour arguments and a defence of the *status quo* on pensions.

Although this tendency to disown the issues most repeatedly emphasized by the other side may simply be a sign of the general rallying of political partisanship under the influence of the campaign, reflected also in attitude movements, it does pre-suppose a knowledge of the proposals of both sides, and an increased awareness of what the parties stand for. Views on national issues are matters of information as well as of opinion, and since the more people saw on television, the more they gleaned of party policies, television may also, as a primary source of information, have affected the emphasis placed on issues. There is nevertheless no indication that television and the other media of communication did more than provide the raw material for opinion-information. People are aware of what is being communicated, and who is communicating it, but they do not necessarily take it at its face value. It is accepted and modified to fit into the whole complex structure of a political attitude and it has no direct effect on a decision. The evidence available suggests very strongly that people think *about* what they are told, if only subconsciously, but at no level do they merely think *what* they are told.

THE ELECTORS' KNOWLEDGE OF PARTY POLICIES

The individual and the community

As with voting, there are a number of powerful determinants of political opinions. There is some dependence on external sources of information but opinions are formed over a good many years, and modifications made in the light of fresh knowledge or new circumstances are likely to be marginal. The formation of views on national issues depends on both personal experience and information and it is clear that a person's social situation plays an important part in this process. Certain issues are more relevant to one individual than to another, and to one class than another, and it is personal experience which is likely to have the most immediate impact. Nevertheless during the three weeks of an election something can be seen of the process which links one interest with another, and enables the individual to see himself as sharing the problems of a much larger community than his immediate family or neighbourhood.

A number of highly significant differences can be found between the issues chosen by men and women, by older people and younger people, and by those in higher and lower occupations.

There appears to be a division between men's affairs and women's affairs which is reflected in their choice of issues. Although the overall priorities do not differ alarmingly, women placed more emphasis than men on housing, the cost of living and juvenile crime, while men attached more importance to international negotiations and to productivity.

Young voters, before the start of the campaign, differed from older voters in their views on the issues facing the Government. They were more concerned about getting an international settlement, about controlling nuclear weapons, about education and employment, and less concerned than older voters about pensions, and the social services. The effect of environment and of immediate experience of life as determinants of these differences is evident, but a comparison with the situation after the election shows the extent to which these subjective interests can be modified by information.

The lack of overall change in the importance attached by the electorate to the campaign issues conceals the adjustments taking place within particular groups. What it amounts to is a process bringing people into line with their fellow-electors, and making them aware of concerns outside their immediate experience. Where a group differed markedly from the whole body of the electorate before the campaign, the tendency was for it to return to the normal view by Polling Day.[18]

Table 46 lists the issues which showed most signs of this readjustment. In each case, before the campaign, the issue appealed disproportionately either to younger or older electors, or to women rather than men.

TABLE 46

Percentages of different social groups selecting certain issues as important before and after the campaign

1. The Cost of Living	Sex	
	Men	Women
	%	%
Before the campaign	59	73
After the campaign	69	70

2. Peace	Age	
	21-44	45 and over
	%	%
Before the campaign	53	39
After the campaign	48	45

3. Pensions	Age	
	21-44	45 and over
	%	%
Before the campaign	42	63
After the campaign	51	57

The percentages are based on the totals in each sub-group. The differences between sub-group percentages before the campaign are significant at the $P = \cdot 01$ level in every case. None of the post-campaign differences is significant.

The issues which showed a marked tendency to appeal to a particular group or sectional interest, and which after the campaign had a more general appeal, are those which received most attention in the propaganda of the parties.

The inference to be drawn from this is of some importance. The attention people pay to a political matter depends primarily on the extent to which an issue touches the individual and secondly on the extent to which he is able to see his own problems in a wider context. Changes taking place during the campaign in the choice of issues reflect the part played by public communication in extending an individual's view of the world. He comes to see his own situation in relation to that of the community as a whole, and to attach an order

THE ELECTORS' KNOWLEDGE OF PARTY POLICIES

of priorities to national concerns which accords with that put to him by his political leaders.

A word of caution is necessary here, anticipating what is discussed in Chapter X. The decisions an elector makes, like his opinions on national issues, do not vary with the *extent* of his participation in the campaign. In the same way, the adjustments between individual interests and the interests of society as a whole take place whether the elector has been fully immersed in the political debate or has only stood on the periphery.

CHAPTER X

The Effects of Television and other Media

During the short period of the election campaign some political changes of real significance took place. A minority of electors changed their minds about the party they intended to vote for. The issues regarded as of first importance changed, often from those with which the elector was personally concerned to those which he came to believe to be of most importance to the community. Already fairly knowledgeable about the policies being put forward by the parties, the average elector enlarged his understanding during the course of the campaign: even on a restricted list of policies he became familiar with one further major item in every eight. In the more sensitive field of attitudes, too, we find a general shift to the Right, complicated as we have seen by re-assessments of parties and leaders.

To get these changes into their proper perspective, we must see them as marginal, not greatly affecting the fundamental allegiances of the mass of consistent party supporters, yet touching in some measure practically every member of the electorate. The question we must now answer, and the one that prompted this study, particularly in its relevance to television, is: what was responsible for these changes? Was it a whole combination of circumstances, or was it one or two, or principally one factor? And did sources of persuasion operate indifferently on all ranks and sections of the electorate, or were some people more influenced by one source while others were more susceptible to another? We tried to answer these questions by setting up an analysis design which we can best illustrate by considering the case of a single elector.

Imagine a hypothetical elector, Mrs Appleyard. She has voted before and she knows which party she intends to support at the General Election, which is announced for a month hence. There is a television set at home. The old radio set, which is now set up in the kitchen so that Mrs Appleyard can occasionally switch on to some music while she works, is usually heard by the whole family round about breakfast time. During the election campaign, Mrs Appleyard hears members of her family talking about the candidates, and there is an occasional argument between her husband and their eldest son as to whether they are 'having it good' or not. They all saw the first two Party election broadcasts and two or three others, though they did not make any special plans to do so. The set was switched on and there was nothing else to see. They also heard news of what the big speakers were saying, on the radio and in the television news. Election addresses came through the letterbox. Mrs Appleyard glanced over the front pages and left them on the mantelpiece for her husband to read. He, too, glanced over them, but they were swept away with the unwanted newspapers at the end of the week. One day, Mrs Appleyard heard a loudspeaker van in the street. She stopped to hear a few sentences but was in too much of a hurry to wait for long. The morning newspaper was full of politics. Sometimes she would pick it up in between jobs and read a few paragraphs. 'They all talk too much', was her usual comment, or 'full of promises when they want your vote'. Canvassers called one evening, when she was getting tea ready, and the youngest boy was watching a television serial. She could not stop to say much to them, though she did say she thought the old age pensioners, like her father, should get a bit more money. Two of their closest neighbours had posters up at their windows but the Appleyards had never been asked and they would not have put one up even if they had been asked. The children were having a mock election at school and her daughter asked her what the Liberals stood for that the other parties did not. She told her to ask her older brother who had been to a political meeting the night before. When Polling Day came along, Mrs Appleyard went on with her daily round of duties, much as she had always done. She voted, with her husband, as she had intended, and as far as she was concerned the business was over for a few more years.

We found, when we interviewed her a second time, that although Mrs Appleyard voted the way she intended, she modified her attitudes both to the party she supported and to the other, and that she got to know rather more about what the parties were representing. But without knowing what was going on in her mind, and what the precise impressions of the campaign were for her, it would be impossible to say which one, if any, of her experiences contributed most to her changed views. But if to her evidence we add that of a cross-section of the electorate, we may then find trends of association between particular sources of influence and the given effects. We could and did ask people if they were aware of any reasons for political changes, but there is ample justification for believing that the more unconscious influences are of greater importance than those which people are conscious of. Introspection is not much of a guide to the deeper levels of attitude and belief, and, until better methods are known, we can only rely on statistical inference. We can establish and measure the degree of association between two processes but we cannot, from those statistics, necessarily infer causation. Occasionally we may be able to isolate the factor we are looking for and reasonably argue that, short of some unobserved third factor operating on both, the correlation must point to the cause. But usually one has to rely on general sense and cautiously interpret what cannot be made clear in any other way.

Even when we have marked out the lines of association between the many campaign influences and changes in the electorate, we need to know whether any one influence may not be merely reflecting that of another. Political discussion may go little further than echo the views printed in the popular Press, and the Press, in turn, may only reflect the more direct, authoritative statements by the parties, which they also express in their broadcasts. How can we disentangle these crossing threads? To some extent this may be done by a process of analysis which measures and separates interaction between the different variables. Our study was designed to be analysed in just this way, partialling out the *independent* effects of television, the Press and the other main channels of information. For this purpose, we planned to process the data for the computer, obtain correlations and calculate regression equations.

The first step was to look at the results for the two constituencies to see whether we were justified in putting them together to form a single basic sample. The two Parliamentary units were chosen to represent different voting combinations and different residential areas, and wherever such factors influenced the results, differences were to be expected. But if these factors were held constant, by taking, for example, the opinions of Conservative voters in the upper occupational levels of each constituency, it was found that the two could safely be put together to form the single, fairly typical population they were intended to represent. We still had to watch local differences closely, as we could see when examining the way the people who were uncertain about their voting intentions divided on Polling Day.

PUDSEY

'Spring Valley', Stanningley, near the centre of the constituency

Corporation flats near the boundary of Pudsey and West Leeds

View of the north-west of the Pudsey constituency, looking towards Rombalds Moor

THE EFFECTS OF TELEVISION AND OTHER MEDIA

Selecting the important factors

Although the number of questions actually used in the survey was kept to a minimum, they still produced a large mass of data, and we had to eliminate from the analysis those sections which were not likely to produce significant results.

A number of the measures were composites – made up from the answers to several questions. 'Local participation', for example, was an amalgam of scores for hearing the local candidates speaking or seeing them, reading election addresses, talking to canvassers and knowing the names of the candidates. Various combinations of exposure measures, and the way they were related to political effects, were sorted by hand, to arrive at the best predictive single variable. As statistical analysis can only cope with numbers, even the presence or absence of some quality had to be quantified, as 1 or 0, or in some other way. The degree of political change involved in moving from a given voting intention to a different act of voting was determined by a group of eight independent assessors whose decisions were combined into a single scale. Details of these and other indexes are given in Appendices A and B.

For the analysis of the whole sample, twenty-two items of information for each elector were chosen. Twelve of them were political changes for which the campaign might have been responsible:

1. Macmillan image, Leadership component change
2. Macmillan image, Personal component change
3. Macmillan image, Policy component change
4. Gaitskell image. Leadership component change
5. Gaitskell image, Personal component change
6. Gaitskell image, Policy component change
7. Labour Party image, increment for Labour voters
8. Labour Party inverse image, increment for Conservative voters
9. Conservative Party image, increment for Conservative voters
10. Conservative Party inverse image, increment for Labour voters
11. Knowledge of party policies increment
12. Political allegiance change, pre- to post-campaign.

The ten campaign influences or personal attributes which it was thought might affect these political changes were:

TELEVISION AND THE POLITICAL IMAGE

1. Television or no television
2. Normal weight of viewing
3. Normal interest in current affairs and news
4. Television exposure to politics during campaign
5. Sound radio exposure to politics during campaign
6. Newspaper exposure to politics during campaign
7. Local participation in politics during campaign
8. Consistency of political allegiance, 1955 - September 1959
9. Age group
10. Occupation group

Men and women were again separated and the correlations between all factors were computed. No regression equations were calculated at this stage, for reasons that will be made plain below.

Finally, three more analyses were completed. The 180 electors who had changed their minds, or only made them up in the course of the campaign, or finally did not vote, were separated from the others and the information was analysed in much the same terms as for the whole sample. The separate image components for Mr Macmillan and Mr Gaitskell were not processed, except for Mr Gaitskell's personal component change which was believed, from a hand-sort, to have possibly significant associations with other factors. A measure for the final 'direction of voting' was included (on a five point scale ranging from $+3$ for Conservative, $+1$ for Liberal with pro-Conservative attitude, 0 for non-voting, -1 for Liberal with pro-Labour attitude and -3 for Labour)[1]. Among the possible causal factors, all but the first three of the items listed above were included. An additional item was one showing the elector's dominant party attitude score before the campaign, a Conservative attitude being listed as positive, and a Labour attitude as negative on the assumption that this would express a person's position on the underlying traditional-versus-radical axis. After the correlations for the changers had been computed, this same material was split into two groups according to constituency, and two further sets of calculations made. This was done to check the significance of any meaningful results that arose among the changers as a whole; if significant figures emerged in both constituency groups, one would have reason to believe that the combined result was valid. So much for the computer operations. What, then, were the results?

TABLE 47

Correlations between individual variables and campaign effects for 180 changers

Individual variables	(a) Macm. incr.	(b) Gaitsk. (pers.) incr.	(c) Gaitsk. incr.	(d) Lab. incr.	(e) Con. incr.	(f) Knowl. policies incr.	(g) Pol. ch. (cmpn.)	(h) Vote (Con+)
1. Voting change (pre-campaign)	—·04	·04	·09	—·01	—·07	—·07	—·08	—·10
2. TV polit. exposure	·08	·12	·09	—·02	·00	**·32**	—·04	—·03
3. Radio polit. exposure	·10	—·04	—·03	—·08	·00	—·07	—·04	·10
4. Press polit. exposure	—·07	·03	·01	·00	—·16	·04	·01	·12
5. Party attitude (Con.+)	—·07	·20	**·25**	**·40**	**—·45**	—·01	—·10	·10
6. Local participation	·03	·12	·08	·09	—·06	·03	—·10	·09
7. Age	·12	·05	·06	—·02	—·07	—·03	—·10	·09
8. Occupation	—·02	·02	—·01	·02	·03	·00	·05	—·10

N.B. Correlations in bold type significant and consistant in both constituency sub-groups.

Individual variables
1. Voting change (1955 – intention 1959) (Appendix B).
2. Total television exposure to campaign politics (Appendix A).
3. Total sound radio exposure to campaign politics (Appendix A).
4. Newspaper reading ef election news (Appendix A).
5. Party attitude score (Cons. +, Labour —).
6. Local participation score (Appendix A).
7. Age group (score increasing with age, 21-9, 30-44, 45-65, over 65).
8. Occupation (score varying inversely with degree of skill, see note to page 137).

Campaign effects
(a) Macmillan attitude increment (post-campaign minus pre-campaign score).
(b) Gaitskell (Personal component) attitude increment (as above).
(c) Gaitskell attitude increment (as above).
(d) Labour Party attitude increment (as above).
(e) Conservative Party attitude increment (as above).
(f) Knowledge of policies increment (as above).
(g) Political change during campaign (Appendix B).
(h) 1959 vote (Conservative +3, Liberal +1 or —1, Labour —3, see page 265).

Television enlarges political knowledge

The results of this study force us to make a sharp distinction between the cognitive level of perception, at which a person consciously augments his knowledge of political policies and programmes, and the deeper levels of attitude and conviction. We are, of course, speaking figuratively, for we know practically nothing about the mental processes involved. If an elector is asked to identify certain policies with the parties responsible for them his answer need not involve his political allegiance at all. He is not being asked to express any opinion on them. In our survey the list of policies was arranged in a random order and it was unlikely that any informant would feel that his answers were reflecting in some way on the party he supported or even on himself, for most people got half of the items right and, in any case, they were not to know whether their answers were right or wrong. Choosing a number of political issues for prime importance is a different sort of function, for it does involve one's political faith. Some issues became strongly identified with one party during the campaign (pensions, for example) and people's choices might be affected by their political attitudes.

It is important to make this distinction because of the line of demarcation that marks off our findings in the cognitive field from those in the attitude field. The General Election campaign added to the electors' knowledge of the party policies in both constituencies alike, and there is a significant association between these increments and the viewing of political programmes on television. There is a progression in the findings so that the more programmes people viewed the more they learned, and this was true whether we confine the comparison to Party election broadcasts, or to political news bulletins, or the whole output. The link with the Party election broadcasts is a little stronger than with the news bulletins. For the whole sample, the correlation is not large, being slightly more significant among men than women, i.e. ·113 (standard error ·05). Among the 27 per cent of the electors who were classed as 'changers', the correlation is ·32, and it is much the same among the sub-samples for each constituency. If one looks at the list of policies presented to electors (p. 166) it is clear that there was not a great deal of room for improvement, since they could correctly identify four out of eight before the campaign started, and of eight listed one was a Liberal policy (about profit sharing) which received little attention during the campaign, and another, 'wait until the colonies are fully ready for self-government before giving it to them' was less a Conservative policy than a statement of the Conservative approach and was scarcely ever discussed over the election. A more sensitive scale might have produced more significant findings.

What of the other campaign influences, how did they affect changes in knowledge of policies? We could find no significant link with any other factor, either in the whole sample, among men or women, or in the changers. The corresponding correlations were: $-\cdot 06$ between increases in knowledge and exposure to political material on sound radio, $\cdot 04$ with newspaper reading and $\cdot 03$ with local participation, none of them anywhere near significant.

How is this difference to be explained? Sound radio was a primary source of news for less than a quarter of Northern electors and this quarter of the population is different from the three-quarters with television, being on the whole, slightly older, poorer and rather less well-educated than the television audience. They would, for those reasons, be less likely to learn quickly, and any small effects would be swamped by the majority of the non-listening public. As a further check, we separated off the people without television who relied on sound radio and plotted out their gain in knowledge of policies against their listening to the political programmes on the radio. Again, we could find no significant connection between the two.

The absence of any comparable link with newspaper reading is more difficult to explain. A far greater volume of political news and comment appeared in the Press than in any other medium; nineteen out of every twenty people read a newspaper and in our constituencies 51 per cent read some political news. The analysis of the Press coverage of the campaign in Chapter IV shows that, although its mass was great, it included a good deal of personal comment and of sidelights on election affairs which may have served to obscure the real political messages of the parties. A more probable explanation is that an entirely different set of associations surrounds political broadcasting compared with Press campaigning. Thirty-eight years of BBC impartiality in controversial matters, the careful balancing of party representation in the broadcasts and the alternation of programmes between parties, all this lends to the television situation an atmosphere of restrained public debate, very different from the partisan campaigning so often associated with the popular Press. This argument is supported by two statistics in our findings which, though small in degree, are of some significance. The people who read about politics in the newspapers tend to be Conservative rather than Labour (the correlation is $\cdot 28$) partly because people in higher grade jobs read more in the Press and such people are also more inclined to Conservatism. Yet the more they read about the campaign in the newspapers the weaker their loyalty to the Conservative Party became; this was expressed by a negative correlation, consistent in both constituencies, of —·16 and this despite the fact that there was an overall strengthening of Conservative attitudes. The inference is that the average reader was slightly repelled rather than persuaded by what often appeared to be a partisan presentation of political news in the Press. And since pro-Conservative newspapers are in a majority and have a larger readership than pro-Labour papers the reaction was anti-Conservative. The point is underlined by the fact that there was a suggestion of a similar (anti-Labour) reaction among readers of a pro-Labour newspaper.[2]

The effectiveness of the local campaign is sometimes underestimated in these days of pre-occupation with mass persuasion. Of our electors, 69 per cent claimed that they had read an election address and 49 per cent received a visit from a canvasser. In the two constituencies, 73 per cent were personally affected by the electioneering efforts of the local parties. How far the parties succeeded in impressing local aspects of the struggle on their electors we cannot say, for our questions were based on national problems and policies, but so far as these were concerned we could trace no significant impact on attitude changes from local sources.

As a result of this outpouring of political persuasion, people saw more clearly not only what the main policies of the parties were; they gained a better understanding of the nature of the parties, of their attitudes to the public and to public problems. And yet, of all the channels through which this information was conveyed, only television produced a direct and progressive effect.

We say 'progressive', because correlation techniques only measure progressive, associated change, which in the present case implies that knowledge went on increasing as people saw more and more television. This is clearly an insufficient measure, for people are not filled with learning as a jar is filled with water. As we shall see in the next section, the process of communication is far from simple.

The insulation of attitudes

Attitudes changed. In all a surprisingly large proportion of the electors (27 per cent) made some change from their voting intention in September 1959. Although political 'swings' are very small in their net effect, they have been shown in earlier chapters to conceal quite considerable cross-movements between parties, even in the campaign period. The two major parties, engaged in an all-out struggle, involved the whole of their supporters in a conflict which resulted in the Right pushing back the Left; different aspects of the party and leader images strengthened and weakened under the impact of the barrage of persuasion. The barrage was fired from every public medium and through many private channels until it fell upon nearly every member of the electorate.

With three incidental and slight exceptions, no medium or source of propaganda or combination of sources, had any ascertainable effect upon any attitude changes. And attitude changes were certainly large enough to be susceptible of effect. However one splits the sample or isolates single groups, like changers, or people heavily exposed to the campaign, no direct connection can be traced between the message and the effect. One might argue that it is a mistake to expect changes to be progressively related to exposure; but, even if we consider merely the presence or absence of some sources of persuasion, like the viewing of Party election broadcasts, still no significance emerges. The attitude measures have been rigorously validated against voting behaviour, and found to be extremely sensitive. The campaign measures have been tested against each other, as for instance, television against sound radio exposure, or age and sex against occupation, and found to show the associations which were to be expected in the population as a whole. The absence of any association is, therefore, not the result of inadequate measures. Perhaps electors' memories or the interviewing techniques were at fault? Yet the informants' recollections of political broadcasts viewed over the three-week period produced estimates of audience proportions which correspond very closely to the national estimates published by the BBC. Having examined every possibility of error and every combination of analysis, we have reached the conclusion that within the frame of reference set up in our experiment, political change was neither related to the degree of exposure nor to any particular programmes or argument put forward by the parties.

The three incidental exceptions to this finding are most clearly seen in the group of changers. One slight tendency to react away from the Conservative campaigning of some newspaper editors has already been mentioned. Another effect (a borderline correlation of ·12, but consistent in sub-groups) was a tendency for electors to rate Mr Gaitskell's personal qualities rather higher after the campaign, the more they had participated in local political activities. One cannot say whether they were cause and effect or whether the sort of person who took an interest in what was going on in his own constituency and also, as we know he did, saw more of political television, and read a great deal more than the average elector of the newspaper reports, and heard more of the party broadcasts on sound radio, revised his views as a general consequence of this exposure or for some more remote reason motivating all of these activities. The third exception was also connected with Mr Gaitskell's personal standing and relates it positively but slightly to the viewing of television political broadcasts (again the correlation is only ·12 – of borderline significance but consistent in sub-groups).

It is, perhaps, not easy to see that what is established here is not merely an absence of cause and effect but *a definite and consistent barrier between sources of communication and movements of attitude in the political field at the General Election.* It is not that the causal connections between television or the sources of information and campaign changes were insignificant – rather that the two were persistently and in a highly significant way disconnected. It is not easy to convey the impression made by table after table of statistics of exposure plotted against statistics of change, the two fields varying independently, so that at every level of exposure one finds every variation in degrees of attitude change.

To put this finding thoroughly to the test, a number of combinations of factors were considered. Thinking that it might be the total weight of the barrage rather than the accurate fire of any particular propaganda that might count in the end, we plotted out the total recorded exposure for each elector in the sample against every type of attitude change, counting not only movements towards or away from either major party, but also total change in any direction. Again, no consistent association could be found. Among the changers we distinguished those who moved from support of one party to another over the period of the campaign, and whose interest in politics and exposure to the campaigning were typical of the solid mass of constant voters; in another category are those who remained doubtful or abstained from voting, whose general level of interest was low, and who tended to avoid or, by some means, see less of the arguments of the parties. By taking these two groups together, one appears to have a small measure of association between political change and exposure to propaganda. But it is not found as a factor operating differentially *within* these groups, building up increasing change with increasing exposure. So far as we can see, it is a group difference which does not form any exception to the principle of resistance found in the sample as a whole.

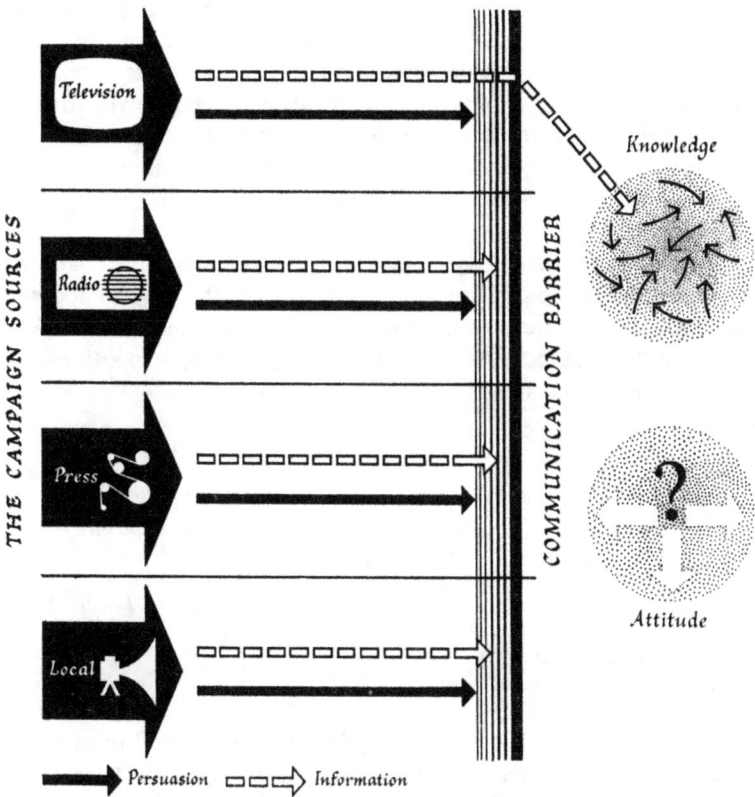

Fig. 7. – The direct impact of the campaign on electors. Knowledge of party policies is increased by television. Political attitudes are not directly affected by any of the campaign sources.

The personal element

Lazarsfeld et al,[3] in their study of the 1940 Presidential Election, speak of a 'two-step flow of communications', first from the formal media to 'opinion leaders' and then from them to the less active members of the population. Could it be that the formal campaign finds fruitful soil only in 'opinion leaders' and that it is they who activize and influence the mass of the electorate? Two-thirds of our electors said they had 'discussed some of the issues with people at work or at home'. These could be 'opinion leaders' or people whose opinions had been led. Presumably the former would talk to more people than the latter and so would be in a minority, but it is more likely that there is no sharply discriminated group at all and that 'discussing' shades off from conscious political advocates to people who are just interested enough to be willing to ask serious questions. The 'discussers', as a whole, lay themselves open to more formal sources of persuasion than the less talkative minority, as the following table shows.

We find almost as many of these discussers among the 'changers' as in the constant party supporters, even among those who appear to have had few opinions of their own with which to lead others. And between their sources of information and their changes in attitude, as with all the others, stands the same barrier.

TABLE 48

Average amount of exposure to the political campaign from three sources (as percentages of total possible exposure) for 'discussers'

	TV %	Newspaper %	Local %
'Discussers' (421)	30	46	44
'Non-discussers' (240)	21	24	34

Lazarsfeld[4] says that 'ideas often flow *from* radio and print *to* the opinion leaders and *from* them to the less active sections of the population'. But his index of exposure[5] shows only about the same variation between opinion leaders and others as we find between 'discussers' and others. He isolates about 21 per cent of his entire sample group as opinion leaders (defined as people who have tried to convince others of their political ideas and have had their advice asked on political questions). There is clearly a continuum in his data as in ours, from the most active to the least. If our 'discussers' include a fair proportion of what he would call opinion leaders, and if, as he suggests, they get their ideas from the formal media, we find no evidence at all that they are directly and progressively affected by that exposure. Whatever it is that screens the others from persuasion through the mass media also cuts off the 'discussers' and, with them, the opinion leaders.

The unexposed

Exposure to the media decreases until at the end of the scale there are a few whose ears are closed to almost every source. In the whole of our sample of electors we found only thirteen people who had apparently avoided any aspect of the campaign about which we enquired. Nine were non-voters of whom five were aged 91, 87, 84, 82, and 70, and the other four were: a housepainter who did not vote in 1955 and never intended to vote; a forty-two year old widow, formerly a millworker, who was ill; the young wife of a storekeeper who was just not interested in national problems; and a thirty-one year old widow whose late husband was a lorry driver and who, as a regular viewer of 'Panorama' and a reader of the *Daily Herald*, and the *Yorkshire Evening Post*, probably saw more of the election than she cared to admit. The remaining four all voted Conservative: one was a sixty-four year old widow who did not take any newspaper and probably was as cut off from outside news as she said she was; one was a forty-three year old labourer who only saw the *Yorkshire Evening Post*, though it is difficult to understand how he could have avoided seeing some political news in it at election time; the third was the young wife of a manufacturer and wholesaler who claimed that she read a fair amount of *The Times*; the fourth was a company director who read, he said, nearly all of the *Yorkshire Evening Post* every day and was a regular viewer of 'Panorama'. Excluding those who were too old or too infirm to follow what was happening in the news, we are left with only six or seven people who evidently had little interest in politics, judging by their opinions and their voting record, and believed that they had not seen anything of the campaign though they had probably received a good deal more than they knew.

We have already suggested that the campaign seemed to have a dynamic of its own and that a good deal of political information was circulated even to those who appear to have little access to it through the public means of communication. It is difficult to see how this could come about except through personal contact and conversation.

Attitudes affect exposure to the campaign

It is clear, then, that in these constituencies nearly every elector had one point of contact, and most had several, with the political messages of the parties. Although people's attitudes and voting intentions did not change in any way that could be associated with what they heard of the campaign, there *is* a connection between their exposure and their attitude position towards the parties. This relationship is not a single linear one, in which, for instance, people see more of the campaign as their attitudes become stronger (i.e. more partisan), which has been the accepted view of social scientists. Lazarsfeld[6] says: 'the more interested people are in the election . . . the more they expose themselves to campaign propaganda'. He had no measure of attitude but he regarded an elector's interest as 'closely related to his involvement in the political scene'. Milne and Mackenzie[7] say that 'the interest and exposure of the opinion leaders was far above the average', and that they 'were in some respects more *partisan* than the average elector'.

Figures 8 and 9 show the total campaign exposure through the mass media (television, plus radio, plus newspaper reading) for each level of partisanship.[8] The average partisanship scores before and after the campaign are indicated by the shaded area.

We see that the intake of campaign material does increase among both Labour and Conservative supporters as their attitudes rise above the average for the whole group, but it also increases correspondingly to nearly double the rate for the average elector where the partisanship is weaker. Presumably, here the elector is coming up against strong cross fire from both parties and is in a state of indecision which induces him to hear more of the campaign than the more assured supporter. At the extremes the level of exposure tends to fall again, where one might suppose the mind begins to close, from deep prejudice at one end and from boredom at the other. There is sufficient similarity between the two graphs to suggest that a bi-modal distribution of this sort is to be expected.

These graphs do not indicate causal effects, for, as we have seen, there is no *progressive* connection between attitude change and exposure. To verify the point, we isolated the Conservative and Labour voters whose partisanship scores lay within the brackets corresponding to the positions of highest exposure, to see whether television or other campaign propaganda could account for any

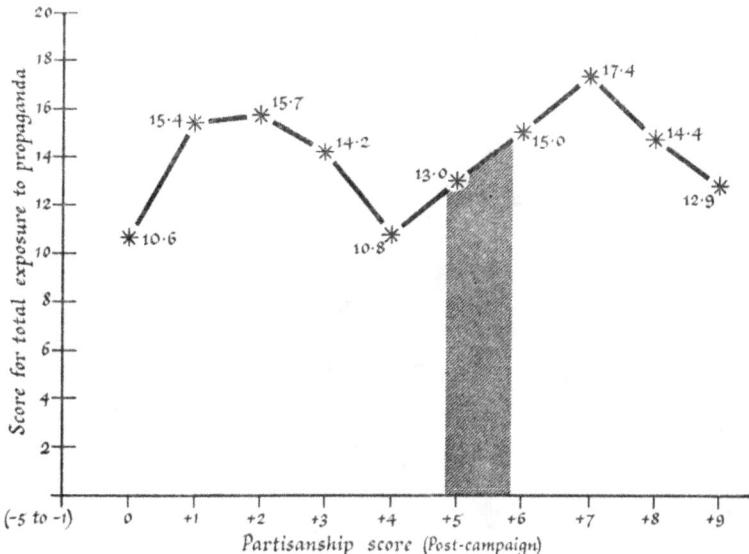

Fig. 8. – Exposure to the campaign at varying levels of Conservative partisanship (post-campaign) towards the Conservative Party. The mean score, 5·70, is indicated by the right-hand limit of the shaded area. (The left-hand limit indicates the mean pre-campaign position, 4·74, not related to exposure scores.)

changes in their attitudes. The results showed that there is no significant relationship. There is only a pattern in the extent to which people follow the campaign; none in its effect. Most of the electors have moderate partisanship scores. It follows, from the evidence of Figures 8 and 9, that the audience for any election propaganda consists mostly of two sorts of elector – those with moderately strong partisan views and those moderately weak in their support of their party, rather than extremists.

Why did the campaign have no direct effect on attitudes?
(a) *Is there a time lag?*
Professor F. C. Bartlett has said that 'there is always a lag between the acceptance of opinions and their incorporation in practice'.[9] The period of time required, he says is 'normally considerable'. He is thinking here of long term propaganda in which 'the opinions of one

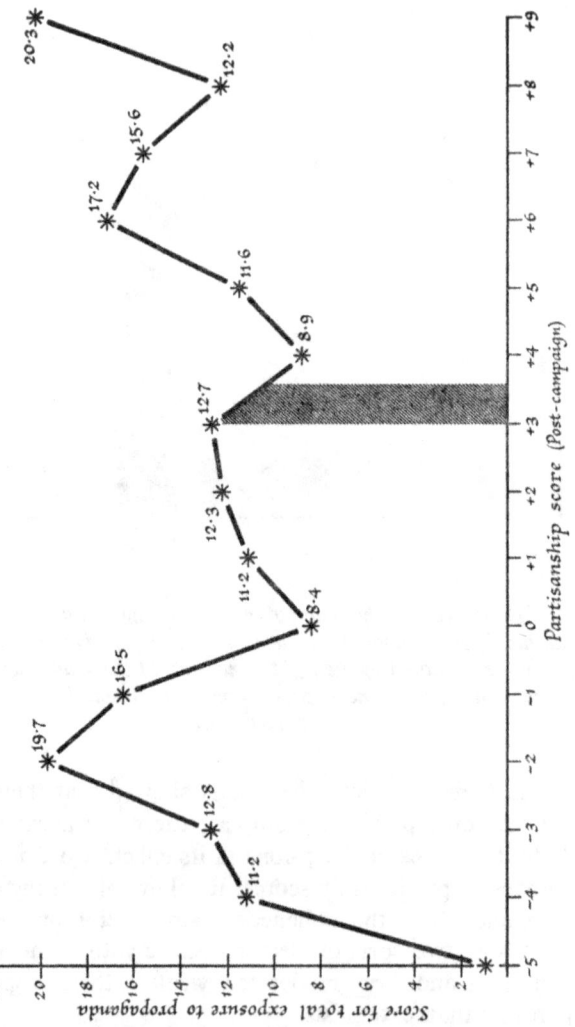

Fig. 9. – Exposure to the campaign at varying levels of Labour partisanship (post-campaign) towards the Labour Party. The mean score, 3·0, is indicated by the left-hand limit of the shaded area. (The right-hand limit indicates the pre-campaign position, 3·50, not related to exposure scores.)

generation become the politics of the next'. To secure short-term effects, he believes 'it is necessary to ferment and maintain a high level of public excitement and the predominant appeals must all the time be to emotion and to sentiment. Among the emotions exploited, fear has generally had, and probably must have, a large part to play.'

If the ultimate effects of the General Election campaign could only be seen in the months to come, it would seem extraordinary that there should be a complete mental lapse at the time, during which no effect is discernible. In other fields of learning, long-term effects are always anticipated by some immediate reaction.

There might well be a time-lag between the electors' perception of changes in a political party and modifications of its image in their minds, just as we saw that there was a time-lag between modifications of attitudes and changes in voting behaviour; for instance, a number of Labour supporters still voted Labour although their attitudes had shifted from pro-Labour to anti-Labour. But one would expect to find differential rates of reaction between individuals, and would expect some part of these reactions to show up in our correlations. We know that attitudes are renewed and revised. Parties and political conditions change. Where an image is no longer supported by the reality it will dissolve.

In the case of the election campaign, we did register quite significant shifts of attitude affecting the whole body of party supporters. If these could not be linked to any campaign exposure how could one expect subsequent measurements to establish any closer connections?

An extension of the time-lag theory is that the attitude changes we recorded were the result of propaganda put out during the months before the election. Butler and Rose[10] give a description of the Conservative advertising campaign, costing just under half a million pounds and extending over the fifteen months leading up to the election, to illustrate their inference that Conservative propaganda assumed that 'people so often decide how to vote long before an election, they must also be exposed to propaganda long before an election'. This advertising campaign was certainly skilfully presented and did conform in several ways to Bartlett's prescription for successful propaganda, including the appeal to fear in 'Don't let Labour ruin it' (i.e. your better life). We can find no means of gauging whether this campaign had any perceptible effect on the outcome of the election. It may have accounted for part of the swing to the Right which took place before the campaign opened. It might also have been responsible for the *general* attitude movement in favour of the Conservatives which we recorded. But not all attitude changes were to the Right and, in fact, the inter-party changers in the period of the campaign included as many conversions to Labour as to Conservative. We also have to account for them.

A refinement of the time-lag theory is that the election campaign simply activated latent attitude changes already determined by some earlier experiences in any direction. If this were so, one would expect to find that as people saw more of the campaign there would be increasing shifts in attitude either to the Conservative or to the Labour Party. To put this theory to the test, we analysed movements in attitude, *regardless of direction*, in terms of exposure to various campaign influences. No significant association came to light. Whether electors had seen very much of the campaign or next to nothing, they showed the same broad distribution of attitude movements. We must therefore conclude that there was no activation effect of this sort. The long-term effects of the Government's record and of the advertising campaigns may have played some part but they cannot account for all the attitude changes.

(b) *Do propaganda and counter-propaganda produce a stalemate?*

It is quite commonly believed that the elector chooses to hear only those political views that will reinforce his own existing convictions. Lazarsfeld *et al*[11] wrote that 'he elects to expose himself to the propaganda with which he already agrees and to seal himself off from the propaganda with which he might disagree'. No doubt there is a general inclination in all of us to look for support for the views we already hold and to look critically at ideas that challenge them. But when we came to examine the way the campaign propaganda and news from all the various sources fell upon the electorate, we were at once struck by the almost complete absence of one-sided exposure.

There is a tendency for people to read a newspaper whose political views roughly coincide with their own; as we saw in Chapter IV only about a quarter of the electors regularly read morning papers the general political slant of which is opposed to their own inclinations. But every newspaper reported something, if only a little, of all the parties' statements, and the Yorkshire evening papers, which are particularly widely read in the constituencies we studied, generally gave a fairly extensive coverage of all points of view.

The audiences for the Party election broadcasts were almost equally divided between followers of the two parties, whatever the party concerned with the programme. The television and radio news bulletins, which – in the 1959 election for the first time – gave almost hourly summaries of the campaign, were scrupulously impartial and managed to balance all points of view expertly in practically every bulletin.

But did electors pay attention to the arguments from the other side? We find that they did. The 'voluntary' viewers (those whose viewing of political broadcasts appeared to be by choice) whose numbers accounted for nearly two-thirds of the audiences for Party election broadcasts, were clearly willing to hear a message with which they expected to disagree. It was clear, too, from the particular issues on which electors changed their views over the course of the campaign, and from the policy points with which they became more familiar, that they had been hearing both sides of the argument.

The theme of Bartlett's essay[12] is that propaganda, to be effective, must be internally consistent. Counter-propaganda will destroy that consistency. This may well be true of the totalitarian societies of which Bartlett was writing. Some experiments carried out in America have compared the relative effectiveness of one-sided and two-sided propaganda in standing up to counter-propaganda. Hovland, Lumsdaine and Sheffield[13] presented some arguments to groups of soldiers on the prospect of an early end of the war with Japan. One group was given only the arguments for thinking the war would be a long one. The other group was given the same arguments with a number of considerations on the other side. They found that the two-sided argument was a good deal more effective with men who were initially opposed to the proposition; those who were already favourable were more affected by the one-sided case. The implication of this experiment in an electoral situation is that, since all propaganda is one-sided, the parties would only have much success with their own supporters. While this might produce something of a stalemate in voting behaviour, the attitude movements within the party groups should then be related to their own party's propaganda.

A further experiment by Lumsdaine and Janis[14] found that counter-propaganda delivered at a later date largely destroyed the effects of earlier one-sided propaganda, but hardly affected the results of a form of presentation in which arguments on both sides were presented. The implication again is that where propaganda and counter-propaganda are both one-sided and are alternately presented each may largely negate the effect of the other.

To put this theory to the test in the election situation, we separated off from the sample all those electors who appeared to have received propaganda from only the party they supported. There were only fifteen electors who had seen two or more Party election broadcasts put out only by the party they voted for; if we also include those who saw one Liberal Party broadcast in addition to two or more of their own, the number goes up to thirty-seven. But some of these saw the television election news fairly regularly or watched the 'Hustings' or 'Last Debate' programmes in which arguments on all sides were presented. All but four, however, read newspapers which supported the same parties as themselves.

The average attitude increment (not partisanship score) for the twenty-eight Conservatives in this group was ·61 towards their own party, compared with an average of ·74 for the whole sample. The corresponding increment for the nine Labour Party voters was −·02 compared with −·03 for the sample as a whole. One Conservative voter was found to have seen one of his party's own party broadcasts, but had neither read a newspaper, nor seen any television news, nor seen any of the public debate programmes. His attitude score showed increments of +2 to *both* the Conservative and the Labour Parties.

This evidence does not support the theory that one-sided propaganda would be effective where no counter-propaganda could cancel out its effect. Of course, the situation in a General Election is not at all like that of a laboratory experiment – there is fire from all sides, and posters, general conversation, loud-speaker addresses and the widespread reporting of every side of the campaign make it very difficult indeed for any individual to escape some of the arguments from the other side. Nevertheless, had the counter-propaganda theory been justified in this context, we would certainly have expected some differential effects with those whose exposure was more one-sided than the general run of electors.

(c) *Group pressures cut across propaganda*

An individual belongs to one or more social or cultural groups and tends to conform to its values. He does not do so unwillingly, under protest as it were. He may be less than half aware of what is happening. In a mining village street the conformity may take the form of joining in the social activities at the pub or welfare, or colour-washing the front doorstep to match the others in the street, or polishing the brass on the hearth, or wearing a cap and not carrying an umbrella. And in a middle-class residential suburb a different pattern will be expected, expressed rather more in terms of what not to do than positively. The individual is quick to perceive the manner of speech, or style of dress or make of car expected by the community. This conformity is not irksome to most members of a group, for it provides them with a sense of security through the stability of the group. At a General Election these group sanctions find political expression, easily detected from the predominant colour of the posters.

Group sanctions act below the level at which people receive political information and think about what they have seen. They reinforce attitudes, accentuating their screening effect against persuasion and driving the non-conformer into isolation. As we saw in Chapter VII working group pressures pull the non-conforming, or uncertain or less politically conscious members towards the group view; in the working class towards Labour, and in the middle class towards Conservatism. The electors who were uncertain how to vote before the campaign divided in the ratio of 2:1 in favour of the dominant party in their constituency – to Conservative in Pudsey and Labour in West Leeds. By cutting across the exposure pattern, group pressures may reduce the direct effect of national propaganda. They may bring about changes which show up as differences between whole groups, but they can hardly produce individual variation within groups. Nor can they account for the swing towards the Conservative Party that took place before the election, nor the general attitude movement in that direction over the campaign.

(d) *The importance of individual judgment*

Group pressures cannot explain the failure of the campaign to connect. The conflicting effects of counter-propaganda cannot account for such changes as did occur. The long-term effects of public impressions of the Government and the Opposition records in the year or so before the election, and the unprecedented advertising campaign, may have been partly responsible for the general movement towards Conservative, but they, too, cannot explain the individual attitude movements which, within the campaign period, seem to be unrelated to the campaign exposure.

We are, therefore, driven to two conclusions. The first is that political attitudes have some protective device which, once the elector has recognized an election campaign as propaganda aimed at persuading him, can apparently screen off and, at least temporarily, suppress any direct effect. Secondly, behind this protective screen there seems to be an element of independent judgment and free choice at work. Free will, which by definition resists persuasion, is usually the last factor to be considered by social scientists, the authors not excepted, if indeed it is considered at all.

Such independence of thought must operate within limits. The individual is subject to many influences. He has inborn tendencies which dispose him to react to events in a particular way and connect him to his antecedents. He is partly a product of his upbringing, in which his early education and his family background are vital factors. He is partly a product of his work or profession which has disciplined and shaped his capacities and activities. He is partly a member of a community in which he lives and works, and it, too, conditions his responses. He is probably a member of a family unit and there are interactions between members of this close group to which he contributes and which affect him. The relative importance of these different factors must vary from one individual to another and will not remain constant in any one. Beyond these factors and beyond the uniqueness of their combinations in him, how far is the individual a distinctive person with independent judgment? Here, we can only say that the evidence we have quoted points to the operation of some quite important factor which is not included in any of the variables we have tried to assess. Its effect suggests that it may be what, for the want of a more precise term, we call individual judgment. In the party image analysis we estimated that about one-third of the variability was accountable to specific acts of judgment. In the larger situation, where voting decisions and shifts of allegiance are involved, one could only speculate on its importance.

In so far as the ordinary elector *is* making up his own mind in an election, how does he view the arguments put before him and what is he looking for?

The comprehensive nature of political judgment

The elector approaches the campaign with an assumption that his political decision, if it has not already been made, is going to be made privately, independently of any persuasion so far as he can manage it. What he is looking for in a political party is a capacity to govern. We see this in the analysis of his attitudes, in listening to his comments on the television broadcasts he saw, from other studies in this field, and from his general approach to the election situation.

He is looking for a whole, coherent policy, for a general picture of what the party as a whole stands for, and it is this general impression, and not particular items of policy, that weigh most with him. This is particularly true of working men and women who are accustomed to look at life in this comprehensive way. Their minds may not be trained to undertake classificatory analysis, as one soon discovers in social studies. They judge situations as a whole, as they judge the merits of a football team or the qualities of the boss or the honesty of a shopkeeper. They look for moral qualities as well as intellectual and they are particularly concerned with the practical working out of any proposals put before them. Their interest in concrete points or particular human illustrations does not contradict this comprehensive view. The concrete items they remember and recount, or fit into an accepted frame of reference. The comprehensive view is an almost involuntary process.

A clue to the nature of these general impressions of the parties is offered by the items in the attitude scales which are least involved in the party images. In the Conservative Party scale,[15] item 9 ('Would make the country more prosperous') has only a low image content compared with the other items, and therefore it has considerable specific meaning for electors. It happens that among Conservative voters this is the item showing the largest increment of endorsement over the campaign. In the Labour Party scale, item 7 ('Has no clear policy') is the one with the lowest image content and this, too, happens to receive the largest increment of endorsement among Labour voters. This would suggest that electors came to associate the Conservative Party with prosperity and the Labour Party with an insufficiently clear policy, in the sense of an alternative Government policy, and that these two general impressions weighed heavily on voters' final decisions.

The consequence of this holistic approach is that the election programmes and individual items of the campaign matter less than the general impression created by a party. We found no connection between what electors believed to be particularly important issues, or even changes in emphasis, and voting or attitude movements. After the election, people tended to choose issues to which the parties had devoted a good deal of attention, but, as with their knowledge of policies, this choice had no direct bearing on their attitudes.

It might be objected that the Conservative Party did not unfold many specific policies by which electors could judge their case. Perhaps they did not need to do so since they were claiming no more than the right to carry on as they had done before. People understood this and were evidently sufficiently satisfied not to want to make a change. A party which has been in opposition for eight years or more has a more difficult problem. It has either to make its case by a process of explanation or wait for a situation in which the electorate is so anxious to get rid of the other party that they are prepared to take it on trust. One of the lessons of this study is that any process of explanation might best proceed on the assumption that the matter is more important than the manner, and that the elector is looking for a simple, coherent and united policy not necessarily identified with his own pocket.

CHAPTER XI

The Characteristics of the 'Changers'

Our total sample produced 180 electors (or 27 per cent) who showed some change during the nineteen days of the campaign period.[1] A further sixty-six people, apart from those who were too young to vote in 1955, had made some change during the 1955-9 period, and did not change again during the campaign. It was this latter group which represented the decisive swing to the Conservative Party which took place between the elections.

This group of 180 changers is clearly not a homogeneous one, although it was treated as a whole in the previous chapter. There are important differences between those who do not vote at all, those who only come to a final decision during the campaign, and those who move from one party to another during the campaign. It turns out in fact that differences in social composition between those who are involved in change during the campaign, and the remainder of the sample are accounted for entirely by the 'don't knows' and the non-voters, and it is the latter who account for the largest differences.

We have distinguished three clear categories among the whole body of changers, each with separate characteristics which can be illustrated in their sex, age and occupations. They are described here as:

(1) *Inter-party changers* — the fifty-two electors (or 8 per cent of the whole sample) who gave their intention of voting for one party and claimed to have voted for another, presumably having changed their minds during, but not necessarily as a result of, the campaign.

(2) *The 'Don't knows'* — numbering sixty-nine electors (or 10·5 per cent of the whole sample) who were uncertain at the start of the campaign. Fifty-nine of these eventually voted for one of the three parties (twenty-three to Labour, twenty-seven to Conservative and nine to Liberal), and ten did not vote. These ten are included amongst the 'don't knows', because their intention at the start of the campaign is thought to be a better indication of their characteristics than their final voting behaviour.

(3) *The Non-voters* – numbering sixty-seven (or 10 per cent of the sample), include the fifty-three voters who stated an intention to vote and abstained, eight others who had no intention of voting, and did not do so, and an additional six who said they would not vote, but eventually did so: here again the position at the start of the campaign is taken as a guide to the category. (Two non-voters, one a 'don't know', are excluded because of incomplete data.)

A total of 188 electors is therefore involved; the discrepancy between this and the figure of 180 changers is due to the inclusion of the eight non-voters who had not intended to vote, and who therefore did not qualify as having undergone any change during the campaign.

The tables below provide comparisons between these three groups and the body of consistent voters in terms of relevant social characteristics.

TABLE 49

Sex and marital status versus voting change

	Men %	Women %		Married %	Single %	
Consistent voters (473)	46	54		83	17	
Inter-party changers (52)	58 +	42	=100%	83 +	17	=100%
'Don't knows' (69)	45	55		76	24	
Non-voters (67)	40	60		70	30	

There is a high proportion of men among the inter-party changers, and a high proportion of women among non-voters. Where there is pressure to change, women seem more likely to react by abstaining, rather than by taking a new course of action.[2] There are more single persons than might be expected amongst non-voters and 'don't knows' (the difference between these groups and the consistent voters is just short of significance at the ·05 level). It seems quite likely that marriage and family ties are strong factors in cementing voting decisions. The more isolated the individual the more likely he or she is to postpone decisions and to lose interest in voting. On the other hand the family as a social unit tends to make for voting in line with the particular social group to which a person belongs.[3] A further point brought out by the comparison is the increased representation of women and single persons, as one moves from the category of

THE CHARACTERISTICS OF THE 'CHANGERS'

inter-party change, through uncertainty, to abstention. A comparison in terms of age produces a similar situation.

TABLE 50

Age and voting change

	% 21-29		% 30-44		% 45-65		% Over 65	
Consistent voters (473)	13		31		41		15	
Inter-party changers (52)	17	+	30	+	45	+	8	=100%
'Don't knows' (69)	15		32		32		21	
Non-voters (67)	16		24		31		29	

There is again a suggestion of a progression here from the inter-party changers who are the youngest group, to the non-voters, who are the oldest. The relation between age and voting behaviour is seen more dramatically in a breakdown of the non-voters, who account for as many as 20 per cent of all electors over sixty-five years of age, but only 8 per cent in the 45-65 age group. A tendency can be seen, which we should not exaggerate, for political allegiances to be lightly held in the first few years of voting life, and to begin to disintegrate after the age of sixty-five, when ties to family, workmates and the community as a whole are weaker, and activity and political interest lessens. The disintegration may result, not in a shift to a new allegiance, but in a tendency to dissociation from all parties.

TABLE 51

Occupation and voting change

	Skilled and highly skilled %		Semi-skilled and unskilled %	
Consistent voters (473)	51		49	
Inter-party changers (52)	45	+	55	= 100%
'Don't knows' (69)	51		49	
Non-voters (67)	33		67	

As one moves from consistency, through changing, to non-participation, so the average occupational level declines. The 'don't knows' are closer to the normal distribution than we would have expected, though 5 per cent sampling errors on a group of this size could account for variations of 12 per cent. We see that, with one exception in the occupational grades, there is a progression among the changers, from inter-party change, to uncertainty, to non-voting. If we move down this descending scale, we find increasing proportions of women, single people, people over sixty-five, and people in less skilled jobs.

These associations between a number of social factors and instability of political allegiance imply that where social bonds are weakest, in early adult life, and in old age, and where the elector is economically and educationally below average (both are strongly associated with the occupational scale), there is a greater likelihood of detachment from the political process. This finding has an important bearing on the part played by public means of communication in an election because the social factors governing political instability and change also affect exposure to the mass media. A comparison between these three kinds of changer in terms of their exposure to political material from all the communication media illustrates this.

TABLE 52

Exposure to political propaganda and news versus voting change

	Percentage with an exposure score equal to or above the average for the whole sample
Consistent voters (473)	49
Inter-party changers (52)	44
'Don't knows' (69)	40
Non-voters (67)	27

Again the categories of change appear in a descending order. In view of the relationships which exist between media exposure and social characteristics[4] this is to be expected. The factors seen to be most strongly associated with low exposure are single status and old age. The extent of this association is brought out later in this chapter where interest in politics, and television in particular, are discussed.

A closer examination of the changers can be made in terms of the movement to Conservative and Labour. For this purpose we shall need to break up the groups classified above and to consider only those changers who eventually voted for one or another of the major parties. Here the smallness of the numbers is a considerable limitation,

THE CHARACTERISTICS OF THE 'CHANGERS'

for they will not allow a separation according to the source of the move; for example, we cannot differentiate between those who were initially undecided and those who supported another party.

TABLE 53

Sex and marital status of those changing to either major party during the campaign

	Men	Women	Married	Single
Electors changing during campaign	%	%	%	%
—to Conservative (53)	51	49	71	29
—to Labour (45)	62	38	85	15

TABLE 54

Occupation and age of those changing to either major party during the campaign

	Age		Occupation	
	21-44	45 and over	more skilled	less skilled
	%	%	%	%
—to Conservative	38	62	54	46
—to Labour	53	47	35	65

Between these two groups of changers taken together and the remainder of the sample there is a difference in the proportion of men represented, just short of significance at the ·05 level, but underlining the point discussed above, that where a voting habit disintegrates, men are more likely than women to change to another party than not to vote at all.

Differences between those changing to Labour and those changing to Conservative which are significant (P = ·05) are in occupational level and marital status. The higher occupational level of those changing to Conservative, consistent with the changes in attitude observed,[5] is also confirmed by previous studies,[6] and is to be expected in view of the greater representation of those in more skilled work amongst Conservative voters. Conversely, those in less skilled work are more drawn towards the Labour Party. To some extent these movements are reflections of the pressures to conform exerted by a group on its deviant members. A previous Labour voter, in a skilled or more responsible occupation, may be more in touch with people of Conservative views, and will have to resolve the conflict either by a move towards the other side or by a reinforcement of his own past opinions. The tendency for single persons to change to a Conservative position must be explained in terms of the attraction the Conservative Party has for older electors, since single people tend either to be young or older than average, and it appears from Table 54 that younger voters tend to change towards the Labour Party, if they do change. The suggestion that it was the younger voters who changed to Labour is interesting in view of the comment sometimes made that the Labour Party is losing its appeal to the younger voter.[7]

Attitude movements of the changers

The measurement of attitudes to the major parties before and after the campaign makes it possible to see what sort of adjustment in political views accompanied voting change among the West Leeds and Pudsey electors. If one is looking for an explanation of change it becomes important to know how far these fluctuations on the fringe of the electorate accurately reflect real changes of opinion. It is useful, too, to know what kind of attitude change accompanies a particular kind of voting decision, or causes a particular voting decision. Does non-voting reflect a genuine disillusion with both parties, or is it caused by conflicting pressures on voting behaviour? Does change from one party to another reflect a move away from the original party, unaccompanied by an increased respect for the other party? Questions like these need to be answered if the causes of change are to be assessed, or even guessed at.

Fortunately, attitude measurements and voting are highly correlated, so that there is good ground for using observed changes in attitudes in any interpretation of the nature of different kinds of change. A movement towards or away from one major party is accompanied by an adjustment of attitude which is in most cases consistent with the direction of the move. For example, although in the electorate as a whole there was actually a slight set-back in attitudes to the Labour Party, amongst the small number (forty-five in all) who moved from uncertainty, or from a different intention, to a Labour vote, there was a significant increment in favourable attitudes to the Labour Party. It might still be questioned whether this is a measure of the favourable change in attitude which caused the Labour vote, or simply a measure of a process of self-justification uncon-

THE CHARACTERISTICS OF THE 'CHANGERS'

sciously, though still not fortuitously, bringing opinion into line with an accomplished action. The evidence strongly suggests, however, that voting change of the kind instanced is not simply blind fluctuation, devoid of any deep significance, and unaccompanied by any political re-thinking. If the character of the voting decision is consistent with the attitudes we measure, even amongst the most unpolitical section of the electorate, then a search for the causes of political decisions and relatively small political changes is meaningful.

How the 'don't knows' reacted to the campaign

Figure 10 is a representation of one kind of political movement during the campaign, as it reflects, or is reflected by changes in attitude.

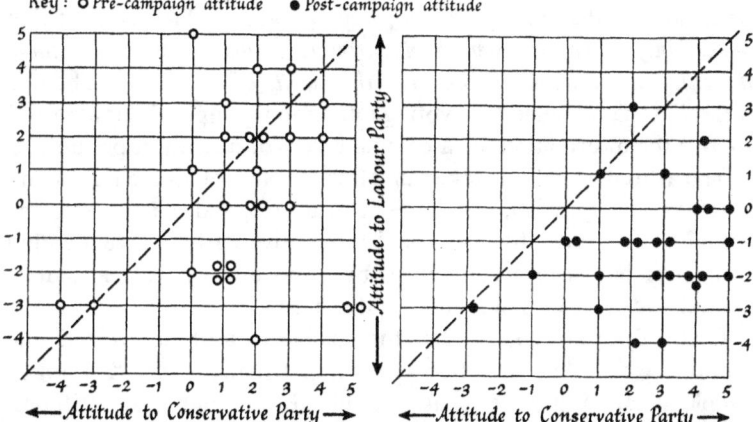

Fig. 10. – Attitude changes of 'don't knows' who voted Conservative. The circles record attitude scores to both major parties before the campaign (left) and after the campaign (right).

The scale on the vertical axis is a measure of the favourableness of attitude to the Labour Party, and along the horizontal axis of attitude to the Conservative Party. If a person's attitude to the Labour Party is scored, and plotted against his attitude to the Conservative Party, the position on the graph represents his position vis-à-vis both parties. A combination of a high positive Labour score and a negative Conservative score would produce a position to the left of the diagonal line, in the top left quadrant. A person strongly pro-Conservative and anti-Labour would appear in the bottom right-hand quadrant. Any position along the diagonal indicates a neutral attitude equally critical or equally favourable towards both parties according to the distance from the origin. Practically all Labour voters appear to the left of the diagonal and Conservative voters to the right.

This figure represents the changes in attitude which took place during the campaign amongst those who were uncertain in their intention, and finally voted Conservative. The outline circles clustering on or close to the diagonal show the attitudes of the 'don't knows' in September, occupying a position between the main parties, not predominantly favourable to either one, but not particularly critical of either. In fact only six of the twenty-six voters represented in the diagram hold predominantly critical attitudes to either party. The implication is that both parties enjoyed a good deal of respect, and that *uncertainty in voting intention is strongly associated with a genuine difficulty in distinguishing between the merits of the parties*. There is little sign that an uncertain voting intention is simply either a refusal to give the information, or a complete lack of interest in politics.

The attitude positions taken up after the election in the right hand diagram of Figure 10, can be seen to correspond closely with the actual vote. A move towards the Conservative Party in actual voting behaviour has been accompanied by a move away from a neutral attitude position to one favouring that party.

It still does not follow that the change in attitude 'caused' the voting decision – the situation as is suggested in Chapter X is not as simple as this. When we speak of political 'decisions' and 'attitudes' we are speculating about mental processes which are largely unexplored. What we do know is that they are not entirely rational, though the irrational element is often over-stressed, and that they are normally resistant to change. At some point the voter who is likely to change his allegiance makes a decision for or against a particular party, and a corresponding realignment of attitudes accompanies this. The decision seems to be a personal one, made on the strength of the situation as seen by the individual voter, and reached apparently independently of any amount of persuasion through political propaganda, by some process of screening that seems to let information pass through into the individual's store of knowledge, but resists evaluation in terms of one or other political party. An immense volume of experiences of political relevance is being accumulated by the electors all the time. Political arguments are not received on a blank slate, as it were, and even their perception is coloured and perhaps distorted by the experiences and attitudes, individual and social, which the elector brings to them. He uses what he wants and in a way that suits his individual requirements, and it is perhaps this individual reaction that seems to make his behaviour idiosyncratic and unrelated to the intentions of the propagandist during the short term of an election campaign.

If the remaining voting changes are plotted in a similar way some further conclusions can be drawn. 'Don't knows' who did not eventually choose one or other of the major parties, differed from those who did. Either their attitudes underwent very little change, or their relative positions vis-à-vis the major parties did not alter. They became less or more critical of both parties to the same extent. The correspondence between the adjustment of attitude and voting behaviour is remarkable.

As a group, the 'don't knows' were less well-informed than consistent voters by as much as 25 per cent on the knowledge of policies scale, showing a general lack of information, and not just an ignorance of particular policies or the policies of one particular party. They also saw fewer Party election broadcasts, and were in general less exposed to possible campaign influence. No explanation can be given for their eventual decision, but twenty-four of the fifty-eight 'don't knows' who had been able to vote in 1955 did in fact revert to the 1955 voting position, and this may represent the re-assertion of old habits, the result of pressure from family, friends or neighbourhood. A further twelve of the fifty-eight voted for a different party in 1959 than the one they had voted for in 1955, and for these individuals the election campaign may have been a time when a previously formed inclination was confirmed, and the indecision may reflect a wish to leave the final choice as late as possible.

The non-voters

It was found in this study, as in most others on the subject, that the electors who are more interested in political matters and listen to political debates or take part in political activities are the better-educated, younger and better-off members of the community and are more often men than women. Since the uncertain and non-voting electors have characteristics in common with the least interested electors, we would expect to find them less involved in the election campaign. One expects to find them apathetic about politics and perhaps more critical of both parties than the average loyal voter. Non-voting is often thought to be a form of protest as well as an expression of disinterest.

Of the fifty-four non-voters in the sample who did express an intention to vote before the campaign, twenty-five had intended to vote Labour, and only three of these held attitudes predominantly pro-Conservative. In this they do not differ from other consistent Labour voters. Similarly, of those who began with a Conservative intention, only one then held an attitude predominantly favourable to the Labour Party. It would have been impossible to predict the final abstention on the basis of their attitude scores, at the start of the campaign. There was nothing, apart from social differences, to distinguish the non-voter from other voters with a similar intention.

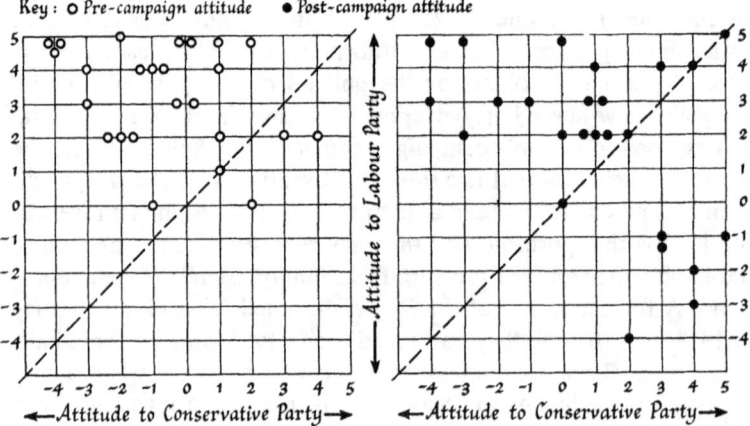

Fig. 11. – *Attitude changes of electors intending to vote Labour who did not vote. The circles record attitude scores to both major parties before the campaign (left) and after the campaign (right).*

Figure 11 illustrates the changes in attitude during the campaign which took place amongst non-voters who originally intended to vote Labour. The unfilled circles represent the attitude position before the campaign, the filled circles the position after the campaign. It is interesting that before the campaign none of the twenty-five held an

THE CHARACTERISTICS OF THE 'CHANGERS'

attitude predominantly critical of both main parties, and that after the election only one did so. Of *all* the non-voters in the sample, in fact only four, either before or after the campaign, are critical of *both* parties.

There is little sign here that cynicism about party politics governs voting behaviour. These non-voters whose original intention was to vote Labour record a general shift in attitude away from the Labour Party much more pronounced than any slight change among the consistent Labour voters. In fact six of the twenty-five became strongly pro-Conservative, and another eight finally expressed attitudes almost equally favourable to both parties. In all, almost two-thirds moved away from Labour and towards Conservative in attitude score. A comparison between the average Labour Party score of consistent Labour voters, before and after the campaign, and that of these twenty-five non-voters further illustrates the point.

TABLE 55

Attitude to Labour Party scores, before and after campaign, of consistent Labour voters, and non-voters with earlier Labour intention

	Consistent Labour voters	Non-voters with Labour intention
Before campaign	2·68	3·0
After campaign	2·65	1·4

(Scale ranges from 5·0 to —4·0)

This seems to dispose of the possibility that in this sample any large amount of non-voting can be the result of pure accident.[8] The general shift in attitude position in a Conservative direction which is associated with non-voting amongst Labour intenders might be explained in terms of conflicting pressures and loyalties. There is a pro-Conservative shift in attitude during the campaign from whatever cause, which generally weakens the intention to vote Labour, without being sufficiently strong, or important, to produce a Conservative vote. Past loyalties and group pressures such as the influence of a working class neighbourhood, or of workmates where the elector is in a less skilled job, are too strong to allow a Conservative vote, and the alternative of abstaining is accepted. It follows that a change in attitude over a three-week campaign period can produce an alteration in voting behaviour. If an abstention were the result of indifference, or was purely circumstantial, there would be no occasion for a reversal or revision of attitude, and such a reversal occurs too often to be coincidental. This particular group of non-voters were not habitual changers – none had voted Conservative in 1955, and only one had voted Liberal.

Among the twenty-six Conservatives who abstained, the shift towards a more neutral position also occurs, but less marked. Among this group of twenty-six, the score towards the Conservative Party falls from an average of $3 \cdot 3$ to $2 \cdot 8$, against a corresponding rise amongst consistent Conservative voters of from $3 \cdot 1$ to $3 \cdot 8$. This, too, suggests that there was an important change of attitudes, as well as any accidental circumstances that may have been responsible. The importance of factors such as age and social isolation as permanent influences of voting behaviour would lead one to expect at least some degree of habitual abstention. A tendency to abstain induced by social circumstances could reinforce other influences affecting attitudes. Such a tendency does seem to exist, since of the seventy-six qualified electors who said they had not voted in 1955 or who had forgotten which party they had voted for, twenty-five eventually did not vote in 1959. Only 11 per cent of the whole sample abstained. Even allowing for the unreliability of the information about the 1955 voting, the difference seems to be significant.

Like the 'don't knows', the non-voters differ from the other voters in their participation in the campaign, since they read less of the political reports in the newspapers, went to fewer meetings and were less aware of the local campaign. They saw fewer television Party election broadcasts, and were in general the least well-informed electors as a group. The absolute differences are still not large, and there is insufficient evidence to conclude that a failure to listen to the views of the parties contributed to their decision to abstain. The evidence referred to above[9] about the penetration of local campaign activities confirms that abstention was not the result of any failure to make contact on the part of the parties, but that withdrawal was seemingly voluntary. One cannot easily go further in explanation of abstention than to suggest the operation of three main factors which have a bearing on the question. One is the effect of cross-pressures which operate at the same time as a change in attitude favourable to the

THE CHARACTERISTICS OF THE 'CHANGERS'

opposing party, and prevent complete apostasy, but which are not strong enough to prevent abstention. Such pressures might be the influence of the family or of workmates or simply habitual loyalty. Another factor is the dissociation from community and national affairs brought about by personal circumstances, and which is more evident amongst old people, single people, and the least educated. These electors tend to be cut off from the pressures of habit and example which impel most people to vote, however that vote is cast. A possibility which cannot be tested here is that the increased neutrality shown by non-voters reflects an inability to make any distinction between the two parties.

The inter-party changers

The third category of electors involved in change during the campaign, those fifty-two who voted for a different party than they had named at the start, also show changes in attitude consistent with the shift of voting allegiance.[10] Thirty-one of these are voters who either intended to vote Liberal and may have been unable to, as in West Leeds, or finally voted Liberal in Pudsey. The numbers are too few to provide clear evidence about change between the two major parties, but the average party scores of the groups involved are given in Table 56.

TABLE 56

Party attitude scores of inter-party changers, compared with consistent voters

Changers from Labour to Conservative (Labour Party scores)

	Changers	Consistent Labour voters
Before campaign	3·6	2·68
After campaign	1·0	2·65

Changers from Conservative to Labour (Conservative Party scores)

	Changers	Consistent Conservative voters
Before campaign	3·4	3·12
After campaign	2·9	3·84

It is noticeable that the initial attitude score towards the Labour Party of the nine Labour intenders who finally voted Conservative is above the average for consistent Labour voters, as it was with the

Labour intenders who finally abstained. The impossibility of making a prediction of a change during the campaign is underlined. The Conservative intenders who changed to Labour were also slightly above average in their Conservative score. Both groups, on the other hand, after the campaign, remained more favourable in attitude to the party that they left than the average supporter of their new party, suggesting that the change was partial. It may be that those who do change in this way are temperamentally more inclined to accompany a marginal attitude change by a new voting alignment, and would be as ready to return to their former position in different circumstances.

It has already been noticed that, as a group, the inter-party changers do not appear to differ in respect of their social characteristics from the body of consistent voters, and that because of this they can be distinguished from the 'don't knows' and the non-voters. This is in part accounted for by the high representation of Liberals among them, but there is a strong suggestion that these electors are quite likely to be politically informed and not below average in their interest and involvement in politics.

The similarity between the consistent voters and the inter-party changers is also evident if the two are compared in terms of their participation in the campaign, and their knowledge of what the parties stand for. All informants were asked before the campaign about their normal viewing and listening to political broadcasts and talks on current events. An index based on this information measures an elector's normal interest in material of this kind. This pre-campaign interest is correlated to the extent of ·34 with later viewing of political broadcasting during the campaign.[11] The average score of the inter-party changers is in fact slightly higher than that of the consistent voters, and 25 per cent higher than that of the non-voters and 'don't knows'. One can infer that these changers brought to the campaign a higher initial interest and awareness of political affairs. This is reflected in the degree of knowledge of party policies before the campaign. The fifty-two who changed from one party to another were slightly better informed than the average consistent supporter, and much better informed than non-voters or 'don't knows'. Table 57 provides a comparison between each group of changers and the consistent voter in terms of their initial disposition to receive political argument and information, their level of knowledge and their exposure during the campaign to television propaganda.

THE CHARACTERISTICS OF THE 'CHANGERS'

TABLE 57

Political interest and participation in the campaign of changers

	(a) Knowledge of party policies (average score)	(b) Disposition to receive political communication (average score)	(c) Average number of Party election broadcasts seen
Consistent voters	4·2	6·0	3·3
Inter-party changers	4·3	6·1	3·2
'Don't knows'	3·5	6·1	2·7
Non-voters	2·9	5·5	2·4

The information we have about the inter-party changers does not explain what brought about the change. The changes in attitude and in voting decisions may have been purely qualitative judgments, relating the impressions made by the parties to a set of expectations which had been maturing, and came to a point during the campaign only because the poll was imminent. It is also possible that the electors who, during the campaign, changed from one party to another represent the small fringe who do in fact weigh up the relative merits of the parties, and vote accordingly, while the non-voters and the 'don't knows' change because they tend to be more unstable in their political behaviour, and are open to influences which consistent voters are sheltered from.

Is voting change habitual?

Previous studies have suggested[12] that the only distinguishing characteristic of changers is their consistent tendency to change. It is thought that there are a small minority of voters who account for the voting change which takes place and that the same voters tend to be involved at successive elections. To test the hypothesis, reliable information about voting at successive elections is needed, and the only comparison that we can make is between change during the campaign, and change since the 1955 election.

Of the total sample, forty-one supported a different party at the start of the campaign from the one they claimed to have voted for in 1955, and of these, fifteen either did not vote in 1959 or voted differently from their intention. Although seven of these changes involved an intention to vote for a Liberal candidate in 1959, which could not have been carried out, there is some indication that those whose 1959 intention differed from their 1955 vote were more likely to change again than the average voter. In other words, of the forty-one who changed their minds since 1955, eight changed again during the campaign (apart from the Liberal intenders without a candidate).

There is no evidence, on the other hand, that the fifty-two voters who changed between parties during the campaign were politically unstable. Although thirteen of them had voted differently in 1955 from their intention in 1959, eight of these were Liberals in West Leeds who were obliged to change their intention during the campaign.

We have already noticed (page 218) a tendency for non-voting to recur and the evidence as a whole tends to confirm the existence of a marginal group of voters who are permanently liable to change or abstain. An estimate based on the number of electors in the sample who differed in their choice of party from their 1955 vote to their 1959 intention, and again over the period of the campaign, or who abstained at both elections, would put the proportion of habitual changers at 6 per cent. As a prediction of voting behaviour, however, evidence of previous change is not very helpful, nor does it add to our knowledge of the reasons for change in a particular case. In addition, it does not seem that it is this group of habitual changers who fundamentally affect the balance of power either way. The vital changes occur amongst a much wider section of the electorate and almost anyone might at one time or another be involved.

CHAPTER XII

Some Implications

The television Party election broadcast has now become the principal platform from which the parties can address the nation. It effectively reaches the largest audience and it makes the greatest impact. The 1959 Party election broadcasts were also a trial of television techniques. The fast moving, fully featurized style of presentation was matched against the more old-fashioned method of the photographed interview or debate. But the electors were not so easily impressed. At least, any slight advantages gained by better methods of presentation were swamped by other factors. For the main advantage of a skilfully contrived programme appears to be that it gives the viewer a better opportunity of understanding what the message is about. It is a means to an end which is the message of the party. The shaping of the programme to suit the requirements of the medium, a visual progression that smoothly and unobtrusively matches the line of thought, a relaxed atmosphere, a lively tempo, these qualities will not convince the doubtful elector any more than they make 'Tonight' the successful programme it is. For, it seems to us, that the elector was looking immediately for concrete, specific points, on which his mind could fasten, and he was looking for a Government. Particular items of policy in isolation mattered less than the overall impression of competence, and, above all, a total policy that was clear and acceptable. The implication here is not that techniques do not matter, but that they are a great deal less important than the selection and shaping of the content.

We find no evidence of the function of the Press being diminished by television nor of any less reading of newspaper reports. The two media fulfil different purposes. The attitude of some newspaper critics has been either to denigrate television or to ignore it. The television services regularly include programmes based on the newspaper reports of the day or week. Press reports on television election broadcasts might help the ordinary viewer to evaluate what he has seen, by constructive criticism of the argument, and by treating the programmes as the major statements of party policy and image projection they in fact are. The public need for explanatory and evaluative criticism of television programmes is still not sufficiently recognized by the Press.

The General Election was, we believe, taken a good deal more seriously by the ordinary elector than many people who are professionally concerned with broadcasting or with politics are inclined to admit. Not all viewers of political programmes were choosing to see them, but millions were. There is not a scrap of evidence in our study which would suggest that the public had had more than enough of them by Polling Day. The period of maximum availability in broadcasting is between the hours of 7.30 and 10 p.m. and no political programme was allowed to intrude on this peak period. Despite the bold and successful first attempt by the television authorities to provide a news coverage of the election, their interpretation of their general political responsibilities as laid down in the Charter and the Act and their view of the importance of the occasion in the life of the nation was such that any direct political broadcasting was subordinated to the normal running of entertainment and other programmes.

If television broadcasting is to be free to fulfil its responsibilities to the electorate, the providing bodies must be given the same facilities as the Press to cover the campaign. This can only be brought about by amending legislation to the Representation of the People Act 1949. A further limitation on television coverage is the section of the Television Act 1954 which requires the Independent Companies to present political material only in the form of debates. The television authorities are also placed at a considerable disadvantage by the short interval between the announcement of the dissolution and the opening of the campaign. If special programmes are to be seen they need to be made known and some programmes can only be prepared after candidates have been nominated.

Political images and television

What of political images themselves? We have seen that what the major parties are consciously projecting is rather different from the images already in the minds of electors. It is highly unlikely that they can bring about any important modifications of their images in the short and artificial period of an election campaign. The ethics of presenting only those aspects of their organizations and policies which they believe to be acceptable, if such were the case, is a matter for the parties, and perhaps ultimately the electors, to judge. There is

SOME IMPLICATIONS

some evidence for believing that the most effective persuasion will be that which, working within the broad features of the party image, presents both sides of an argument and does not shrink from a certain amount of self-criticism.

The Conservative Party's goodwill, as reflected in its political image, rests on its claim to tradition, its claim to represent the nation as a whole, its resolution of purpose and its defence of individual rights. It is not so much in any particular programme of improvement as in the maintenance of an accepted tradition that its campaigning strength lies.

The Labour Party has a more difficult task to sustain its morale. Its concern with the welfare of the ordinary person seems widely accepted. It is likely to be more difficult for it to reconcile its willingness to act in the national interest with its working-class foundation. Its strength lies in its radicalism, which is perhaps only sustained by its constant challenging of the accepted order. Its supporters regard disunity and irresolution as inimical to their purpose. It is on this ground that it appears to have lost support.

In a viable democratic community, the organs of communication should be used, not to project an artificial political façade to a docile electorate, but to enable Governments and political parties to present themselves as they are and to learn from the images they see mirrored in the public eye.

Implications for future research

In most election studies it is the people who change their intentions during the campaign who form the important part of the sample. In our research we were exploring new factors and wanted to compare the effects on consistent as well as changing voters. As we have shown, changers are of three sorts. Two of these, the 'don't knows' and the non-voters to some extent, could be isolated before the campaign (since some non-voters have been non-voters before). By confining a large sample to these two categories (eliminating all others with a couple of preliminary questions) one could make a more detailed study of their behaviour. The third category, the inter-party changers, could not be identified from preliminary questioning, at least not on the basis of present knowledge.

In working over our material, we have felt the lack of a more intimate knowledge of our electors. We needed to know much more about their background, their temperament, the influence of people they work with and of other members of their families. We would like to have known what qualitative effects some of the campaign appeals had upon them, when and by what means a change of allegiance came about. We were curious to know how much of the campaign was really getting through to those elusive electors who managed to avoid so much of the overt propaganda. Did they see the posters? Did they overhear chance conversations, and were they interested to know what other people were thinking? The sample survey gives one a broad panoramic view. One also needs a magnified close-up to see the processes of change at work. Another time, it would probably be worthwhile trying to supplement an interviewing survey with a close study of a number of individual families, preferably in their own homes.

In view of the important connection between television viewing and what people learn about the parties, it would be useful to have much more sensitive tests of political knowledge. We expected to find the more significant effects on attitudes and concentrated our preliminary studies on this field, confining our knowledge questions to short lists of policies and issues. One would like to know why some policies are more easily communicated than others and which particular viewing experiences contribute to wider understanding.

We have only started to explore party images. Behind the attitudes lie allegiances to broad ideologies which could best be investigated outside the artificial climate of a General Election campaign. The features we have sketched out in the political images need to be delineated in greater detail through further experiments on scales constructed around each feature. It would also be interesting to try to relate these image features to other identified social attitudes.

It is highly probable that the period of a year or so before a General Election is more formative than the three weeks of intensive campaigning. We need to know how much weight to attach to advertising schemes, Government legislation, industrial unrest, conference decisions, and the like. Another election study might well start a year or more before the dissolution, taking a series of readings of attitude levels at significant points of time over the whole period. Such a study might also consider the impact of political and topical programmes on television over the preceding months, in view of the findings of the present research.

CHAPTER XIII

Summary of the Findings

To help the reader to get a general picture of the whole complex, we have prepared the following summary statements of the principal results. They are signposts rather than inventories, but they may help to indicate the nature of the ground covered.

What are the public images of the parties and their leaders? (Chap. III)

By sifting opinions actually expressed by electors and submitting them to correlational analysis, a number of unitary features were revealed. They may be said to represent public attitudes, lying behind and largely governing individual and specific opinion. The largest element is a traditional-versus-radical feature, dividing off Conservative from Labour supporters. The former expresses a general loyalty to traditional features with an emphasis on the upper levels of society; the other is identified with a general reforming or radical attitude to society, and has some association with the working class.

Further analysis of the features of the Conservative Party image among its supporters reveals three common elements, identifying the party's aims with the interests of the nation as a whole, with strength of purpose, and with individual rights, in that order of priority.

The Labour Party image also has three common features beyond its radical basis. They are associated with the betterment of the lot of the ordinary person, with a sense of disunity, and with a concern for national interests, in that order.

The same radical-versus-traditional factor divides attitudes to the leaders of the two major parties. In addition, the Conservative image of Mr Macmillan is shaped by three features in descending order of magnitude: a recognition of strength of leadership, general cultural characteristics, and thirdly, a criticism on grounds of being unsuitable. The Gaitskell image has three components, beyond the general radical foundation, again in descending order of importance: first, is a general leadership idea, compounded of strength and cultural characteristics; secondly, there is the common idea of a trusted, straightforward individual; thirdly, a criticism of unsuitability. Although personal qualities figure fairly prominently in the leader images, there is no indication of an overwhelming *personal* following for either leader. Both are liked, but as figures generally suited to their rôle rather than as strongly individual characters.

These common traits occur in varying strengths in every individual attitude. They represent about two-thirds of the total discrimination, beyond which there are specific notions, varying from one person to another. When we consider the attitudes of electors to the parties and leaders they do *not* support, quite a different set of images emerges.

In addition to the stereotypes embodied in the political images, some degree of tolerance of political ideas is almost universal. It is rather more marked among Labour than Conservative supporters, but among both there is a general willingness to see some points to the credit of the other party and to voice a few criticisms of one's own.

What was the nature of the campaign? (Chap. IV)

There is a very close resemblance between the proposals set out in the manifestoes of the parties and what was conveyed by the mass organs of communication to the electorate. Peace, pensions, Commonwealth and Colonial problems, the national economy, and prosperity – these were the principal questions and in that order.

Detailed content analyses of the scripts and recordings of the election broadcasts on television and sound radio and a further analysis of the Press coverage show a broad similarity between emphases on the main issues. About 15 per cent of the output was devoted to discussion of Peace, 12 per cent to pensions and about 8 per cent to prosperity.

The average amount of space given to political news by the Press was a little under 20 per cent of the editorial columns, or about 10 per cent of the whole newspaper including advertisements, varying from about 4 per cent in the *Daily Sketch* to about 17 per cent in the *Daily Telegraph*. Nearly half of this reporting was concerned with news of the campaign in the local constituencies, apart from the reporting of policy questions raised by candidates in their speeches. A further 18 per cent was given over to personal descriptions of politicians or to personality gossip.

Under 6 per cent of the BBC television output in the North was devoted to political material during the campaign, and this mostly after peak viewing hours. About 18 per cent of the total news bulletin time dealt with the election. On ITV the proportion of total time given to the campaign was higher, 10 per cent, because of the 'Election Marathon' series. This series presented 229 candidates in 100 Northern contituencies, a total of about two-thirds of the candidates in the area covered.

Both networks exercised exacting impartiality in their own presentations, maintaining a strict balance between the parties in the amount of time given to each. Compared with the Press, they were severely handicapped in their coverage of the campaign by the Representation of the People Act 1949 and the Television Act 1954. The time allocated to political broadcasts was insufficient to allow anything like the full coverage afforded by the national newspapers.

In sound broadcasting, the proportion of time given over to the election was under 1 per cent. Even if the basis of comparison is confined to the hours in which television is transmitted and to the Home and Light programmes, the ratio is still only 2 per cent.

How far did the campaign reach the electors? (Chap. V)

A comparison with studies of the three previous General Elections shows no change in the proportions of the electors attending political meetings (about 10 per cent). Increasing proportions read election addresses. A constant proportion of nearly 70 per cent were reached by the Party election broadcasts, through sound radio in 1950 and 1951, and through both broadcasting media in 1955, and now mainly by television.

Each Party election broadcast on television was viewed by over one-fifth of the entire adult population. The television news bulletins on both networks were seen by about half the population during the campaign, and altogether 73 per cent were in touch with the national campaign either through television news or the daily Press.

A phenomenon of broadcasting is that all of the election programmes, especially those on television, reach almost equal numbers of the supporters of both major parties. 49 per cent of the normal audience for any given Party television broadcast were intending supporters of the other party. About 60 per cent of all these viewers were *choosing* to watch the programmes. As with other forms of political activity, viewing of the Party broadcasts varied from one type of person to another. Married people viewed far more than single, men slightly more than women, and the 30-65 age bracket more than younger or older people. Those in more skilled occupations viewed rather more than those in lower grades.

Rather more Labour than Conservative viewers consistently see ITV programmes and rather more Conservatives see the BBC's.

Granada's 'Election Marathon' programmes were seen by about one-fifth of the electors in the sample. These viewers were a fair cross-section of the local electorate. Only a third of them saw their own candidates and there is no evidence that interest was chiefly focused on this purely local aspect of the series.

Just over half of all voters were looking at television on the evening of polling day. The proportions were much the same among voters for all three parties and not significantly higher among non-voters.

The Party election broadcasts on sound radio reached 16 per cent of the electors; 6 per cent of the electors saw them on television and also heard the separate sound radio programmes. Local campaign activities reached much the same audience as was addressed through the public means of communication. Only about 7 per cent actually saw their local candidate at a meeting, and these electors were the more politically interested. 69 per cent claimed to have read some or all of the campaign addresses, and half the sample had been visited by a canvasser. Abstention is not associated with any failure by canvassers or candidates to reach electors personally. There is an inference that television has not materially affected the extent of local participation. Those who were above average in their interest in the local campaign also saw more election broadcasts on television.

What changes took place during the campaign?

(a) *Changes in party allegiance* (Chap. VII)

During the campaign itself the sample as a whole showed no decisive swing towards either party. In West Leeds there was a pro-Labour swing of about 3 per cent, and in Pudsey a pro-Conservative swing of about 3 per cent. These changes were measured from an intention expressed before the campaign, to a vote in the election. The movements are accounted for largely by final decisions made by 'don't knows', or by abstentions. There was on the other hand, a decisive swing between 1955 and 1959 in a Conservative direction based on the direct conversion of a number of former Labour supporters. The evidence points to the much greater importance of the longer period of time as an influence on political allegiance.

SUMMARY OF THE FINDINGS

Expected associations were found between party allegiance and social characteristics like occupation, age and sex, and a comparison between the two constituencies in terms of voting change pointed to the importance of local circumstances, and of an elector's immediate environment as an influence on voting. In Conservative Pudsey every form of voting change showed the influence of a dominant leaning towards Conservatism, and in West Leeds which has always been, and remained Labour, the pull towards the dominant party affected even those outside it.

The sample produced 10·5 per cent of 'don't knows', of whom one in seven did not eventually vote. Those who did vote divided 2:1 in favour of Labour in West Leeds, and 2:1 to Conservative in Pudsey.

11 per cent of the sample did not vote. Both parties lost equally through abstention, though more Conservative intenders abstained in the Labour constituency, and more Labour intenders in the Conservative.

(b) *Changes in attitudes to the parties and leaders* (Chap. VIII)

The analysis of political images produced finely graded scales on which to measure shifts of attitude too slight to result in any changes of voting intention. Scale positions are very highly correlated with voting behaviour and they change as voting intention changes.

Attitudes were found to be extremely stable, even over a period of intense propaganda like an election campaign. Such movement as there was produced two distinct trends. One was a slight changing of attitude within the ranks of party support, the extremer views tending to be modified, a tendency to consolidation among Conservatives and a possible scattering of Labour views. The second overall movement reflected the struggle between the contending parties. As a whole, Conservative attitudes gained in strength and Labour attitudes lost ground very slightly. Almost the whole body of supporters was affected by this movement, not merely a vulnerable fringe.

Attitudes vary in strength and direction according to certain social or personal characteristics of the elector. People in more skilled occupations differ from those in less skilled, and men differ somewhat from women in political attitude. These same characteristics affect changes. Among Labour voters it was men in more skilled jobs whose political morale suffered the greatest loss, because the group of skilled male workers as a whole tended to be Conservative. In the same way,

Conservative men in lower level employment showed less gain in morale, than men in higher level jobs.

The peculiar features of the Labour Party image affect these general shifts in attitude. Over the period of the campaign the favourable features increased in strength, but the critical component became even more marked, so reducing the net effect. The problem created by contradictory forces within the Labour Party image are discussed in Chapter VIII.

Attitudes to Mr Macmillan generally became a little more favourable over the campaign. Mr Gaitskell's personal qualities gained in favour significantly as did other aspects of his function as party leader. He lost ground somewhat on his strength of leadership.

(c) *Changes taking place in the electorate's knowledge of party policies, and in the relative importance of national issues* (Chap. IX)

There was a significant increase in political knowledge during the campaign and, as far as comparisons could be made, these increases were consistent with the emphasis placed by the parties on different aspects of their policy. It seems, as previous studies have shown, that the attempt to convey information does not meet with the same resistances as does the attempt to persuade, but that material designed primarily to influence opinion may also increase knowledge. Men were found to have a higher political knowledge than women, but women learned more during the campaign. Non-voters were below average in information before and after the campaign. A minority of the electorate, who appeared to be less well-informed and less interested in politics, were hardly reached by the election campaign, which may even have increased their isolation from the main body of electors. A comparison between those least exposed to influence through the public means of communication and the remainder of the sample showed the former to have much smaller increments in knowledge, or none at all.

The issues electors thought important before the campaign were almost identical with those they thought important after it, and none of the small changes showed any correspondence with the content of party propaganda or election news. Neither major party appeared to have persuaded its own supporters that the issues it concentrated on were overwhelmingly important. There was, however, a significant tendency for electors to react away from issues emphasized in the propaganda of the opposing side.

Those who had had almost no contact with propaganda during the campaign did not, as a group, differ in their opinions on national issues or in the adjustments made during the campaign from those who were most exposed.

The overall lack of change conceals certain important adjustments in opinion. Before the election there was a tendency for certain electors to regard an issue as important because of its bearing on their own circumstances. A younger person, for example, was much less likely than an old person to regard the question of old age pensions as a vital issue. After the campaign there were signs that the individual was more inclined to form his opinion in the light of the whole community's needs.

What was the bearing of political propaganda, and particularly that conveyed by television, upon these changes? (Chap. X)

Effects of the campaign on knowledge are clearly differentiated from those on attitudes. Of all the sources of political persuasion, only television is found to add significantly to electors' knowledge. There is a very significant association between the amount of political news and propaganda an elector received through television and his better understanding of the policies the parties were putting forward. This is most marked among those who changed their voting intentions during the campaign, who were a little less well-informed to start with than the rest of the electorate.

In the field of attitudes a highly significant screening effect separates exposure to the campaign from changes in strength or direction of attitude. This is true of every aspect and every combination of political attitudes and of the campaign influences. Among 'changers' there is a slight link between the improved regard for Mr Gaitskell's personal qualities and television viewing; and there is a similar weak connection between reading about the campaign in the newspapers and attitude movement away from the Conservative Party – possibly a slight reaction against what they felt were pro-Conservative editorial policies of the Press, since the association among readers of the Labour press is slightly, but not significantly, the other way. These are exceptions, of borderline significance, to the universal rule that the electorate was *not* influenced directly in its voting or political attitudes, either by the amount of the political campaign to which it was exposed, or by the presence or absence of any part or of virtually all the campaign.

By way of explanation, four factors emerge. First, there is an intensification of political awareness which affects almost every elector regardless of what he sees of the election campaign. The propaganda output is so considerable that it builds up pressure within the electorate which is rapidly communicated. Secondly, the elector is exposed to cross-fire from several parties which is so extensive that hardly anyone does not see something of the other party's case and most people see nearly equal amounts of each. There is some cancelling out effect as a result, but separate consideration of those electors who saw little except their own party's propaganda indicates that this is not the most important factor. Thirdly, at an election, group or social pressures become more important and influence some voters independently of rational argument. Lastly, there is fairly strong ground for believing that changes of political attitude are the result of independent, personal judgments acting upon information partly taken in from the campaign. These decisions rest upon assessments of a general nature concerning the case put forward by the parties, rather than upon acceptance of any particular programme or policy advanced. The elector is looking for a coherent and convincing policy for government.

What sort of people were involved in voting change, and what factors are associated with it? (Chap. XI)

The 27 per cent of the sample involved in some voting change during the campaign, fall into three broad categories: changers between parties, the 'don't knows', and those who finally did not vote. If the groups are compared in terms of relevant social characteristics, they form a consistent hierarchy – the inter-party changers being most normal and the non-voters the least normal.

Non-voters are more likely than 'don't knows' to be women, over 65, single, and in the less skilled occupations, while the 'don't knows' themselves are more likely to show all these same characteristics than the inter-party changers. The latter do not significantly differ from the consistent voters. Political interest and political knowledge show the same progressive tendency to decline through the three types—from straightforward change, to uncertainty, to non-voting.

SUMMARY OF THE FINDINGS

Those who change to a Labour vote from any other intention differ significantly from those who change to a Conservative vote, in being in less skilled occupations and in including more married persons. They also tend to be younger than changers to Conservative.

The measured changes in attitude reflect (or are reflected by) the voting changes. Those who did not vote moved to positions of neutrality between the parties, and the 'don't knows' who voted moved away from their previous intermediate attitude positions. Neither uncertainty nor abstention was associated with criticism of the two major parties, but rather with an equally favourable view of each.

Apart from the combinations of social characteristics which are associated with certain kinds of voting behaviour, there is no known way of predicting voting change. Of the few who changed at all, those who changed from Labour to Conservative began the campaign slightly more pro-Labour than is usual in their attitude, and those who changed from Conservative to Labour were slightly more pro-Conservative than the average at the start of the campaign. It is possible that one is dealing here with the small minority who really make a considered choice between the two parties during an election. The evidence of the survey as a whole suggests that the irrational or chance element in political behaviour is often too strongly stressed. Although non-voters at a previous General Election are likely to abstain again, an estimate of habitual changers would put the proportion at not more than 6 per cent of the electorate.

How did the television audiences react to the Party election broadcasts? (Chap. VI)

Groups of electors were invited to view recordings of the first two Party election broadcasts of the campaign. The aim was to see how successful the broadcasts were in creating the right impression and conveying information, and how far the widespread comment provoked in the Press and elsewhere by the opening election broadcasts was borne out by a fairly typical audience.

Technical competence in production is expected, and where it is shown it is appreciated. It is not, all the same, as important as the content of the broadcasts. The Conservative broadcast was criticized by the audience for the uneven quality of the production, and for its lack of clarity, but viewers did not object as many of its critics had done to what has been described as a rather forced air of informality and bonhommie. There is no sign at all that the more sophisticated production of the Labour broadcast earned it any disfavour. It dealt unambiguously with a limited number of subjects, and was found easy to understand and interesting to watch. Both Conservative and Labour supporters believed that it would be more likely to influence people than the Conservative broadcast.

As a speaker, Mr Gaitskell evoked much less critical comment than Mr Macmillan, particularly on grounds of greater clarity and directness. Criticism of the Labour broadcast centred primarily on its tendency to attack the other side; the lack of partisanship in the Conservative broadcast appeared to be generally appreciated.

Notes on the Chapters

CHAPTER I · Election Television – An Unknown Factor

Page 14

[1] The National Opinion Polls Ltd. undertook a sample survey of the Rochdale electorate on this occasion and estimated that 36 per cent saw the Granada programme of whom nearly a third believed that it had 'helped them to make up their minds about voting'.

[2] Himmelweit, H. T., Oppenheim, A. N., and Vince, P., *Television and the Child* (Oxford University Press, 1958), p. 258.

Page 16

[3] *The Twentieth Century*, November 1959.

CHAPTER II · Method

Page 17

[1] With biological experiments there are nearly always great advantages in using the same sample for two or more sets of measurements over intervals of time. In social surveys there is some danger of conditioning a sample of informants at the first interview and the statistical accuracy varies with the changes in responses between the two interviews. With responses of the sort obtained in this study, independent samples of more than three times the size would have been needed to obtain information of corresponding statistical accuracy. See Ehrenberg, A. S. C., *The Relative Merits of Independent Matched Samples and of the Panel Technique for Before-and-After Studies*, LPE Research Paper No. 1, privately circulated by the London Press Exchange, 1959.

[2] Gray, P. G., Corlett, T., and Frankland, P., *The Register of Electors as a Sampling Frame* (Central Office of Informatiom, 1950).

Page 19

[3] Gray, P. G., Corlett, T., and Jones, Pamela, *The Proportion of Jurors as an Index of the Economic Status of a District* (Central Office of Information, September 1951).

[4] We are indebted to the Director of the Social Survey, Central Office of Information, for tables of polling areas with juror-indices.

Page 22

[5] Using the term in its common sense and not in the stricter sense in which R. A. Fisher designates confidence in statistical inferences; see *Statistical Methods for Research Workers* (Oliver and Boyd, 1950), pp. 10–15.

Page 23

[6] Kendall, M. G., 'Technical Note on the Sampling Error', in *Explanatory Manual to the National Readership Survey of the IPA*, London, 1958.

Page 25

[7] Cronbach, L. J., 'Response Sets and Test Validity', *Ed. Psy. Meas.*, 1946, pp. 475–94; 'Further Evidence on Response Sets and Test Design', *Ed. Psy. Meas.*, 1950, 10, pp. 3–31.

[8] Adorno, W. T., et al., *The Authoritarian Personality* (Harper, New York, 1950).
Page 27
[9] The principal axis transformation which we used is often attributed to Hotelling but was first described by Karl Pearson in 1901, see Burt, C., 'Alternative Methods of Factor Analysis and their Relation to Pearson's Method of Principal Axes' (*Br. Journal Stat. Psy.* II, 1959, p. 98).
Page 29
[10] Thurstone, L. L. *Multiple-Factor Analysis* (University of Chicago Press, 1947); also Guilford, J. P., *Psychometric Methods* (McGraw-Hill, 1936) pp. 496–502.
Page 30
[11] Thurstone, L. L., *Multiple-Factor Analysis* (University of Chicago Press, 1947) p. 128.
Page 31
[12] Stouffer, S, A., Guttman, L., etc. *Studies in Social Psychology in World War II, Vol. IV, Measurement and Prediction* (Princeton University Press, 1950).
[13] Trenaman, J., 'Guttman's Scalogram Analysis of Attitudes' in *Attitude Scaling* (The Market Research Society in association with Oakwood Press, 1960).

CHAPTER III · Political Images

Page 36
[1] R. H. S. Crossman, MP, with the Rt. Hon. Viscount Hailsham, QC, and David Butler in 'The Gentle Art of Making Voters', Third Programe, January 22, 1960.
[2] Milne, R. S., and Mackenzie, H. C., *Straight Fight* (Hansard Society, London, 1954).
[3] Benney, M., and Geiss, P., 'Social Class and Politics in Greenwich', in *Br. Journal of Sociology*, December 1950.
[4] Lazarsfeld, P. F., Berelson, B., and Gaudet, H., *The People's Choice* (Col. University Press, New York, 1948).
[5] Wallas, G., *Human Nature in Politics* (Constable, 2nd ed., 1910).
A party, Wallas wrote, 'is primarily a name, which, like other names, calls up when it is heard or seen an "image". . . . It is the business of the party managers to secure that these automatic associations shall be as clear as possible, shall be shared by as large a number as possible, and shall call up as many and as strong emotions as possible' (p. 84). Wallas also anticipated the possibilities of manipulating the 'image'. On p. 5 he wrote 'if the rich people in any modern state thought it worth their while . . . to subscribe a third of their income to a political fund, no Corrupt Practices Act yet invented would prevent them from spending it. If they did so, there is so much skill to be bought, and the art of using skill for the production of emotion and opinion has so advanced, that the whole condition of political contests would be changed for the future'.
[6] Mitchell, A., *The Brand Image and Advertising Effectiveness*, Associated Television Ltd., Research Library, London, 1959.
[7] Mitchell, A., op. cit.

NOTES ON THE CHAPTERS

[8] Butler, D. E., and Rose, R., *The British General Election of 1959* (Macmillan & Co., 1960), p. 17.

Page 37

[9] Crossman, R. H. S., MP, in *The Gentle Art of Making Voters*, op. cit.

Page 39

[10] Thurstone, L. L., and Chave, E. S., *The Measurement of Attitude* (University of Chicago Press, 1928).

[11] Allport, G. W., *The Nature of Prejudice* (Addison-Wesley, Camb., Mass., 1954).

[12] Allport, G. W., 'Attitudes' in *A Handbook of Social Psychology* ed. Murchison, C. (Clark University Press and Oxford University Press, 1935).

Page 42

[13] In 1944 Eysenck analysed responses to thirty-two statements of attitude and found 'radicalism-conservatism' as the first, and therefore, the strongest factor. All the items, however, were statements of attitudes towards definite policies, like 'In the interests of peace, we must give up part of our national sovereignty', many of which were unlikely to be endorsed by Radicals and Conservatives alike. See Eysenck, H. J., 'General Social Attitudes', *J. Soc. Psy.*, XIX, 207–27; also *The Structure of Human Personality* (Methuen, 1953) p. 227; also *The Psychology of Politics* (Routledge, 1954).

[14] Johnson, M., summary of thesis, *Br. J. Ed. Psy.*, XII, 1942, p. 183.

[15] Sanai, M., 'An Empirical Study of Political, Religious, and Social Attitudes', in *Br. Journal Psychology* (Stat. Sec.) V, Pt. II, 1952, pp. 81–91.

CHAPTER IV · The Nature of the Campaign

Page 60

[1] *The Public and the Programmes*, BBC, 1959, estimates that 35 per cent of the 'sound only' public and 20 per cent of the television public are over sixty years of age and the corresponding proportions of retired people are 12 per cent and 5 per cent.

Page 62

[2] cf. Butler, D. E., and Rose, R., op. cit. Chapter IX.

Page 67

[3] We are indebted to Professor Asa Briggs for permission to make use of this quotation from his forthcoming *History of the BBC*.

[4] Reith, J. C. W., *Broadcast over Britain* (Hodder and Stoughton, 1924) p. 112.

[5] BBC Handbook 1959, p. 19.

Page 72

[6] *A First Report on Constituency Television in a General Election*, Granada TV Network, Manchester, 1959.

[7] *A First Report on Constituency Television, etc.*

Page 74

[8] Newspapers vary in readership, format and size. For example, the column width of *The Times* is $2\frac{3}{8}$ inches, while *The Sketch* and *The Mirror* have a column width of only $1\frac{1}{2}$ inches. Column lengths vary from 21 to 13 inches, and the number of columns is either seven or eight. There is also variation in the number of pages between different newspapers and within any one paper,

depending in most cases on the day of the week and the amount of advertising carried. The ratio of advertisement space to editorial space averages out at about 55 per cent to 45 per cent in favour of the advertising. Friday appears to be the peak day for advertisement content. The average of the Press coverage on the selected three days (Monday, Wednesday and Friday) has been taken as an index of the average weekday issue over this period.

[9] If in the course of a reported speech a politician mentioned more than one point, the total column inches were divided by the number of subjects dealt with and allocated accordingly.

Page 78

[10] The proportions of editorial space in election newspaper coverage devoted to 'Personalities' are listed below:

	%
Daily Express	55·2
Daily Sketch	54·0
Daily Mirror	38·5
News Chronicle	35·5
Daily Herald	16·9
Daily Mail	15·1
Daily Telegraph	11·2
Yorkshire Evening Post	9·4
The Guardian	7·3
Yorkshire Post	4·8
The Times	3·7
Yorkshire Evening News	0

CHAPTER V · How the Campaign Reached the Electors

Page 80

[1] Benney, M., Gray, A. P., and Pear, R. H., *How People Vote* (Routledge & Kegan Paul, 1956).

[2] Butler, D. E., *The British General Election of 1955* (Macmillan, 1955) p. 52.

Page 81

[3] *The General Election*. An Audience Research Report (BBC, 1959), p. 33.

[4] Some of these figures must be qualified. Election addresses were said to be 'read' by these proportions. When Milne and Mackenzie asked electors just how closely they had read the party literature only about two-fifths claimed that they had read it through; there is no reason to believe that the semantic ambiguities of 'reading' are any greater in Bristol than in Leeds. Some Bristol electors in 1955 must have heard *both* radio and television broadcasts and this overlapping is not known. The 38 per cent of electors seeing Party election broadcasts in 1955 represents only the Conservative and Labour voters seeing their own party broadcasts. Proportion of opposing party's supporters in election broadcast audiences means the proportions of the *actual audiences*, seeing or hearing at least one Party election programme put out by a party other than the one they voted for.

NOTES ON THE CHAPTERS

[5] The corresponding figures issued by the Gallup Poll were:

	1955	1959
Radio	57%	27%
Television	33%	61%

Page 82

[6] Nicholas, H. G., *The British General Election of 1950* (Macmillan, 1951) p. 234.

Page 83

[7] The average amount of viewing of all political broadcasting during the campaign for different types of electors is represented numerically in the following table. The averages are for the divisions of the whole sample, including non-viewers; the figures would be about one-third as large again if they were based on viewers only. A viewer scored 2 marks if he saw the late political news bulletins at least three times a week, 2 for each Party election broadcast seen, and so on. A score of 6 could therefore represent the fairly regular viewing of news bulletins and two party broadcasts.

	Mean viewing scores
Men	
married	10·5
single	7·4
Women	
married	9·4
single	5·0
Age group	
21-9	9·4
30-44	10·4
45-65	10·2
Over 65	6·8
Occupations	
more skilled	10·2
less skilled	8·8

As with exposure to other forms of campaign propaganda, there are significant differences between the groups. The largest variation is between married and single people. Men saw more than women. Among the age groups the oldest saw least. The difference between higher grade and lower grade occupations is less than one would expect from the correlation between occupation and education.

[8] The Gallup Poll asked people in the weekend after Polling Day about viewing of Party election broadcasts. 61 per cent had seen at least one; 58 per cent one or more Conservative, and 56 per cent one or more Labour.

[9] Electors with television sets were classified into light, medium or heavy viewers according to a record of their viewing of a scale of serial items of different types during the week preceding the interview (see Appendix A). There were 30 per cent of viewers seeing under a third of the selected programmes, 29 per cent seeing about half, and 41 per cent seeing from 60 per cent to 100 per cent. The Granada Viewership Survey conducted by Hobson, Bates & Partners in conjunction with Research Services Ltd. in 1959 found a similar flat distribution

curve in intensity of viewing, 26 per cent of owners of ITV sets viewing up to seven hours a week, 46 per cent viewing eight to twenty-one hours and 28 per cent viewing from twenty-two to thirty-six or more hours per week. The BBC Audience Research study, reported in *The Public and the Programmes* (BBC, 1959), found much the same distribution, with individual viewing ranging from a few minutes per night to five hours or more.

Page 84

[10] *The Public and the Programmes* (BBC, 1959), p. 9. These and other figures are quoted by permission of the BBC.

Page 85

[11] TAM have provided evidence to support their conclusion: 'At the same time in 1958 (10 p.m.) the ITV News was broadcast over a slightly shorter period but was a comparable programme. It was preceded and succeeded by the same sort of light entertainment material as preceded and succeeded the Election broadcasts. During the period September to October 1958 the fall-off in the ITV audience from the start to the end of the news was 12 per cent in the North, and, again in the North, the drop was 11 per cent over the whole of September to October 1958. In 1958 there was one fairly popular programme "The Larkins" which succeeded the News, and, of course, the News is slightly shorter than the Party Political Broadcast.' These and other TAM figures are quoted by permission of Television Audience Measurement Ltd.

[12] *The Public and the Programmes* (BBC, 1959), p. 40, estimates that 46 per cent of predominantly BBC viewers received full education up to fifteen and beyond, compared with 29 per cent of ITV viewers.

[13] In our sample viewers divided as follows according to the television service they viewed most:

	BBC		ITV	
Conservative	40	+	60	=100%
Labour	25	+	75	=100%

(There is a considerable overlap between viewing of the two services.)

Page 86

[14] The Index of 'Total disposition to receive current affairs and information' (see Appendix A) gave us a convenient measure for this purpose. A borderline between 'interested' and 'not interested' was decided by independent inspection by the two authors of individual cases and placing them into two groups representing high and low political interest. This established a score of 7 out of 12 as a reasonable minimum. The proportion of viewers of Party election broadcasts with a score of at least 7 then gave us our second estimate of relatively selective viewers.

[15] cf. Gallup Poll estimate of 59 per cent of the audience for these broadcasts viewing 'because they wanted to'.

Page 89

[16] *The General Election* (BBC, 1959), p. 15.

NOTES ON THE CHAPTERS

Page 93

[17] *A First Report on Constituency Television in a General Election*, Granada TV, Manchester, 1959, p. 14.

[18] *A First Report on Constituency Television* etc., p. 38.

[19] Butler, D. E., and Rose, R. op. cit. p. 83

Page 95

[20] At this point it is relevant to include some evidence from the study about the normal viewing habits of the different political groups. The following table shows how the preferences for one service or the other vary between the political parties. There is a significant ITV bias among Labour supporters, a bias for the BBC among Conservatives, and, as with the viewing on Polling Day and so many other characteristics, the Liberals take up a midway position. Preferences were judged from actual viewing of six assorted BBC and six ITV programmes during the week preceding the first interviews (see Appendix A).

Party supporters	Viewing BBC mostly %	Viewing both %	Viewing ITV mostly %
Conservative	25	37·5	37·5
Labour	15	40	45
Liberal	29	42	29
Non-voters	19	33	48

The reason for these differences almost certainly goes back to preferences identified with different social class or occupational groups. The occupational differences clearly mark off one party's supporters from another's, and so their preferences appear as politically differentiated.

A BBC Audience Research Study *The Public and the Programmes* (BBC, 1959) showed a consistent movement in 'patronage' from BBC to ITV as the occupational level changed from highly skilled with 41 per cent preferring ITV to unskilled with 72 per cent.

[21] The BBC pamphlet *The Public and the Programmes* estimates that 95 per cent of the adult population have sound radio.

[22] IPA 80 per cent of adult population in the North and North-East Region (IPA, 1959). If Sunday papers are included the percentage goes up to 92 per cent.

[23] The estimates of readership of the national dailies in Fig. 2 (*Times, Guardian, Telegraph, Daily Mail, Express, News Chronicle, Herald, Mirror* and *Sketch*) have been taken from the IPA National Readership Surveys 1959. As the corresponding figures for the Yorkshire papers are averages over the whole region, and readership varies widely within this area, it was decided to use the proportions of our own survey sample claiming to read these papers regularly as estimates of local Leeds and Pudsey readership. The proportion of *Yorkshire Evening Post* readers in West Leeds and Pudsey appears to be several times greater than that of other parts of the county.

Page 98

[24] Trenaman, J., 'Education in the Adult Population', *Adult Education*, XXX, 3, 1957, p. 220. 'The various educational opportunities are found to overlap. The reading of books, the reading of the more significant items in the newspapers, the listening to talks and discussion, the visiting of museums and concerts,

going to classes or local study groups – all go together and reinforce each other.'
Page 102

[25] Butler, D. E., *The British General Election of 1955* (Macmillan,1955) p. 3. 'A veteran agent's chance remark, "no candidate is worth 500 votes" was echoed around the country during the 1955 election, and the results showed very few candidates who seemed to have been worth any more.'
Page 103

[26] 36 per cent of the 22 per cent who saw any 'Marathon' programmes.

[27] Milne & Mackenzie, *Marginal Seat*, found that the 63 per cent of local constituents who claimed to have read an election address were made up of 35 per cent who 'read it through' and 28 per cent who 'glanced at it'.
Page 104

[28] Lazarsfeld, P. F., Berelson, B., and Gaudet, H., *op. cit.*
Page 106

[29] Mr Crouch answered a number of our questions in great detail on the impact of television from the candidate's point of view, and we are grateful for his permission to allow us to quote.

CHAPTER VI · Television Electioneering – The Viewers' Response

Page 107

[1] Groups numbering eighty electors in all saw the two Party election broadcasts. Further evidence on general questions of matter and method in party broadcasts has been taken from the views put forward by 186 Leeds electors who saw a Conservative Party film and a Labour Party political broadcast in group meetings held shortly before the campaign. Invitations to attend all group meetings were sent to a randomly selected list of addresses in two wards of the North West Leeds constituency. Actual attendance was therefore dependent to some extent on the degree of interest in television. Test conditions are also not strictly comparable with home viewing conditions. A BBC Audience Research report – 'An Inquiry into the comprehensibility of "Topic for Tonight" (1952)' compiled by W. A. Belson, found that viewing under special experimental conditions increased attention and comprehension. On 'attention', listeners at home scored about three-quarters as much as studio listeners. The composition of the final group of eighty electors is as follows: men, 47 per cent; women, 53 per cent; skilled and highly skilled, 66 per cent; semi-skilled and unskilled, 34 per cent; aged under forty-five, 45 per cent; forty-five and over, 55 per cent; aged fifteen or under on leaving school, 74 per cent; educated after fifteen, 26 per cent; Conservative supporters, 44 per cent; Labour supporters, 31 per cent; Liberal and undecided, 25 per cent. The audience is therefore fairly representative, though it has the expected biases: somewhat older, better educated, more highly-skilled people than in the population as a whole.

[2] Some earlier work (unpublished) by one of the authors has shown that a second, as compared with a first, viewing of a television programme makes virtually no difference to attitudes and comprehension.

[3] Broadcast, September 19, 1959.

NOTES ON THE CHAPTERS

Page 108

⁴ In the broadcast discussion referred to above (Chapter III, note 1) LordHailsham agreed with David Butler that the Conservatives began the election at a low tempo.

Page 110

⁵ cf. J. Trenaman, 'Television: the Nature of the Medium and its Impact' – *Lo Spettacolo*, X, 1, January-March 1960 – 'Much the most significant factor (in increasing the comprehension of the viewer) proved to be the concreteness of the subject'. This fact emerged from a series of experiments, involving large numbers of viewers, on the nature of the television impact.

⁶ See Chapter VIII, p. 179.

Page 112

⁷ BBC Audience Research Report – *The General Election* (BBC, 1959) para. 53 – seems to corroborate this. The anti-Conservative and uncommitted groups amongst the audience reaction groups 'seem to have been impressed by Mr Macleod'.

Page 113

⁸ cf. *The General Election* (BBC, 1959) para. 60 – 'The uncommitted group (amongst audience research panels) ... were often impressed by Mr Gaitskell'.

Page 114

⁹ cf. *The General Election* (BBC, 1959) para. 53 – 'The anti-Conservative and uncommitted groups tended to be irritated by a "mutual admiration society" atmosphere in the first broadcast'.

Page 117

¹⁰ cf. *The General Election* (BBC, 1959) para. 58 – Speaking of reaction by pro-Labour viewers to this broadcast the report says: 'The general view seemed to be that the broadcasts were to be commended for their professional approach to the medium, that they were entertaining as well as interesting and easy to follow'. And para. 60 – 'The uncommitted group and, grudgingly or wistfully, the anti-Labour group conceded that these broadcasts were skilful and ingenious and Mr Benn effective'.

CHAPTER VII · Changes of Allegiance during the 1959 Campaign

Page 125

¹ See Chapter III, note 1.

Page 126

² We are grateful to National Opinion Polls for permission to quote the size of sample used. This is as large or larger than the normal sample used in market and public opinion research. The *Daily Express* Poll of Public Opinion also bases its findings on a quota sample of at least 3,000 people.

³ Gallup Poll normally employs quota samples of between 2,000 and 3,000, and the immediate pre-election poll in October 1959 included 2,500 interviews (Gallup Political Index, March 1960). Increases in sample size beyond levels of this kind only very marginally affect the expected sampling errors.

[4] A margin of about 2–3 per cent must be allowed to eliminate the effect of chance variations in the sample, and this is on the assumption that the sample is an unrestricted random one, which quota samples are not. Estimated moves of 0·5 per cent or 1 per cent cannot in isolation be significant when the effect of chance variation is allowed for.

Page 128

[5] The table is based on the entire before-and-after sample of 661. In six cases information about voting behaviour was either refused, or was not obtained by the interviewer. So that information about the sample should be as complete as possible, an estimate of the voting behaviour of these six was made on the basis of their attitude scores to the two major parties. Since there is a correlation of ·98 between voting and attitude score, this seemed to be justified, although it is still possible that the people involved had not in fact voted, even where they said they had. Three votes have been allotted to Conservative, two to Labour, and one counted as a non-voter.

Page 130

[6] The definition of 'swing' we have used is: the average of one major party's loss plus the other party's gain, expressed as a percentage of the total vote cast for the two major parties on the earlier occasion. (See *Marginal Seat*, p. 41, and D. E. Butler's appendix to Nicholas, *The British General Election of* 1950, p. 315).

This statistic is not really applicable to a sample survey like the present one. One constituency had a Liberal candidate in 1955, but not in 1959, so that former Liberal voters are redistributed over the two major parties. Any comparison between the Conservative and Labour shares of voters over the two elections would therefore be estimating changes within major party supporters and also the effects of Liberal redistribution. A further difficulty is that although our 1959 sample could tell us how they voted in 1955, it could not represent a true sample of 1955 voters. The electorate changes considerably in four and a half years. See also Milne & Mackenzie, *Marginal Seat*, 1955, p. 42. Over 20 per cent of 1955 voters in Bristol had their previous vote in another constituency.

Page 131

[7] Milne & Mackenzie, *Marginal Seat*, 1955, pp. 41–3.

[8] See Milne & Mackenzie, *Straight Fight*, p. 155, and *Marginal Seat*, 1955, p. 203. The 1951 Bristol sample overestimated the Conservative share of the vote by 2 per cent, and in 1955 by 3·1 per cent. The Droylsden survey (Campbell, P., Donnison, D., and Potter, A., *The Manchester School*, January 1952) also slightly underestimated the Labour vote. Benney, M., Gray, A. P., and Pear, R. H. *How People Vote*, (Routledge, London, 1956, p. 207) report an overestimation of the Labour vote, but Greenwich is a Labour stronghold, with areas of almost total Labour support where the factors we have mentioned would be reduced. Some evidence of the cause of the anti-Labour bias in our survey is provided by the 5 per cent of the original sample who were interviewed before the campaign, but who refused or could not be reached after the election. One can infer that what is true of these applies to some extent to the initial failures. They were predominantly older, more in manual occupations, and were overwhelmingly Labour in their support. There was also no sign of any

NOTES ON THE CHAPTERS

swing between their 1955 vote and their 1959 intention. If more of these had been interviewed a second time, or if more of the initial failures had been reached there would have been a higher representation of the solid Labour vote. For further details see Appendix C.

[9] Where questions are being asked about past behaviour an additional source of error is fallibility of memory. Benney, etc. (op. cit. p. 218) report that in Greenwich over 10 per cent of a group of 200 voters who were asked about the way they had voted five years previously, in the 1945 election, gave different answers on two separate occasions. They found that the effect of the election campaign was 'to make people project their present allegiance into the past'. What may well have happened with the present sample is that some of them projected on to the post-1955 period changes from Labour to Conservative they had made in 1950 or 1951. The general trend to Conservative over the whole period would make this understandable. There were also thirty-three electors in the sample who could not remember their previous vote. From their behaviour in 1959 the majority appear to be Conservative, and if they had been so in 1955, this would partly redress the balance, and make the sample swing between elections accord more with the swing in the constituency.

Page 133

[10] $\chi^2 = 37\cdot3$ (1 d.f.), $P = \cdot001$.

[11] *The People's Choice*, p. 107.

[12] cf. Lazarsfeld, *et al.* op. cit., p. xvii, who find that the party with the dominant machine in a particular area was most likely to succeed in gaining last minute votes.

Page 134

[13] See Chapter II, p. 17.

[14] See Appendix C, p. 268.

Page 135

[15] See D. E. Butler's appendix to Nicholas, *The British General Election of 1950*, p. 318. The median turnout in constituencies with a majority of under 10 per cent was $85\cdot6$ per cent, and where the majority was over 30 per cent it was $84\cdot5$ per cent. Labour seats showed even less tendency for turnout to be affected by the size of the majority.

Page 136

[16] Nominations did not close until during the campaign, so that at the time of interviewing there was still a possibility of a Liberal standing.

Page 137

[17] Electors were asked to describe their occupations in detail. They were then classified into one of six groups on a scale worked out by W. A. Belson for the BBC Audience Research Department in 1952. The scale, Belson says, 'had its beginnings in one presented by Spielman and Burt (1926), was influenced by research data giving mean intelligence test scores in various occupations (Foulds & Raven, 1948, Lingwood, 1952, Vernon, 1949).' The norms divided the population into seven (here compressed into six) occupational groups of fairly even size. The Census classification is less suitable if only because one group (Class III) is as large as $52\cdot5$ per cent of the adult male population. Belson, in a later private communication, says that the grading has a $\cdot74$

correlation with general intelligence as measured by P. E. Vernon's Abstraction Test. Occupations are fitted into Belson's classification according to descriptions of skill and training required at each level. The chief difficulty in grading, as in all such scales, is to know where to place housewives whose jobs before marriage were very different from their husband's. Belson has described the scale in 'The Construction of an Index of Intelligence', *Br. Jnl. Psy.*, Vol. XLVI, Pt. 1, February 1955, p. 47, and in 'The Comprehensibility of "Topic for Tonight" ', an Audience Research Dept. (BBC) duplicated report, 1952.

The six grades of occupation used, with an example of each were:

1. Professional and administrative (solicitor)
2. Highly skilled (bank clerk)
3. Skilled (lithographer)
4. Moderately skilled (bricklayer)
5. Semi-skilled (bus-conductor)
6. Unskilled (labourer).

[18] This is a consistent finding of previous election studies, and public opinion polls. No conclusive explanation has been reached, but Milne & Mackenzie (*Straight Fight*, pp. 54–7) have attempted an explanation in terms of differential birth and mortality rates between social classes, which have some effect on the age composition of party support. Labour gains from differential birth rates, Conservatives from death rates. They conclude: 'differential birth rates among different social classes probably accounted to some extent for the preponderance of Labour voters among the under-fifties, particularly among the youngest voters. The larger birth rate among the lower social classes in the 1920s would result in a relatively larger number of young Labour voters in recent years'. It has also been suggested (*Straight Fight*, p. 58) that the greater Conservative support among the older electors arose because the views of many older electors were formed before the rise of the Labour Party as the alternative Government.

Page 138

[19] See Milne & Mackenzie, *Marginal Seat*, 1955, p. 61: '... in so far as there is an "age" effect, it consists of the strong tendency for electors in the 21–9 group to vote Labour'. A tendency was also noted for the Labour advantage among those voting for the first time, to be less pronounced than in the previous year. See also *Straight Fight*, p. 32.

[20] Gallup Poll Political Index, February 1960.

Page 140

[21] See, for example, Milne & Mackenzie, *Marginal Seat*, p. 54. The association, though consistent, was not found to be statistically significant.

[22] Gallup Poll Political Index, February 1960.

[23] cf. Chapter VIII, pp. 154–5. Although Labour's women supporters were less partisan in their support than their husbands, their pro-Labour attitude strengthened slightly during the campaign, while that of their husbands weakened.

Page 141

[24] Comparable evidence over a long period about the voting of different social classes is not available, largely because no common method of classification has

NOTES ON THE CHAPTERS

been used. Some figures can, however, be given to show how constant the extent of working-class Conservative support appears to be. Comparable figures for the 1955 and 1959 elections are given in the Gallup Political Index for Feburary 1960: in 1955, 34 per cent of their 'lower middle and working class', and 31 per cent of their 'poor' category voted Conservative. In 1959, the comparable figures were 34 per cent and 19 per cent, a gain for Labour amongst the latter category. Benney, etc., op. cit., using the same Gallup ratings found that in 1950 27 per cent of the lower middle and working class voted Conservative and 18 per cent of the 'poor' category. Greenwich was, however, a firm Labour constituency, so a smaller Conservative ratio could be expected. Milne & Mackenzie in 1951, using a rating based on the Hall-Jones scale of occupations (see *British Journal of Sociology*, Vol. I, 1, 1950), estimated that 34 per cent of the 'working class' voted Conservative. In 1955, using the Registrar General's classification, they found that of grades IV and V, 35·8 per cent voted Conservative. Our own estimate, in W. Leeds and Pudsey, puts the proportion of the lower occupational groups who voted Conservative at 39 per cent. The category of 'lower occupational groups' (i.e. moderately skilled, semi-skilled and unskilled workers) used by us comprises 52 per cent of our population, whereas the Gallup categories of 'lower middle and working class' plus the 'poor' comprise 75 per cent. If any conclusion can be drawn from these different estimates, it is that since the war the Conservative Party has enjoyed a constant share of at least a third of the working class vote.

CHAPTER VIII · Changes in Political Attitudes

Page 146
[1] Abrams, M., *Why Labour Has Lost Elections*, Socialist Commentary, May and June 1960; also Abrams, M., and Rose, R., *Must Labour Lose?*, (Penguin Books, 1960).
Page 147
[2] Lazarsfeld, *et al.*, op. cit.
[3] op. cit., p. 186
[4] Milne & Mackenzie, *Marginal Seat*, p. 91.
[5] Lazarsfeld, *et al.*, op. cit.
Page 148
[6] Milne & Mackenzie, *Marginal Seat*, 1955.
Page 150
[7] Lazarsfeld, *et al.*, op. cit.
[8] Crossman, R. H. S., MP, Lord Hailsham, Butler, D. E., op. cit.
Page 151
[9] The possibility of a rebound after the declaration of the poll, or the reverse of the bandwagon effect, cannot be ruled out. The justification of Conservative claims and the dashing of Labour hopes may have had some effect on the morale of both sides. Lazarsfeld, Berelson and Gaudet, who carried out a succession of seven interviews on a sample of electors, including one as close as possible to the eve of the election and another shortly after the election, do not report

any noticeable effect, in *The People's Choice*. The Gallup Poll in Britain was sounding public opinion immediately after the 1959 General Election and showed only a fractional difference between voting in the October election and fresh intentions in early November 1959, i.e. excluding 'don't knows' and non-voters, Poll: Conservative 48·8 per cent, Labour 44·5 per cent; November intention: Conservative 48 per cent, Labour 44 per cent. The Gallup Political Index, based on measures of approval of the Government and Opposition to a number of issues showed a parallel decline, from a baseline of 100 in December 1959 to a figure of 70 representing the standing of the Government among Government voters and 69 for the Opposition among Labour voters. Voting intention figures for both parties also declined after November 1959 – but not before. Taking this evidence, with what has been shown of the stability of underlying political attitudes, *once they are roused*, our impression is that any rebound effect would be slight in the immediate post-election period.

Page 154

[10] Milne & Mackenzie, *Straight Fight*, p. 60, say they found 'no clear evidence in Bristol North-East' of a movement to a higher objective social class causing voters to change more readily from Labour to Conservative.

CHAPTER IX · The Electors' Knowledge of Party Policies and National Issues

Page 165

[1] See Klapper, J. T., in *The Process and Effects of Mass Communication*, ed. Schramm, Urbana, Illinois, 1955, p. 294, who summarizes the findings of research undertaken by the US War Department ' . . . all media products and all devices investigated were found to be highly effective in communicating information and imparting skills. All, however, were found to be very much less effective, and at times wholly ineffective, in modifying opinions or in increasing motivation . . . Products designed to affect opinion and motivation also succeeded in imparting the *facts* which it was hoped would stimulate the formation of the desired attitude.'

[2] Milne & Mackenzie, *Marginal Seat*, p. 121, employed a scale of four policies to see how far voters could attribute them to the correct party. The fifteen policies used by us were submitted to the party headquarters for checking. For obvious reasons the parties could not, shortly before the election campaign, specify the actual policies they would put forward in their manifestoes.

Page 166

[3] See Ehrenberg, H. S. C., 'The Relative Merits of Independent Matched Samples and of the Panel Technique for Before-and-After Studies'. LPE Research Paper No. 1, 1959, for a note on sampling errors.

Page 167

[4] The higher educational standards of Conservative voters would lead one to expect this to be the case.

Page 168

[5] See below, Chapter XI, p. 210; cf. also Milne & Mackenzie, *Marginal Seat*, p.

NOTES ON THE CHAPTERS

122. Using a short but similar scale of propositions attributable to one or other party, the authors came to similar conclusions about the factors associated with the lack of knowledge. Working-class people, older electors and women are less correct in attributing a proposition to the correct party.

[6] All those with a total exposure score to campaign propaganda of 0, 1, 2 or 3 were included in this sub-sample. (See Appendix A.) This produced a total of 141 electors.

Page 173

[7] *Daily Telegraph*, September 17, 1959. The issues volunteered to its interviewers came in the following order of importance: 1. Cost of living, 2. Pensions, 3. Unemployment, 4. Summit talks, international affairs, 5. Productivity, economic prosperity, 6. Housing and rents, 7. H-bomb, 8. Education.

[8] Milne & Mackenzie, *Straight Fight*, p. 103, report a similar finding: 'very little change in opinion occurred and the issues regarded as most important by all voters in the sample *before* the election – peace, cost of living, housing, and the health service were placed in the same order *after* the election'. cf. also *Marginal Seat*, 1955, p. 111.

Page 174

[9] The percentage of TV time is based on an analysis of all time given in television to politics. See Chapter IV, Table 8, for details of the analysis.

[10] This percentage of Press space was based on an analysis of space given in the national daily Press to election material. See Chapter IV, Table 8 and p. 58 for details of the analysis.

Page 176

[11] Only where the difference between Conservative and Labour support for an item is significant at ·05 level is it quoted here.

Page 178

[12] A similar tendency was noted in the 1951 election by Milne & Mackenzie (*Straight Fight*, p. 103) who found that issues particularly associated with one party were less likely after the campaign to be thought important by political opponents.

Page 180

[13] This tendency is still limited by the political situation. For example, people in highly-skilled or more responsible jobs show no significant or consistent tendency to adopt, as a result of the campaign, an issue previously more favoured by those in less-skilled occupations. Here the party loyalties associated with occupational divisions are dominant.

CHAPTER X · The Effects of Television and Other Media

Page 186

[1] There was no particular significance in attaching a positive value to Conservative scores. Had we reversed the signs and given them a negative value the results would have been the same.

Page 190

[2] We looked at the 113 electors in the sample who read the *Daily Herald* and

TELEVISION AND THE POLITICAL IMAGE

plotted their changes in attitude towards the Labour Party over the period of the election against the amount they read of the political reporting in that newspaper. As a group, their Labour Party attitude scores declined by 0·40 points which was a larger decrement than was found in the sample as a whole. There was a slight negative correlation ($-·03$) but it was too small to achieve statistical significance.

Page 193

[3] Lazarsfeld, *et al.*, *The People's Choice*, p. 151.

Page 194

[4] Lazarsfeld, *et al.*, op. cit., p. 151.

[5] Lazarsfeld, *et al.*, op. cit., p. 51 – their index of exposure scores:

	Greater interest		Less interest	
	opinion leaders	others	opinion leaders	others
Newspaper	15·8	12·3	14·8	6·6
Radio	14·6	12·3	13·0	7·6

Page 196

[6] Lazarsfeld, *et al.*, op. cit., p. 42.

[7] Milne & Mackenzie, *Marginal Seat*, pp. 149–50.

[8] 'Partisanship' being defined here as the increment of an elector's attitude score towards the party for which he voted over his score towards the other major party.

Page 197

[9] Bartlett, F. C., *Political Propaganda* (Cambridge, 1940), p. 131.

Page 199

[10] Butler, D. E., & Rose, R., op. cit., p. 17.

Page 200

[11] Lazarsfeld, *et al.*, op. cit., p. xx.

Page 201

[12] Bartlett, F. C., op. cit.

[13] Hovland, C. I., Lumsdaine, A. A., and Sheffield, F. E., *Experiments in Mass Communication* (Princeton University Press, 1949).

[14] Lumsdaine, A. A., and Janis, I. L., quoted in Hovland, C. I., Janis, I. L., and Kelley, H. H., *Communication and Persuasion* (Yale University Press, and Oxford, 1953), p. 110.

Page 205

[15] See Table 35, Chapter VIII, for list of items in the scale.

CHAPTER XI · The Characteristics of the 'Changers'

Page 207

[1] As far as comparisons can be made with other panel studies, the proportion of electors involved in change during an election campaign, using similar definitions, does not appear to vary. Benney, etc. op. cit., p. 170, found that 23 per

NOTES ON THE CHAPTERS

cent changed in the weeks before the 1950 election; Milne & Mackenzie found the corresponding proportion of changers in Bristol to be 26 per cent in 1951 (op. cit., p. 27) and 20 per cent in 1955 (op. cit., p. 41). The variations could be accounted for by differences in method and in the areas sampled, and by sampling errors.

Page 208

[2] Lazarsfeld, Berelson, Gaudet, op. cit., p. 48, make a similar point: 'If a woman is not interested, she just feels there is no reason why she should vote. A man, however, is under more social pressure and will therefore go to the polls even if he is not "interested" in the events of the campaign.' The authors explain this in terms of the time-lag between the lifting of legal restrictions on women's voting and changes in women's attitude to politics. Even forty years after the granting of voting rights to women a tendency remains to regard voting as a man's affair.

[3] See Milne & Mackenzie, *Marginal Seat*, p. 93, and Benney, *et al.*, op. cit. p. 184. Both these studies emphasize the important influence exerted by the political opinions of the family, friends and workmates. Milne & Mackenzie found the influence of the elector's family particularly important immediately before the election, and that of workmates in the longer period between elections.

Page 210

[4] See Chapter V, p. 99.

Page 211

[5] See Chapter VIII, p. 155.

[6] Lazarsfeld, *et al.*, op. cit., p. 70. 'The party changers resembled the adherents of the party they changed *to*, more than the party they changed *from*.' See also Milne & Mackenzie, *Straight Fight*, 1955, pp. 49–50. The authors conclude that those who change have more in common with the party they change to, than the party they leave, and this is particularly true of their social class, both objective and subjective.

Page 212

[7] Certainly both parties do not make an equal appeal to the entire community. Labour's main election plank was its superannuation scheme; before the campaign opened, 70 per cent of those in the least skilled occupations felt this to be amongst the most important national issues; only 30 per cent of those in the highest occupational group felt this to be so.

Page 217

[8] See Lazarsfeld, *et al.*, *The People's Choice*, p. 45. The authors concluded that although lack of interest and non-voting are associated, 'two out of three cases of non-voting were intentional and premeditated, according to the voter's own statement'.

Page 218

[9] See Chapter V, p. 103.

Page 219

[10] Of these fifty-two, nine changed from a Conservative intention to a Labour vote, nine from Labour to Conservative, nine from Liberal to Labour, fifteen from Liberal to Conservative, eight from Conservative to Liberal, and two from Labour to Liberal.

Page 220
[11] cf. Milne & Mackenzie, *Marginal Seat*, p. 39, and Lazarsfeld, *et al.*, *The People's Choice*, p. 79. Interest in politics and exposure to political information are interlocking, and neither can be isolated as the cause of the other.
Page 221
[12] cf. Lazarsfeld, *et al.*, op. cit., p. 70; Milne & Mackenzie, *Marginal Seat*, p. 41.

Glossary

A few technical terms have been used in this study and sometimes common words in a special sense. Although nearly all such terms are described in the text as they arise, it may not always be convenient for the reader who is dipping into these pages to find the original definitions. The more important ones are therefore listed below:

ATTITUDE SCORE. An index of strength of attitude towards one of the two major political parties or their leaders. A score represents a position on scales ranging from $+5$ to -4 for the parties, and $+8$ to -6 for each leader.

CAMPAIGN. A period of nineteen days extending from the day following Dissolution, Saturday, September 19, 1959, to the day before Polling Day, i.e. October 7.

CHANGERS. All electors in the sample whose final voting position differed from their intention expressed at the beginning of the campaign. Changers therefore include most non-voters, all 'don't knows' and changers between parties.

CHI-SQUARE. An index of dispersion, with which a difference or a similarity between observed and expected frequencies may be tested for significance.

COMMUNALITY. A measure in any single item or test of the total amount of variability accounted for by all the factors in a principal component or factor analysis. It is obtained by summing the squares of the factor loadings.

COMPONENT. A common factor among attitudes; here used to describe an underlying unitary feature of a political image.

CORRELATION. A measure of association, or of simultaneous change between one variable and another. The correlation coefficient is the index used and it varies from $+1\cdot0$ to $-1\cdot0$.

EXPOSURE. In the context of this study, reception of campaign material from any given source acknowledged by an elector. Degrees of exposure are measured and explained in the text.

ISSUE. A matter in contention or requiring action by any Government and distinguishable from party policies.

MONITORING (of programmes). Scrutiny and appraisal of political television broadcasts during the campaign by six assessors working independently.

OCCUPATION. A classification into six grades of job based on the skill and training required (see note 17, Chapter VII, for description of grading).

PARTISANSHIP. A measure of the extent to which strength of attitude towards the party supported by an elector exceeds that towards the other major party. It is expressed as an index representing the difference between the two party attitude scores.

PARTY ELECTION BROADCAST. A programme on television or radio sponsored by a political party and broadcast during the campaign, under an arrangement agreed between the three political parties, the BBC and the ITA. It is distinguished here from 'Party political broadcasts' which are transmitted between elections.

PROBABILITY. Used only in the statistical sense (e.g. probability sample).

SIGNIFICANCE. Used here generally in the strict statistical sense.

SPECIFICITY. A measure of the extent to which the meaning of an attitude item is *not* governed by the common image factors. The higher the specificity the more an item has unique meaning for electors.

SWING. A convenient measure of the advantage gained by one major party over the other between two General Elections. As used by D. E. Butler it can be defined as the average of one major party's gain and the other party's loss expressed as a percentage of the total votes cast for both parties.

VARIANCE. Used here only in the statistical sense.

Reference Table of Sampling Errors

Sampling errors show the margins within which a statistic produced by a sample is likely to vary from the 'true' figure for the original population. What such a margin of error is really telling us is that if we continued to draw further samples of the same size from the same population the corresponding statistics would mostly lie within its range. The limit within which nineteen out of twenty figures would fall is roughly twice the calculated standard error, and it is a convenient convention to regard this as the first limit of 'significance'. If we compare a statistic from one sample with a statistic from another, we must take both margins of error into account before claiming a significant difference. Such margins can be calculated from averages (or means), percentages, etc. Errors based on percentages will vary not only with the sample size but also with the size of the percentage itself.

Standard errors vary as the *square root* of the sample size, which is why we can often obtain nearly as much information from a sample of, say, 500 as from one of 5,000, provided the sample is well drawn. All such calculations of error assume that the sample is an unrestricted random sample, by which we mean that every member of the population had an equal chance of being selected. Complete random samples are practically never obtained in social surveys. In the present study, over 85 per cent of the original sample was reached and although, in the short time available, this was something of an achievement for the interviewing force, it does mean that the sample was not a completely random one. A further limitation is that statistics derived from verbal statements can never be as reliable as physical measurements. The sampling errors quoted in this table are, therefore, minimal.

Where comparisons are made in the text between statistics obtained from the *same* sample, before and after the campaign, very much smaller errors apply and separate significance tests have been calculated and are used in discussing the results.

The table shows sampling errors expressed as percentages. They represent twice the standard errors, and imply that there is about a 95 per cent chance of statistics lying within this range of the true, population figure, or a 5 per cent chance of their not doing so (i.e. P=·05).

Percentage	Size of sample					
%	50	100	250	661	1000	3000
10	8·5	6·0	3·8	2·3	1·9	1·1
20	11·3	8·0	5·1	3·1	2·5	1·5
30	13·0	9·2	5·8	3·6	2·9	1·7
40	13·9	9·8	6·2	3·8	3·1	1·8
50	14·1	10·0	6·3	3·9	3·1	1·8
60	13·9	9·8	6·2	3·8	3·1	1·8
70	13·0	9·2	5·8	3·6	2·9	1·7
80	11·3	8·0	5·1	3·1	2·5	1·5
90	8·5	6·0	3·8	2·3	1·9	1·1

APPENDIX A

Construction of Indices of Exposure

The study made use of a number of indices of exposure to different sources of information and persuasion during and prior to the election campaign. The method involves weighting the degree to which informants were open to possible influence.

1. *Weight of viewing*

All informants were asked about their viewing of a selected list of six BBC and six ITV programmes in the seven days preceding the first pre-election interview.

The number of items viewed by each informant was entered on a continuous distribution scale. The distribution was conveniently divided into three roughly equivalent parts. The lines of demarcation were used to classify informants with television as 'light', 'medium' or 'heavy' viewers.

2. *Viewing of current affairs and informational programmes (pre-campaign)*

Informants were asked if they ever viewed programmes dealing with party politics, and how often, and were asked to name speakers they had seen recently. They were also asked if they had seen 'Tonight', 'This Week' or 'Panorama' in the preceding week.

Scores within a range 0 to 6 were allotted as follows:

Seeing	Score
This Week	1
Tonight	1
Panorama	1

Watching programmes about politics:

	Score
Nearly always	3
Fairly often	2
Occasionally	1

3. *Exposure to politics and current affairs through newspapers (pre-campaign)*

Our concern was with the amounts of political and topical information which an elector was likely to have obtained from any newspaper source in the period before the election campaign. The newspaper regularly read was scored as follows:

	Score
The Times, Daily Telegraph, Guardian or *Yorkshire Post*	3
Daily Express, Daily Mail, Daily Herald, News Chronicle or evening papers	2
Daily Mirror, Daily Sketch	1
No paper read regularly	0

In addition to this score a weight of 1 was added if 'nearly all' the political news was read in the daily paper. Range: 0-4.

4. *Exposure to political news and information through sound radio (pre-campaign)*

Informants were asked which news broadcasts they heard, and if they listened to evening talks and discussions.

Scoring

Morning news	1
Midday news	1
Evening news	1
Evening talks and discussions	2

(Range: 0-5)

5. *Total disposition to receive current affairs and information (pre-campaign)*

This score is a sum of the three preceding scores and ranges from 0-15. It was used as an index of general political interest.

6. *Viewing of Party election broadcasts*

Electors were asked which of the twelve broadcasts they had seen, and were reminded of the content of each one. A score of 2 for each broadcast was given, so the score could range from 0-24.

7. *Viewing of other television election programmes*

A total score for seeing other programmes dealing with the election was given to each informant, as follows:

	Score
ITV *'Election Day-by-Day'*	
If seen – Most evenings, 3 or 4 a week	2
1 or 2 a week, or less often	1
BBC 10.15 p.m. election news	
Scores 2 or 1 as above	
Granada's *'Election Marathon'*	
If 3 or more seen	3
If 2 seen	2
If 1 seen	1
BBC *'Hustings'*	
If any one seen	3
Other election programmes	
Granada's 'The Last Debate'	3
Granada's 'Now is the Time'	1

APPENDIX A

The total score for these television programmes ranged from 0-14.

8. *Total television exposure to politics*
This score is the sum of the two preceding scores, and has a range 0-38.

9. *Newspaper reading of election news*
Electors were asked if they had read reports of election speeches in a newspaper, and how often, and how much of the reports they had read.
  Scoring was as follows:

	Score
(i) For reading reports:	
Fairly regularly	3
About 2 or 3 times per week	3
Only occasionally	1
(ii) For amounts of the reports read:	
Nearly all	2
About half	1
Just a little	—

These two scores were added together to give a maximum of 5, but an additional weight of 2 was added if the papers happened to be *The Times, Daily Telegraph, Guardian* or *Yorkshire Post*.

10. *Listening to election broadcasts on sound radio*
A question was asked about the number of Party election broadcasts heard on sound radio, and the extent of listening to news bulletins during the campaign. A score in the range 0-8 was given, made up as follows:

	Score
(i) Listening to Party election programmes:	
Most of them	5
About 4 or 5	4
Only 1 or 2	2
(ii) Listening to evening news bulletins:	
Fairly regularly	3
About 2 or 3 a week	2
Only occasionally	1

11. *Total exposure to propaganda*
This score is a sum of the scores for exposure to the three media, television, sound radio and the Press during the campaign and has a range 0-53.

12. *Local participation*
The score indicates the extent to which the informant was canvassed, saw local candidates, knew their names, read any of the electoral addresses, or heard any candidate speak.

The range is from 0-5, made up as follows:

Talking to canvasser	1
Seeing any of the local candidates	1
Correctly naming at least one candidate	1
Attending an indoor or outdoor meeting	1
Reading any of the local election addresses	1

13. *Political discussion*

Electors were simply asked if they had had any opportunity during the election of discussing any of the issues with other people at work or at home.

* * *

In all these indices there is a large element of subjective judgment. It is assumed, for instance, that reading a more literate and serious newspaper indicates a high political interest, or that Party election broadcasts are more important than news and discussion programmes. It was also assumed, where exact information was not asked for, that expressions like 'nearly all', 'about half', or 'just a little' mean the same thing to all informants. The need to keep the length of the interview to a minimum imposed a good deal of restriction, and we had to rely on the experiences of previous surveys in making decisions of this sort.

APPENDIX B

An Index of Political Change

There are varying degrees of voting change. There seems, on the face of it, a qualitative difference between a switch from, say, a Labour vote to a Conservative vote, and a switch from a Labour vote to uncertainty of voting intention. The concepts of a 'major party' and a 'minor party' had been used by Milne and Mackenzie in both Bristol studies and we hoped to extend this distinction so as to produce a scale giving values to differing kinds of change. Numerically weighted, it could then be used to estimate the relative effects of the different influences on voting stability.

The method used was to ask a number of judges to rank, in order of political deviation, a list of representative types of change. For this purpose, the Labour and Conservative Parties were given equal status as 'major' parties, and distinguished from the Liberal Party, on the, perhaps presumptuous, grounds, that there was no immediate possibility of the Liberal Party forming a Government, so that a decision to vote Liberal might be more lightly taken. The analysis of political images had also shown that the Liberal position stood mid-way between Conservative and Labour positions on the basic attitude dimension.

The complicating factor was that the crucial period of the campaign involves a comparison, not between one voting position and another, but between an intention to vote and an actual vote, and the preceding period involves a similar comparison in reverse. It was decided to equate a voting intention with a vote, and to assume that change in one direction should be given the same weight as its reverse. The period between elections was also divided into two, and change from a vote to a voting intention was not differentiated from change from an intention at the start of the campaign to a vote at the end of it.

On this basis a list of seven different types of change was compiled which is here given in the order in which they were finally placed, and the scores allotted:

Change	Score
Major party to other major party	7
Major party to Liberal	6
Major party to non-voting	5
'Don't know' to major party	4
Liberal to non-voting	3
'Don't know' to Liberal	2
'Don't know' to non-voting	1

The first item is regarded as showing the largest change, the last the smallest.

Amongst the eight judges there was a high measure of agreement. The coefficient of concordance calculated is ·94 which is highly significant (P= ·001).

In order to score the change over both periods from the 1955 election to the 1959 election, the separate scores from 1955 vote to 1959 intention and from the 1959 intention to actual vote could not always be added together. Consider, for example, the following two types of change:

1. Labour vote, to 'Don't know', to Conservative vote.
2. Conservative vote, to 'Don't know', to Conservative vote.

The move from either major party to 'don't know' or vice versa on our judges' ranking would score 4 points, the total being 8 for each overall change, but change no. 1 probably represents a consistent movement in a direction away from the original position – from one major party to the other. Change no. 2 represents only a temporary uncertainty, but no change of allegiance. In order to establish additional weights for double movements of this sort, judges were asked to rank four examples of double change (it being understood that in each change the other major party could have been substituted) with the results shown in the column headed 'score'.

	1955 *vote*	1959 *intention*	1959 *vote*	*Score*
1.	Labour	'Don't know'	Conservative	4
2.	Conservative	'Don't know'	Conservative	1
3.	Liberal	'Don't know'	Conservative	2
4.	Didn't vote	'Don't know'	Conservative	3

The highest score is given to the largest degree of movement.
As a result the scoring system for changes over the two consecutive periods, vote-intention-vote, was awarded as follows:

I. 1955 (vote) to 1959 (intention)

Change

From (to)	*To (from)*	*Score*
Major party (Con., Lab.)	Other major party	7
Major party	Liberal	6
Major party	Non-voting	5
Other major party	'Don't know'	4
Same major party	'Don't know'	1
Liberal	Non-voting	3
Liberal	'Don't know'	2
Non-voting	'Don't know'	1
No change		0

APPENDIX B

II. 1959 (intention) to 1959 (vote)
    Change

From (to)	*To (from)*	*Score*
Major party	Other major party	7
Major party	Liberal	6
Major party	Non-voting	5
'Don't know'	Major party	4
Liberal	Non-voting	3
'Don't know'	Liberal	2
'Don't know'	Non-voting	1
No change		0

To score the total change over the period, scores (1) and (2) are added together.

Scoring for 1959 vote
In order to be able to correlate exposure and other measures with the 1959 vote it was necessary to allot scores to represent the various voting positions as follows:

Conservative vote	+3
Liberal vote (dominant Conservative Party attitude)	+1
No vote	0
Liberal vote (dominant Labour Party attitude)	−1
Labour vote	−3

APPENDIX C

Fieldwork and a Note on the Elusive Elector

Recruitment and briefing of interviewers

On the first round of interviews, thirty-seven paid interviewers were employed. These were recruited by public advertisement, and included a number with professional market research experience. Six of them were students at the University. The number was reduced to thirty-two for the second round as there were fewer calls to be made. As far as possible the same interviewers were used, and given the same people to re-interview. In about two-thirds of cases this was possible.

A pilot survey was undertaken by four experienced interviewers to test the draft questionnaire, and for this, twenty-four interviews were taken outside the constituencies selected for the main survey. Training of interviewers was undertaken by a professional fieldwork organizer.[1] Briefing meetings were held, where the questionnaire was explained in detail, and a demonstration interview given, and throughout the interviewing period the work was supervised. As far as possible, all interviewers were accompanied on at least one interview by the supervisor of fieldwork. All the first completed forms were checked with the interviewers, and interviewers were kept informed of any changes to be made, or of any difficulties which had arisen.

Payment was by the hour, no distinction being made between travelling time and interviewing time.

The first round of interviews

Starting at a random point on the first page of the register, every 150th name was chosen from the West Leeds electoral register, and every 125th from the Pudsey register, giving a total sample of 820 – 401 of them in West Leeds, and 419 in Pudsey.

The thirty-seven interviewers, some working part-time, and some full-time, were given eight days in which to complete their quota of interviews. No interviews were to be carried out after the start of the first election broadcast on September 19.

This 820 *includes* the seventy-six substitutes who were allowed where the original informant was known to have removed from the district. The name chosen as a substitute was that appearing ten places further down in the register. Of these substitutes fifty-seven were actually interviewed and are included amongst the 701 successfully interviewed.

[1] We are indebted to Messrs. Research Services Ltd. for the temporary secondment of Miss C. Seabrook for this purpose.

APPENDIX C

Interviewing results (pre-campaign)

Successfully interviewed (3 subsequently discarded because of inadequate information)	701
Refused	61
Died since compilation of register	13
Not found	32
Too ill	13
	820

If the substitutes are included, 85·5 per cent of the initial sample were successfully interviewed. Excluding the substitute interviews, 78·5 per cent of the 820 were successfully interviewed.

The second round of interviews

Briefing was carried out on the day after the poll and interviewing began the next day. The operation was terminated after ten days, and by the end of the week following Polling Day 85 per cent of the interviews had been successfully completed. There were twenty-five particularly elusive electors on whom several recalls were made, extending over a further two weeks, before being successfully interviewed.

Interviewing results (post-campaign)

Successfully interviewed	661
Refused	25
Too ill	2
Not found	7
Other (e.g. wrong person interviewed, spoilt form)	3
	698 (=701−3 discarded above)

95 per cent of the interviews attempted in the second round were successfully completed.

80·5 per cent of the original sample were interviewed both before and after the election including substitutes.

The elusive elector

In all, thirty-seven electors were interviewed before, but not after the campaign, twenty-five of them refusing the interview in the second round. An analysis of their characteristics provides some valuable evidence about the nature of those who are missed in surveys of this kind:

(a) *Characteristics of 'failures' at second interview*
(*Refusals, ill, not found, spoilt questionnaires, etc.*)

Voting intention		Sex		Occupation		TV ownership		Age	
Labour	18	Men	14	Skilled & highly skilled	19	TV	25	21-44	14
Conservative	7	Women	23	Semi-skilled & unskilled	18	No TV	12	45 plus	23
Liberal	4								
'Don't know'	4								
Refused and no vote	4								
	37		37		37		37		37

The 'refusals' are the largest category of failure at this stage of the survey (not at the first round) and separate breakdowns are given of these twenty-five:

(b) *Characteristics of refusals*

Voting intention		Sex		Occupation		TV ownership		Age	
Labour	13	Men	8	Skilled & highly skilled	13	TV	15	21-44	9
Conservative	3	Women	17	Semi-skilled & unskilled	12	No TV	10	45 plus	16
Liberal	3								
'Don't know'	2								
Refused	4								
	25		25		25		25		25

The attitude score of these Labour supporters to the Labour Party was slightly below average at 2·5 and the Conservatives' score to their own party a little above average at 4·2. Conservative intenders, like those in the before-and-after sample, were thus more partisan than Labour intenders.

The average score of the thirty-seven, based on their pre-campaign disposition to receive information through broadcasting and the Press, is 4·9 against an average for the sample interviewed before-and-after of 6·1. This average of 4·9 is lower even than that of the non-voters, and together with the social characteristics is a pointer to voting behaviour. It seems likely that a high proportion of these 'failures' eventually did not vote.

The number of 'failures' is too small to be at all conclusive, but the figures reveal important characteristics of those who were not reached by the survey. Amongst all 'failures' there was a statistically significant over-representation of Labour voters, and of women. Treating refusals as a separate category, these features are accentuated. No fundamental difference in occupation is shown, and the higher age of refusals must also only be regarded as a tendency, which would need to be validated in a larger sample.

APPENDIX D

Voting in the Sample and in the Constituencies

The percentage of votes cast for each party in each constituency at the General Election, and as recorded in the sample.

The sample percentages are based on the number in each constituency who claimed to have voted for one of the three parties at the election.

It is noticeable that the greatest under-representation of Labour support occurs in the Conservative constituency. This is consistent with our other evidence that there is local pressure to conform to majority behaviour, which accentuates the common tendency to underestimate the left-wing vote.

WEST LEEDS

Party	Sample	Standard error	Population
	(279)	(×2)	(47,163)
	%		%
Conservative	46·2	±6·0	45·1
Labour	53·8	±6·0	54·9

PUDSEY

Party	Sample	Standard error	Population
	(309)	(×2)	(45,422)
	%		%
Conservative	56·6	±5·6	50·1
Labour	29·8	±5·2	35·8
Liberal	13·6	±3·9	14·1

COMBINED CONSTITUENCIES

Party	Sample	Standard error	Population
	(588)	(×2)	(92,585)
	%		%
Conservative	51·7	±4·1	47·6
Labour	41·2	±4·1	45·5
Liberal	7·1	±2·1	6·9

Voting in the two constituencies, 1959 and 1955

PUDSEY

1959 *General Election*
   (Population 52,285; turnout 86·9 per cent)
   J. Hiley (Conservative) 22,752; V. P. Richardson (Labour) 16,241;
   J. S. Snowden (Liberal) 6,429. Conservative majority 6,511.

1955 *General Election*
   Banks (Conservative) 20,445; Payton (Labour) 15,881; Wainwright (Liberal) 6,526. Conservative majority 4,564.

WEST LEEDS
1959 *General Election*
(Population 60,269; turnout 78·3 per cent)
   T. C. Pannell (Labour) 25,878; D. L. Crouch (Conservative) 21,285. Labour majority 4,593.
1955 *General Election*
   Pannell (Labour) 24,576; Hiley (Conservative) 18,312; Hudson (Liberal) 3,699. Labour majority 6,264.

APPENDIX E

The Social Composition of the Sample

	Complete sample (661) %		Whole population (U.K.) %
Sex			
Men	46·2	Men	47·0
Women	53·8	Women	53·0
	100·0		100·0

	%		%
Age			
21-29	13·9	21-29	16·5
30-44	30·9	30-44	30·0
45-65	38·4	45-65	36·6
Over 65	16·8	Over 65	16·9
	100·0		100·0

Occupation groups (see Chapter VII, page 137 and note 17)

	%
Professional and administrative	9·7
Highly skilled	15·7
Skilled	22·6
Moderately skilled	23·3
Semi-skilled	20·2
Unskilled	8·5
	100·0

Age distribution and voting

Male electors (302)

	All men (302) %	Conservative (150) %	Labour (109) %	Non-voters (27) %
21-29	16·3	18·0	11·9	18·0
30-44	28·2	25·6	32·1	22·0
45-65	38·4	42·7	36·7	30·0
Over 65	17·1	13·7	19·3	30·0
	100·0	100·0	100·0	100·0

Women electors (359)

	All women (359) %	Conservative (154) %	Labour (133) %	Non-voters (46) %
21-29	12·0	9·1	15·8	13·0
30-44	33·0	29·9	36·8	30·5
45-65	38·5	44·1	36·1	26·0
Over 65	16·5	16·9	11·3	30·5
	100·0	100·0	100·0	100·0

APPENDIX F
Estimates of Press Space devoted to the Campaign
TABLE 58

Editorial space in column inches devoted by national and local (Leeds) newspapers to election campaign issues on September 25, 28, October 7, 1959

Issues	Totals	%
Cost of living	201	8·8
Nationalization	135	5·9
Permanent peaceful settlement between great powers	168	7·4
Spend more on education	150	6·6
More houses, fair rents	147	6·5
No return of unemployment	154	6·8
New approach to question of old age	265	11·6
Improve health and social services	21	0·9
Ensure greater productivity	72	3·1
Help people of poorer Commonwealth countries	75	3·3
Control H-bomb testing	62	2·7
* Suez, Egypt, Cyprus etc. Criticism and defence of policy	96	4·2
* Agriculture	128	5·6
Roads	32	1·4
* Take-over bids, capital gains tax, expense accounts, reform company laws	475	20·9
* Anti-semitism	13	0·6
* Unions, strikes, etc.	83	3·7
Total (all issues)	2,277	100·0

* Issues marked with an asterisk were not included in the survey list. The percentages differ from those listed in Table 8 (p. 59), because references which applied particularly to party policies on some of these issues have been separated into a further table.

TABLE 59

Editorial space in column inches devoted by national and local (Leeds) newspapers on September 25, 28, October 7, 1959, to election campaign policies selected for the survey

Policies	Column inches	%
Provide for more people to buy their own houses	62	10·4
Stop spread of H-bomb to other countries	44	7·5
More freedom to individual enterprise in business	68	11·6
Immediately increase old age pensions	265	45·0
Abolish 11-plus exam	87	14·9
Wait until colonies are fully ready for self-government before giving it to them	61	10·3
Introduce schemes to enable workers to share in the profits of their own firms	2	0·3
Total	589	100·0

APPENDIX G

Analysis Tables of Political Images

The six tables in this appendix set out some of the results of the principal components analyses of political images, carried out as a preliminary to the main study. The first two tables (60 and 61) are derived from attitudes of the whole sample, Conservative and Labour included, to each of the two major parties and their leaders. The remaining four tables (62–5) are derived from attitudes of each group of party supporters to its own party and leader.

TABLE 60

Attitudes to the political parties (whole sample). Percentages of the whole sample endorsing each item, first factor loadings and communalities

Attitude item	Conservative Party			Labour Party		
	(a) %	(b)	(c) %	(a) %	(b)	(c) %
1. Would try to abolish class differences	26	+·58	48	53	+·48	34
2. Talks too much	34	−·68	50	47	−·63	40
3. Too much internal squabbling	21	−·41	28	56	−·27	39
4. Would get things done in a forthright way	37	+·60	37	28	+·72	58
5. Really respects British tradition	54	+·40	49	34	+·59	40
6. Too much afraid of America	45	−·53	47	25	−·26	38
7. More interested in people abroad than at home	29	−·32	37	13	−·37	38
8. Will give more chances to the individual who wants to better himself	37	+·50	33	39	+·58	39
9. Stands mainly for the upper classes	55	−·48	48	10	−·25	49
10. Would really work to prevent a nuclear war	58	+·57	34	63	+·54	34
11. Would extend the welfare services	26	+·58	42	58	+·53	54
12. Would take nationalization too far	10	−·18	41	56	−·38	55
13. They have a bad past record	25	−·58	38	30	−·52	40
14. Stands mainly for the working class	8	+·26	48	54	−·33	96
15. Out for the nation as a whole	49	+·64	54	30	+·59	40
16. Out to raise standard of living for man in the street	36	+·64	46	54	+·66	50
17. Would keep prices down	34	+·52	41	30	+·48	52
18. Don't keep to their promises	42	−·62	55	46	−·56	45
19. Fair treatment of all races and creeds	49	+·68	61	51	+·60	43
20. Has no clear policy	17	−·59	47	27	−·49	66
21. Would be too free with public money	20	−·47	35	49	−·53	47
22. Keeps too rigidly to party line	29	−·47	36	38	−·24	38
23. Would make country more prosperous	51	+·67	47	31	+·69	54
Mean variance			47			44

Key: (a) % of electors endorsing, (b) first factor loading, (c) communality.

APPENDIX G

TABLE 61

Attitudes to party leaders (whole sample). Percentages of the whole sample endorsing each item, first factor loadings and communalities

Attitude item	Mr Macmillan			Mr Gaitskell		
	(a) %	(b)	(c) %	(a) %	(b)	(c) %
1. Interested in the welfare of the people	53	+·68	47	68	+·63	49
2. Has some distinguishing qualities of greatness	59	+·48	45	23	+·33	15
3. Out to secure world peace	69	+·60	45	50	+·57	44
4. Not vigorous enough	29	−·32	38	35	−·50	48
5. A clever man	69	+·55	53	60	+·49	42
6. Strong-willed and firm	49	+·69	54	37	+·59	37
7. Straightforward and frank	46	+·69	54	45	+·65	45
8. Practical and down to earth	46	+·61	41	44	+·58	36
9. Not a pleasing personality	13	−·52	45	27	−·62	54
10. Not the best man in his party for the job	13	+·55	53	25	−·52	36
11. Fair-minded and unbiased	37	+·65	64	33	+·58	47
12. Only interested in one class	38	−·51	67	37	−·46	44
13. Puts his party interests first	47	−·05	31	46	+·04	28
14. Well educated	85	+·42	73	63	+·42	31
15. Humane and kindly	57	+·59	40	37	+·61	63
16. Speaks very well	64	+·52	35	52	+·61	48
17. Too full of his own importance	18	−·55	51	25	−·62	49
18. Not always sincere	27	−·57	47	30	−·55	56
19. Really honest	47	+·64	53	37	−·69	57
20. A strong leader	51	+·54	34	39	+·61	40
21. Has a sense of humour	58	+·56	36	44	+·59	39
22. Not really strong enough	23	−·55	39	32	−·49	52
23. Strong enough to make even unwelcome decisions	52	+·55	36	30	+·16	15
24. Looks too much to past events	20	−·55	51	28	−·47	42
25. Concerned with rich and poor alike	41	+·71	57	35	+·66	47
26. Out of touch with the needs of ordinary working people	42	−·63	53	13	−·40	27
27. Has wide political experience	68	+·38	34	52	+·53	44
28. Tries to restore Britain's greatness	65	+·52	60	27	+·59	43
29. Relies too much on those around him	23	−·65	52	23	−·36	43
30. Puts good of country before party politics	35	+·55	45	25	+·42	45
Mean variance			48			42

Key: (a) % of electors endorsing, (b) first factor loading, (c) communality.

TABLE 62

Attitudes to the Conservative Party (Conservative supporters). Percentages endorsing each item, factor loadings, communalities (proportions contributed to variance by the three factors) and specificities

Attitude item	Percentage endorsing %	Factor loadings I %	II %	III %	Communality %	Specificity %
1. Would try to abolish class differences	41	+59	+34	+07	47	53
2. Talks too much	16	−65	+22	−09	48	52
3. Too much internal squabbling	9	−18	+12	+36	18	82
4. Would get things done in a forthright way	57	+46	+54	−04	51	49
5. Really respects British tradition	74	+62	−02	−24	44	56
6. Too much afraid of America	24	−23	+58	−19	42	58
7. More interested in people abroad than at home	16	+37	−16	+11	18	82
8. Will give more chances to the individual who wants to better himself	55	+51	+53	−03	54	46
9. Stands mainly for the upper classes	36	−22	+61	+24	48	52
10. Would really work to prevent a nuclear war	79	+35	−06	−34	24	76
11. Would extend the welfare services	42	+46	+08	+39	37	63
12. Would take nationalization too far	7	−24	+34	−16	20	80
13. They have a bad past record	7	−21	+40	−44	40	60
14. Stands mainly for the working class	13	+24	−08	+30	15	85
15. Out for the nation as a whole	71	+57	−21	+30	46	54
16. Out to raise standard of living for man in the street	58	+45	+22	+05	25	75
17. Would keep prices down	47	+67	+24	−20	55	45
18. Don't keep to their promises	21	−50	+02	+38	39	61
19. Fair treatment of all races and creeds	72	+61	−21	+50	67	33
20. Has no clear policy	3	−39	+23	+57	53	47
21. Would be too free with public money	8	−20	+13	−19	09	91
22. Keeps too rigidly to party line	12	−24	+08	+45	27	73
23. Would make country more prosperous	80	+25	+18	+20	14	86
Mean variance		19	09	09	37	64

APPENDIX G

TABLE 63

Attitudes to the Labour Party (Labour supporters). Percentages endorsing each item, factor loadings, communalities (proportions contributed to variance by the three factors) and specificities

Attitude item	Percentage endorsing %	Factor loadings I %	II %	III %	Communality %	Specificity %
1. Would try to abolish class differences	70	+79	+11	−00	64	36
2. Talks too much	17	−10	+54	−37	44	56
3. Too much internal squabbling	33	+10	+61	−02	38	62
4. Would get things done in a forthright way	51	−61	−34	+10	50	50
5. Really respects British tradition	54	+42	−21	+29	30	70
6. Too much afraid of America	19	−06	+53	+25	35	65
7. More interested in people abroad than at home	4	−03	+25	+40	22	78
8. Will give more chances to the individual who wants to better himself	56	+56	−12	+02	33	67
9. Stands mainly for the upper classes	10	−30	+13	+68	59	41
10. Would really work to prevent nuclear war	82	+67	+21	−13	51	49
11. Would extend the welfare services	75	+88	+19	−17	84	16
12. Would take nationalization too far	29	+31	+48	+25	39	61
13. They have a bad past record	10	−13	+49	−04	26	74
14. Stands mainly for working class	78	+76	+14	−20	64	36
15. Out for the nation as a whole	47	+58	−20	+30	47	53
16. Out to raise standard of living for man in the street	81	+87	+06	−15	78	22
17. Would keep prices down	44	+57	−29	+04	41	59
18. Don't keep to their promises	19	+05	+74	−07	56	44
19. Fair treatment for all races and creeds	72	+85	−17	−11	76	24
20. Has no clear policy	6	−02	+24	+25	12	88
21. Would be too free with public money	17	+20	+31	+60	50	50
22. Keeps too rigidly to party line	22	+27	−16	+53	38	62
23. Would make country more prosperous	54	+67	−19	+13	50	50
Mean variance		27	12	08	47	53

TABLE 64

Attitudes to Mr Macmillan as a party leader (Conservative supporters). Percentages endorsing each item, factor loadings, communalities (proportions contributed to variance by the three factors) and specificities

Attitude item	Percentage endorsing %	Factor loadings I %	II %	III %	Communality %	Specificity %
1. Interested in welfare of people	80	+60	−06	+28	44	56
2. Has some distinguishing qualities of greatness	70	+48	+40	−03	39	61
3. Out to secure world peace	81	+66	+50	−09	69	31
4. Not vigorous enough	26	−36	+50	−21	42	58
5. A clever man	79	−65	+32	−33	63	37
6. Strong-willed and firm	62	+71	+18	+31	63	37
7. Straightforward and frank	63	+59	+04	+15	37	63
8. Practical and down to earth	61	+68	+22	+09	52	48
9. Not a pleasing personality	6	−44	+31	+43	48	52
10. Not best man in his party for job	6	−33	+65	−03	53	47
11. Fairminded and unbiased	55	−61	+68	+18	87	13
12. Only interested in one class	19	−43	+49	+01	43	57
13. Puts party interests first	43	+09	+40	−09	18	82
14. Well educated	91	+59	+17	−53	66	34
15. Humane and kindly	68	+54	+26	−26	43	57
16. Speaks very well	78	+50	+18	−48	51	49
17. Too full of own importance	5	−43	+58	+17	55	45
18. Not always sincere	12	−55	+32	+23	46	54
19. Really honest	64	+69	+14	−04	50	50
20. A strong leader	69	+59	+04	+43	54	46
21. Has a sense of humour	72	+39	+33	+54	55	45
22. Not really strong enough	15	−64	+17	−04	44	56
23. Strong enough to make even unwelcome decisions	68	+65	+11	+26	50	50
24. Looks too much to past events	9	−49	+52	−03	51	49
25. Concerned with rich and poor alike	62	+67	−05	+23	50	50
26. Out of touch with needs of ordinary working people	20	−46	+50	+22	51	49
27. Has wide political experience	81	+49	+35	−33	47	53
28. Tries to restore Britain's greatness	82	+43	+28	−20	30	70
29. Relies too much on those around him	6	−45	+62	+03	59	41
30. Puts good of country before party politics	48	+52	+10	+37	42	58
Mean variance		29	14	07	50	50

APPENDIX G

TABLE 65

Attitudes to Mr Gaitskell as a party leader (Labour supporters). Percentages endorsing each item, factor loadings, communalities (proportions contributed to variance by the three factors) and specificities

Attitude item	Percentage endorsing %	Factor loadings I %	II %	III %	Communality %	Specificity %
1. Interested in welfare of people	90	+37	−42	+30	40	60
2. Has some distinguishing qualities of greatness	29	+35	+12	−09	15	85
3. Out to secure world peace	65	+27	−43	+03	26	74
4. Not vigorous enough	24	−53	+36	+25	47	53
5. A clever man	68	+37	−07	−29	23	77
6. Strong-willed and firm	49	+63	+33	−13	52	48
7. Straightforward and frank	68	+61	+12	+02	39	61
8. Practical and down to earth	59	+45	+37	+15	36	64
9. Not a pleasing personality	11	−54	+29	−06	38	62
10. Not best man in his party for job	15	−39	+26	+43	41	59
11. Fairminded and unbiased	47	+42	+22	+17	25	75
12. Only interested in one class	24	−24	+37	−41	36	64
13. Puts party interests first	43	+15	+43	−42	38	62
14. Well educated	68	+35	+22	+05	17	83
15. Humane and kindly	49	+66	+25	+11	51	49
16. Speaks very well	62	+56	+12	−22	38	62
17. Too full of own importance	10	−36	+37	−21	31	69
18. Not always sincere	14	−27	+46	−13	30	70
19. Really honest	54	+62	+37	+28	60	40
20. A strong leader	53	+53	−07	−39	44	56
21. Has a sense of humour	57	+67	+04	−07	46	54
22. Not really strong enough	21	−39	+33	+35	39	61
23. Strong enough to make even unwelcome decisions	37	+48	+32	−02	33	67
24. Looks too much to past events	11	−42	+35	−06	30	70
25. Concerned with rich and poor alike	51	+57	+21	−10	38	62
26. Out of touch with needs of ordinary working people	7	−43	+58	−39	67	33
27. Has wide political experience	60	+49	+06	+09	25	75
28. Tries to restore Britain's greatness	46	+39	+41	+21	36	64
29. Relies too much on those around him	7	−16	+43	+50	46	54
30. Puts good of country before party politics	41	+30	+14	+52	38	62
Mean variance		21	10	07	38	62

Index

ABC Television, 90
Abrams, Dr Mark, 146
Abstention, *see* Non-voting
Adorno, W. T., 25
Addresses, election, 81–2 and n, 103, 183, 190
Advertising, political, 15, 36, 199
Age:
  and campaign exposure, 99
  first voters, 138–9
  and national issues, 179–80
  and voting behaviour, 137–8 and n, 209, 211, App. E
Allport, G. W., 39
Amory, D. Heathcoat, Rt. Hon., MP, 61, 112–3
Attitudes, political (*see also* Images, Partisanship and Scales):
  of changers, 212–3
  changes in, 142 ff, 190–1, 192, 199, 200, 202, 212–3, 219–20
  Conservative, to own party, 42–4, 148–9, 152, 154–5, 156, 227, App. G
  Conservative, to Labour Party, 47–8, 52, 54, 156
  Conservative, 'don't knows', 213–5
  Conservative, first voters, 139
  Conservative, inter-party changers, 219–21
  Conservative, non-voters, 215–9
  consistent with voting, 35, 142
  consolidation, 152
  and cross-pressures, 153–5, 202–3
  delayed changes, 199
  and exposure to election campaign, 196–7
  extent of toleration in, 39, 52–4, 150
  insulation of, 190–3, 203–4
  item endorsements, 145, 161
  items listed, App. G
  Labour, to own party, 40–1, 45–7, 52, 148–9, 151–2, 153–6, 227, App. G
  Labour, to Conservative Party, 44–5, 52, 54, 157–8

Labour, 'don't knows', 213–5
Labour, first voters, 139
Labour, inter-party changers, 219–21
Labour, non-voters, 215–9
Liberal, to major parties, 42, 52, 145–6
to party leaders, 158–64, 185, 227
to party and leader, compared, 158–60
re-appraisal of, 149
regression effect, 149
relation to voting, 142, 212–3
scales, 33–5, 142–4
score defined, 255
stability of, 146–9
Audience, sound radio, 81, 95, 189
Audience, television (*see also* under names of programmes):
  characteristics of, 83, 201, 223
  characteristics of, compared to sound radio, 189
  compared with Press readership, 95–6
  interest in political broadcasts, 86–7, 91, 201, 224
  losses estimated by TAM, 85
  national coverage, 13, 82
  political composition of, 87–8, 91, 95n
  on Polling Day, 94–5
  reaction to first two election broadcasts, 107ff
  and voting change, 221
Authoritarian tendencies in political attitudes, 158–9
Axes, principal, analysis, *see* Factor analysis

Bartlett, F.C., on propaganda, 197–201
BBC (*see also* 'Hustings', News broadcasts and Television authorities)
  Audience Research, 80, 117, 107n, 137n;
  Charter, 224

BBC (contd)
  editorial policy, 224
  election policy, 14–15
  estimates of audiences, see Audience
  impartiality, 71, 189
  Report, *The General Election*, 1959, 81n, 89n, 112n, 113n, 114n, 117n
  Report: *The Public and the Programmes*, 60n, 95n
Beavan, John, 16
Belson, W. A., 107n, 137n
Benn, Anthony Wedgwood, MP, 109, 113
Benney, M., and Geiss, P., 36
Benney, M., Gray, A. P., Pear, R. H., 80n, 131n, 147
Braddock, Bessie, MP, 113
Briggs, Asa, 67n
Bristol studies (see also Milne, R. S., and Mackenzie, H. C.), 81, 131
Burt, Sir Cyril, 42, 137n
Butler, D. E., 36n, 81, 84n, 102n, 108n, 125, 130n, 135n
Butler, D. E., and Rose, R., 36, 93, 199
Butler, R. A., Rt. Hon., MP, in first election broadcast, 112

Campbell, P., Donnison, D., and Potter, A., 131n
Campaign, see Election
Candidates, local, 104, 106
Canvassing (see also Local campaign), 103, 183, 190
  effect of television on, 105, 185
Castle, Barbara, MP, 69, 90
Changers:
  separate analysis for, 186, 192
  attitudes of, 212–3
  characteristics of, 207 ff
  to Conservative and to Labour compared, 210–2
  defined, 255
  effect of television on, 186–7, 188, 191–2
  and local participation, 105
  persistent changers, 221–2
  and political discussion, 194
  need for research into, 225
Changers, inter-party:
  attitudes of, 219–21
  characteristics of, 207 ff
  exposure to propaganda, 210
  political knowledge and interest of, 220–1
  proportion of, 207
Changes of allegiance, 123 ff, 207 ff
  constituencies compared, 130–1, 135–6
  habitual nature of, 221–2
  scoring degree of, 185, App. B
Changes in political attitudes, see Attitudes
Changes in political knowledge, see Policies, knowledge of
Changes in selection of election issues, see Issues, election
Chave, E. S., 39n
Chi-square, defined, 255
Class, see Social class
Communality, in factor analysis, defined, 255
Communication (see also Press, Sound broadcasting, Television):
  barrier, 192–3
  and social factors, 210
Community and group pressures:
  on attitudes, 152–5, 202–3, 204
  and election issues, 179–81
  on voting, 133, 135, 209, 217, 219
Component, image defined, 255
Confidence limits, see Scales
Conservative Central Office, 118
Conservative Party:
  advertising campaign, 15, 36, 199, 203
  age, sex and occupation of voters, 137–41
  changers to, 211–2
  election manifesto, 56
  general nature of image, 53, 55, 205, 225
  issues associated with, 176–8
  partisanship, 152, 154
  policies, knowledge of, 167–8
  reasons for election victory, 100–2, 206
  swing to, between elections, 128–34, 203
  toleration of Labour Party, 149
  women voters, 139–40, 171
Constituencies, choice of, 18–21, 184
Corlett, T., 17n, 19
Crawford Committee, 67
Cronbach, L. J., 25

INDEX

Crossman, R. H. S., MP, 36, 37, 109, 113, 125
Cross-pressures on voters:
  influence of, 153, 158, 202–3, 217, 218
Crouch, David, 93 and n, 106

Daily Express, 63, 76, 120, 124, 126 and n, 127, 147
Daily Herald, 61, 76, 88, 190n, 195
Daily Mail, 76, 124, 126–7
Daily Mirror, 64, 74n, 76, 88, 89, 95, 147
Daily Sketch, 74n, 76, 120
Daily Telegraph, 64, 65, 66, 74, 89, 124, 126, 173n
Discussion, political, 184, 194–5
'Don't knows':
  attitudes of, 132, 213–5
  causes of uncertainty, 134
  characteristics of, 207 ff, 213–5
  influences on, 133–4
  later voting of, 133, 203
  need for research, 225
  opinion poll estimates, 124, 126
  political knowledge and interest of, 220–1
  previous voting of, 132
  proportion of, 132, 207
  young voters, 138
Droylsden Survey, 131n

Education and channel preference, 85n
  and voting, 167n
Ehrenberg, A. S. C., 17n, 166n
Election (*see also* Issues, Policies and Local campaign):
  campaign dates, 18
  campaign defined, 255
  campaign, television coverage, 57–60, 66–74
  changes during, 150–1, 188, 199
  compared to preceding period, 127, 130–1, 226
  exposure to campaign and partisanship, 196–7
  exposure to mass media, 98–9, 168–70
Exposure to propaganda (*see also* Propaganda, Audience and Election): defined, 255
  constructing indices of, App. A

Eysenck, H. J., 26, 42 and n

Factor analysis:
  choice of method, 26–7, 39
  description of method, 27–31
Family, influence of, 204, 208, 209
First voters (*see also* Age), 138–9
Fisher, R. A., 22n
Forster, Peter, 119
Frankland, P., 17n
Free will, *see* Individual judgment

Gaitskell, Rt. Hon. Hugh, MP (*see also* Images, party leader), 66
  attitudes to, items listed, App. G
  changes in attitude to, 163, 191–2
  in the first election broadcast, 108, 113, 117–8, 120
  opinions of, 101
Gallup Political Index, 126n, 141n, 151n
Gallup Poll, 83n, 86n, 126 and n, 138, 140, 141n, 151n
Galton, Sir Francis, 149
Granada TV, *A First Report on Constituency Television*, 72n, 93n
Granada TV Network Ltd (*see also* 'Marathon, Election', 'Last Debate'), 14
Granada Viewership Survey, 83n
Gray, P. G., 17n, 19
Greenwich study, *see* Benney etc.
Group pressures, *see* Community
Guardian, The, 61, 76, 88
Guilford, J. P., 29n
Guttman, L., 31

Hailsham, Lord, 36n, 65, 108n, 112, 119, 125, 150
Himmelweit, H. T., 14
Holt, Arthur, 69, 90
Hotelling, H., 27
Hovland, C. I., et al., 201
'*How People Vote*', *see* Benney, Gray, etc.
'Hustings' programmes, BBC, 14, 59, 60, 68, 69, 92, 202
  audience size, 86, 89

Images, brand-, 36, 37
Images, party (*see also* Attitudes):
  Conservative, 30, 40, 42–5, 55, 227
  Conservative, changes in, 149, 151, 155–8

Images, party (contd)
  Conservative, components, 42–4, 44–5
  Labour, 30, 40–1, 53, 55, 205, 225, 227
  Labour, changes in, 150, 151, 155–6
  Labour, components, 45–7, 47–8
  traditional-versus-radical component, 28, 32, 40–2, 52, 142, 143, 159, 160, 186
Images, party leader (see also Attitudes):
  distinguished from party image, 160
  Gaitskell, 37
  Gaitskell, among own supporters, 48–9, 162–3, 227, App. G
  Gaitskell, among Conservative supporters, 49, 162
  items listed, App. G
  leadership component, 33, 40
  Macmillan, among own supporters, 50–51, 158–9, 162, 227, App. G
  Macmillan, among Labour supporters, 51, 162–3
  personal component, 33, 40
  policy component, 33, 40
  traditional-versus-radical component, in the leader image, 42n, 159, 160
Images, political (see also Scales), 36 ff, 51–4
  definition of, 39
  method of analysis and construction of scales, 23–35
  and political judgment, 150–1, 205
  projection of, 55
  and reality, 199
  and television, 224–5
Independence of political thinking, see Individual judgment
Independent Television Authority, editorial policy (see also Television authorities), 70
Independent Television Companies: (see also ABC and Granada), 224
Independent Television News, see News broadcasts
Individual judgment, 43, 203–4, 214–5
IPA (Institute of Practitioners in Advertising), 95n
Interest in election, 208n, 215–6, 221, 224
  and exposure, 86n, 196, 220, 224
  of first voters, 139
  index of, App. A
  and non-voting, 215–6, 218
  and uncertainty, 214, 218
Interviewers, recruitment of, App. C
Interviewing of electors, App. C, 17, 21–2, 34
  characteristics of 'failures', 268
Issues, election (see also Policies), 171 ff, 188
  changes in selection of, 173–81
  and the community, 179–81
  discussion of, 194
  distinguished from policies, 172, 255
  and occupation, 154, 180n
  order of importance, 62, 173n
  press coverage of, 59, 76, 174–6, App. F
  sound broadcast coverage of, 59
  stability of opinion on, 173
  television coverage of, 59, 174–6
  and young voters, 139, 179–80

James, William, 42
Jennings, Sir Ivor, 72
Johnson, M., 42
Jones, Pamela, 19
Juror index, 19, 24

Kendall, M. G., 23
Klapper, J. T., 165n
Knowledge of policies, see Policies

Labour Party (see also Images, party, and Attitudes)
  age, sex and occupation of voters, 137–41
  and BBC/ITV preference, 85 and n, 95 and n
  changers to, characteristics, 211–2, 219–20
  election manifesto, 56
  issues associated with, 176–8
  loss of support, 47, 128–34, 199, 212
  partisanship, 131, 151
  policies, knowledge of, 167–8
  radicalism of, 53, 158, 225
  reasons for election loss, 100–2
  support in West Leeds, 130–1
  tolerance, 149
  women voters, 139–40, 171

INDEX

'Last Debate, The', Granada, 69, 90, 122, 202
Lazarsfeld, P. F., Berelson, B., and Gaudet, H., 36, 80, 104, 133 and n, 147–8, 150, 151n, 153, 158, 193–4, 196, 200, 208n
Leaders, party (*see also* Attitudes and Images), qualities, 158–60
Leeds, West, constituency (*see also* Local campaign):
    choice for survey, 18–19
    votes cast, in, App. D
Liberal Party:
    candidates, 19
    election manifesto, 57
    policy, 188
    sex and occupation of voters, 137
Liberals:
    attitudes to major parties, 42, 52, 145–6
    as inter-party changers, 220
    knowledge of party policies, 167
Lloyd, Selwyn, Rt. Hon., MP, 63, 69, 90, 107
Local campaign (*see also* Election), 102–6, 190, 218
    and attitude change, 192
    effect on political knowledge, 189, 190
    effect of television on, 92–3
    measurement of participation, 185, App. A
Lumsdaine, A. A., and Janis I. L., 201

Marital status:
    and campaign exposure, 99
    and voting change, 208, 211–2
Mackenzie, H. C., see Milne, R. S., and Mackenzie, H. C.
Macmillan, Rt. Hon. Harold, MP (*see also* Images, party leader):
    attitude to, 227, App. G
    changes in attitude to, 162–3
    in first election broadcast, 107, 111–2, 115
'Marathon, Election', Granada, 14, 68, 71–4, 86, 90–3, 103
Macleod, Rt. Hon. Ian, MP, 112, 115
Meetings, election, 81–2, 103, 106
Men voters, *see* Sexes
Method (*see also* Sampling), 17 ff, Appendices A, B, C, D

definition of terms used, 255–6
fieldwork and results, App. C
image analysis, 23–35, 38–9
measuring degree of political change, App. B
measuring direction of vote, 186
measuring effect of television and other media, 184–6, 191
measuring exposure to propaganda, App. A
measuring opinion on national issues, 172–3
measuring political knowledge, 165
monitoring of programmes, 58, 255
selection of sample, 18–22
Milne, R. S., and Mackenzie, H. C., 15, 36, 80, 81n, 103n, 131, 137n, 141n, 147, 148, 153, 165n, 168n, 173n, 178n, 196, 210n, 220n, 221n
Montgomery, Lord, 77
Must Labour Lose, 146n

National Opinion Polls (*see also Daily Mail*), 14n, 126n
Nationalization, 56, 59, 100, 174, 272
News broadcasts (*see also* Audience):
    effect on knowledge of policies, 188
    sound, 69, 95, 98, 201
    television, 69–71, 85–6, 89, 97, 201
News items, influence on election, 99–100
News Chronicle, 61, 76, 88, 119, 120, 124, 126
Newspapers, *see* Press
Nicholas, H. G., 82, 130n, 135n
Non-voting, 130, 134–5
    and attitude change, 212, 215–9
    characteristics of non-voters, 207 ff
    constituencies compared, 135–6
    extent of, 208
    habitual nature of, 221–2
    and knowledge of party policies, 167–8, 220–1
    political interest of, 220–1
    reasons for, 218–9, 222
    need for research, 225

Occupation:
    as a cross-pressure, 153–4
    and campaign exposure, 99
    distribution in sample, App. E
    grading of, 137 and n, 141

Occupation (*contd*)
  and voting behaviour, 140–1, 141n, 209–10, 211, App. E
Opinion leaders, 193–5
Oppenheim, A. N., 14n

Pannell, Charles, MP, 106
Partisanship (*see also* Labour and Conservative Party):
  and degree of exposure to campaign, 87–8, 150, 196–7
  description of, 144, 151, 196n, 256
  scores before and after campaign, 151
  and selection of national issues, 179
Party election broadcasts, 13, 60, 68, 191, 221, 223, 256
  audience for, 82–6, 191, 200, 215, 218, 223
  and changes in political knowledge, 188
  press reaction to, 118–21
  reaction to, 107 ff
Pearson, Karl, 27n
Pensions, 59, 63–5, 100, 110, 212n
People's Choice, The, see Lazarsfeld, etc.
Policies, party (*see also* Issues and Policies, knowledge of):
  electors' knowledge of, 165 ff
  measuring political knowledge, 165 and n
  press reporting of, 61 ff, 77, Table 9, App. F
Policies, knowledge of (*see also* Scale of):
  of changers, 220–1
  changes in, 166
  description of scale, 165–7
  of 'don't knows', 215
  and exposure to communication media, 168–70, 187–90
  extent of, 165–7
  of non-voters, 220–1
  scale, items, 166
Polling, effect of television on, 93–5
Polls, public opinion (*see also* Gallup Poll):
  estimates of voting intentions, 123–7
  and issues, 173
Press, the (*see also* Issues and Policies):
  coverage of campaign, 60–1, 74 and n, 82, 189, 228
  editorial policy, 15, 60–1, 78–9, 189–90 and n
  effect on political knowledge, 189
  and election issues, 59, 74–6, 174–6, App. F
  and election policies, App. F
  measuring exposure to, App. A
  as a medium of communication, 79, 89
  reaction to first election broadcasts, 118–21
  readership of, 95–7, 190
  relation to television, 223–4
Press Council, 78
Propaganda, party (*see also* Audience and Election campaign):
  effect of, 191, 192, 197–202, 214–5
  effect on non-supporters, 178
  exposure to, 195, 202
  exposure to different media compared, 96–7
  exposure and voting change, 210, 214–5, 220–1
  and group pressures, 202–3
  measurement of, App. A
  and national issues, 172, 173–81
  penetration of, 80 ff
Prosperity, 45, 61–2, 149, 151, 205
Pudsey (*see also* Local campaign):
  choice for survey, 18–19
  votes cast in, App. D

Radicalism, 53, 158
Radical, traditional-versus-, component, *see* Images, political
'Rawhide', effect on polling, 94
Readership, *see* Press
Rebound effect, 151n
Register of electors, 17, 131
Reith, Lord, 67
Representation of the People Act 1949, 14, 60, 62, 67, 77, 91, 93, 224
Research, future, 225–6
Rochdale by-election, 1958, 14, 72
Rose, R. (*see also* Butler, D. E., and Rose, R.), 146n

Sample, composition of, App. E
Sampling errors (*see also* Method), 23, 131, 257–8
  on attitude scales, 144
  in opinion polls, 126

INDEX

Sanai, M., 42
Scale of political knowledge, *see* Policies, knowledge of
Scales, image (*see also* Attitudes, political, and Method), 33–5, 142–4
Scalogram analysis, 31–2
Selectivity, *see* Audience
Sexes (*see also* Women):
  and attitude change, 153–5
  and campaign exposure, 99
  and choice of national issues, 179–80
  and partisanship, 140n
  and political knowledge, 167, 170–1
  separate analyses, 186
  and voting, 139–40, 208 and n, 211, App. E
Significance, statistical, 126, 144, 186
Social class, 137, 141n, 154n, 210n
Socialist Commentary, 146n
Sound broadcasting (radio):
  audience for election programmes, 81, 95, 189
  effect on political knowledge, 189
  election policy, 15
  exposure index, App. A
Spectator, The, 119, 120
Sunday Times, The, 64, 118, 120
Swing:
  between parties 1955–9, 128, 130–1, 132–4, 191
  defined, 130n, 256

TAM (Television Audience Measurement Ltd) (*see also* Audience), 82–5 and n
Television (*see also* News broadcasts, Party election broadcasts, Election, campaign coverage, etc.):
  audience compared to sound radio, 189
  compared to other media, 58–60, 89
  coverage and changes in political knowledge, 166
  coverage and election issues, 174–6
  coverage of election, 66–74
  effect on political knowledge, 187–9
  effects of, 182 ff
  exposure to, and voting change, 220–1
  nature of medium, 14, 89, 92, 121–2
  overlap with other media, 95, 96–7, 104
  and partisanship, 148, 196
  and political images, 224–5
Television Act 1954, 14, 67, 72, 224
Television authorities (*see also* BBC, Granada and Independent TV Companies), 14, 66–72, 189, 224
Television and the Child, 14n
Thurstone, L. L., 29, 30, 39
Times, The, 66, 74n, 76, 195
Tolerance, political, 148–9
'Tonight', BBC, 13, 120
Traditional-versus-radical component, *see* Images, political
Trenaman, J., 98n, 110n
Turnout, 94, 135n
Twentieth Century, The, 16n

Ullswater Committee, 67
Uncertainty, *see* 'Don't knows'

Vicky, 109
Vince, P., 14n
Viewing, *see* Audience
Voting, *see* Polling
Voting change:
  and attitude change, 212–3
  habitual nature of, 221–2
  measuring degree of, App. B
  and participation in the campaign, 220–1
  prediction of, 222
Voting figures, App. D
Voting, predicting from attitude score, 35, 142, 212

Wallas, Graham, 36 and n
Winning, John, 106
Women voters (*see also* Sexes):
  political knowledge of, 167, 170–1
  tendency to abstain, 208–9
Working-class, 40, 45, 53, 205, 225
Wyatt, Woodrow, MP, 109

Yorkshire Evening News, 74, 76
Yorkshire Evening Post, 74, 86, 95 and n, 195
Yorkshire Post, 74, 120
Young voters:
  and selection of national issues, 179
  and voting change, 138, 211–2

For Product Safety Concerns and Information please contact our EU
representative GPSR@taylorandfrancis.com
Taylor & Francis Verlag GmbH, Kaufingerstraße 24, 80331 München, Germany

www.ingramcontent.com/pod-product-compliance
Lightning Source LLC
Chambersburg PA
CBHW061434300426
44114CB00014B/1681